FUELIN' AROUND

A Fast-Paced Life in Motorsports

J.K. KELLY

ISBN: 978-0-9994099-2-3 (paperback)
ISBN: 978-0-9994099-3-0 (ebook)

Published by:

JK Kelly Consulting LLC
P.O. Box B
Media, PA USA 19063
Jk.kellyconsulting@gmail.com

JKKelly.com

DEDICATION

This book is dedicated to my parents, the great Mom and Dad who picked me out of a crowd of screaming basinets. They gave me the foundation that helped launch this wonderful life.

APPRECIATION

A very special and sincere thank you must go to Fred Morrison and to Steve Burns. They gave me an opportunity decades ago and provided me with the vehicle that would carry me on all sorts of adventures and experiences here at home and around the world.

Brett Deyo was quoted as saying,
"Everyone has a Jim Kelly story."
This is mine.

CONTENTS

Chapter One
SOMETIMES CHANGE IS GOOD

BAM! STUNNED BY the loud gunshot, the girl fell backward and onto the floor as the chair rolled out from under her. BAM! The second shot rang out. "What the hell are you doing?" she yelled as she cowered from her place on the office trailer floor. Her ears were ringing and for a moment she thought she had gone deaf. The gunman pulled the .357 caliber handgun back from the open window and the summer heat and set it down on his desk.

"Just chasin' the stray dogs," he laughed, reaching over to help her up from the floor. Flustered from the commotion and embarrassed that she fell, she tried to hold in her laugh and just looked at him as she brushed herself off and fixed her skirt.

"I was told working here would be a lot of fun, but next time give me a heads-up, okay?" she demanded with a smile. He nodded. "Is the boss coming in today?" she asked as he walked out the door.

"You just never know. He might show up every day for two weeks or we might not see him for a month," he replied.

That was the young girl's first day on the job at VP. I laughed really hard the first time I heard that story and to this day remember it fondly. The owner had hired her to answer the phones and keep the books but had never offered in the interview any hint of how present or absent he might be. Little did anyone know from that small site located thirty miles south of the Alamo in San Antonio, a young man named Steve Burns would lead a classic American success story that would take me on the ride of a lifetime. His VP Racing Fuels would evolve and grow to wage epic David versus Goliath battles and wars that continue today. Miles away, while the history of VP's earliest days in the racing fuel business were being written in Texas, I was living a much different life in the Northeast.

On a particularly cold winter night in the suburbs of Philadelphia I found myself in a precarious position, carrying precious cargo. The evening had started out awkwardly enough. As I entered the warmth of that family's living room my eyeglasses immediately fogged over and I couldn't see a damn thing. I quickly took them off as I began to introduce myself but it left me legally blind and struggling to read the faces of the people who were greeting me. To make matters worse, the weather was turning. While we were inside the house attending to the grieving family and the deceased, a frosty mist had fallen and everything outside had begun to freeze over with ice. So there I was, backing down the front steps of a row home, wrestling with the heavy end of a stretcher. Not only were the steps very steep but also there seemed to be a small mountain of them. We were headed for the silver station wagon that we'd double-parked in the street.

Suddenly I started to slip and slide on the steps, and this caused the guy on the other end to stumble too. Off we went, very quickly and somewhat unprofessionally down the steps. I managed to jump backward onto the hood of a car parked at the curb as my end of the stretcher slammed hard into the front fender. How my helper managed to maintain his footing I will never know. Luckily, our precious cargo was unharmed. The family and many of the neighbors had been watching and seemed relieved none of us were hurt. One of the relatives slipped his way down the steps and checked his car for damage but there was surprisingly not even a scratch. The best thing about the funeral business, and especially just then, was that the person left in your care never complained. Okay, they rarely did. On the drive to the morgue, after laughing off the tension, I reminded myself, "This is only short term. I won't have to do this forever."

My father owned a very successful funeral home and encouraged me to be a part of it. He had always wanted me to follow in his footsteps and hoped that by working in it I would take a greater interest. When I wasn't in school, working a regular job, or out trying to have a good time, he paid me to put on a suit and go to a hospital, nursing home, or private residence. There, I'd essentially do what was referred to in the business as a removal. If we were moving someone that had died at home, I would be the family's first contact. I was the son of the funeral director who they knew and trusted, and since I'm a very compassionate person I believe I handled things very well - one family helping another. My being there gave the surviving family and friends the reassurance that their loved one was being taken care of with the respect and dignity they deserved. I would carefully place the remains of someone who had just died on a stretcher for transfer to the morgue. Sometimes people would want to help. Other times they were too overwhelmed with grief. It might sound like a pretty messed up job, but someone had to do it, and for doing this sort of thing the money was *very* good. That winter night, with the fogged up glasses and the ice follies on the front steps, was not a typical one but reminded me to always maintain a sense of humor.

I might have been very good at helping people through difficult times but it would take a toll on me and I wanted to be living life, not watching people mourn the loss of one. One morning in particular I had to drive into Philly to do what I considered was the toughest part of my job. There I was, standing in the morgue at the Philadelphia Medical Examiner's Office, literally picking up the remains of an infant who had died suspiciously under the care of a babysitter. Three days later I would help the baby's mother place him in a little white casket and physically support her as she said goodbye. My heart broke for her. She and everyone in her family were crushed. Funerals are tough enough but when it came to children, and in this case, an infant, all of us hurt. All of us were numb. Luckily I was always able to keep my emotions in check and do what I was there to do. Help. That was the day I knew I had to get as far away from that business as possible and in *my* life, timing has been everything. I needed to get *back* into racing.

One of my best high school buds, Glen Sides, introduced me to live motorsports in the '70s. I had watched some racing on television but when he took me to a NASCAR race in Pocono, Pennsylvania I was hooked. I didn't give any thought to what fuel the cars were racing on, I only recognized the familiar day-glow red stripes and STP logos on Richard Petty's blue #43 and the Purolator #21 Ford that David Pearson was driving. Glen and I went to high school together and had after-school jobs as custodians. It was there that I met Fred Morrison and before long the three of us we were getting into all sorts of things. We'd pile into someone's car and drive non-stop to Gainesville, Florida every March for the NHRA Gatornationals drag race. Gas ups and pee breaks were the extent of our few pit stops. Counting down the endless billboards along I-95 touting the South of the Border food and gas was the only thing that kept whoever was driving entertained once everyone else nodded off. They called it the Gators, not only because you could find them in the state, the track also had a few resident alligators that often made things interesting for the onsite campers and their barbeques. They have gators at Volusia Speedway near Daytona but that's a dirt oval and an entirely different animal from drag racing. The National Hot Rod Association sanctions drag strips across North America. They put on over twenty events across the U.S. featuring the best of the best in the professional classes, and some of the best local, regional, and touring sportsman racers. Back in the '70s, we were thrilled to escape the cold, wet weather and head to North Florida where the temperature was in the 80s and sunny. The fact that a drag race was going on made the trip even more worthwhile. We'd bake in the sun at the track for a few days and then haul ass north on the interstate so everyone would be back in class, or work, on Monday morning. It was our Spring Break and we loved every minute and mile of it.

After high school, just about everyone headed for college. I wasn't completely sure of what I wanted to study, or if I wanted to study at all, so I took the year off to try to figure that out. I hate to waste time. So many of my friends who jumped right into college switched majors about five times and today aren't even working in the fields they were degreed in. Fred started at West Chester University nearby and got a part time job working with Bobby Thompson at his auto body shop in Havertown, Pennsylvania. "BT" specialized in corvette repairs and restorations by day but by night and many weekends all focus turned to Thompson's beautiful '67 canary yellow B/MP Corvette drag car. It was the first race car I was ever involved with. In all honesty, I was tasked with keeping that beauty clean while trying to learn as much as I could from the real gear heads that tended to her like a baby. The shop was one of many in this little industrial park. It seemed everyone was doing tune-ups and bodywork by day and working on their own race cars by night, a scene that takes place in little racing "villages" like that one all across the country.

I grew up discovering the world through the pages of *LIFE* and *National Geographic* magazines and developed an interest in photography. Yes, the topless native women were a curiosity for any boy at that age but the photos captured moments. They captured people and events, history. Being a part of that intrigued me. When my grandmother died she left me $100, and with it I bought my first 35mm single lens reflex camera. On one of our excursions to Gainesville, I took some candid photos of drivers like professional drag racers Don "The Snake" Prudhomme and Shirley Muldowney. Prudhomme was already a legend and Muldowney was the first woman to win national drag race competitions. Her amazing story was told in the film *Heart Like a Wheel*. I was also fortunate enough to capture a few action shots of nitromethane fueled "funny cars" doing what they seemed to do best, go really fast and sometimes – blow themselves up. I sent them off to *Super Stock & Drag Illustrated* magazine to see if they were good enough for publication. The late Steve Collison, the editor for SS&DI at the time, must have liked what he saw. He was the first guy to give me a break in motorsports photojournalism and for that I will be forever grateful.

In no time I was traveling to the NHRA Nationals with credentials that got me into the races for free, but more importantly they were all-access passes. I could go into restricted areas and snap away. For a race fan and a novice at what I was now into, I remember one time in particular that took place early on that was pretty cool to me. Prudhomme's U.S. Army Monza funny car had just made a fast pass down the quarter mile but the driver had used one of the early exit roads to pull off the track and wait for his crew to retrieve him and tow him back to their pit. The NHRA Safety Safari trucks were on site as always, strategically parked at various points down track, able to react to an emergency as quickly as possible. From their vantage points they could see that Prudhomme didn't seem to be in any trouble so they remained where they were and waited for the next set of cars. There I was taking photos of the funny car as it rolled pretty much right to me. Inside it I saw two gloved hands making a lifting gesture so I slung the camera straps over my shoulder, pulled the body release handle, and raised the fiberglass body up high enough to let the driver climb out from behind the sizzling hot engine. I got the cameras back to work and snapped away as he removed some very cumbersome safety gear. It was pretty cool. I guess at this point I can say The Snake popped my cherry. There would be many other times to come when I found myself in the same spot but got to hear some language much different from Prudhomme's words of appreciation. I actually learned some four-letter ones I had never, ever heard before. A few would become my favorites and anyone who knows me well can attest to that.

There were plenty of ways for me to get to the races. Either Glen, Fred and I would drive non-stop to a race or I'd go by myself. I'll never forget driving all night to cover the IHRA National Event at Darlington in South Carolina. I remember pulling into the parking lot of a Waffle House, a road warrior's favorite. It was a few hours before dawn so I crawled into the back seat of my midnight blue Dodge Charger and caught a few hours before the racing would begin. Nothing like brushing your teeth in one of those bathrooms and then crushing a plate of waffles, grits, home fries, and whatever kind of "meat" that sausage patty was supposed to have been. Other times, BT would drive his race car hauler to an event and Fred and I would ride along. We'd take turns in the bunk that lay just behind the front seat. You'd climb though the area where the back window used to be and hope for a smooth ride when it was your turn to snooze. Hopefully the radio or the 8-track tape player would take it easy on anyone trying to sleep but quite often it was called on to overcome the intriguing sounds of someone snoring. This was all long before iPhones and iPads and ear buds and such. Each day at the track, I'd be off taking pictures while Fred would be helping BT with his car. We'd reconnect when the racing was done and then head home again. At some point though I realized that I needed to get serious so I enrolled at a local college and then moved to Penn State's main campus at University Park. I'd always had an interest in helping people, protecting people, especially those being picked on or bullied by the bigger or more powerful.

I wanted to be involved in law enforcement in some way but I had no interest in writing traffic tickets. I like to listen and observe. Assess things, design a game plan, anticipate reactions to my actions, and so on. A friend at the FBI in Quantico suggested the path I should take to becoming a Fed. The courses were fascinating and I really got into it. I also pursued a minor in accounting at their recommendation; that would help with going after white-collar crime. But with the suddenness of a guillotine my dream was dumped in a bucket. It had turned out that my uncorrected vision wasn't good enough to get me into the FBI or Treasury and I was devastated. Contact lenses may have given me 20/20 but that didn't matter. This was all years before they developed corrective laser surgery. I may have moped around a bit but I got to abandon the accounting minor and thank God for that. Boring! I switched majors and pursued another passion, journalism. I've always had an investigative curiosity, something that drives some of my family crazy to this day. I don't miss a detail, remember more than I should, and have a keen sense about people. That particularly endeared me to my two daughters much later in life as I got to screen, I mean meet, a few of the boys they were dating.

I figured if I couldn't put a bad guy in jail with a badge then perhaps I would use my talents to go after them in another way. I had paid attention as the Nixon nightmare unfolded and watched the Watergate hearings on TV throughout the summer of '73. I was impressed with the investigative, never-give-up attitude of Woodward and Bernstein and thought that might be for me. However, two things happened at Penn State. First, I partied more than studied. We turned the off-campus condo into party central. We'd do things like place a large bowl on a table inside the front door and to gain entry you had to pay the toll. Pills of all sorts, bags of what is now legal in many states, and loose change would fill the damn thing pretty quickly. It would always seem that half the house would be wired and the other half would be extremely mellow but there was never a dull moment. For me, I learned quickly that one of my inner demons would be excess. It's part of my personality. Remember the potato chip commercial, "bet you can't eat just one?" In years to come that trait would be an asset to any employer but a troublesome one for me. I would take everything to excess. Chasing sales contests, going after the Goliaths, drinking, connecting with the ladies, whatever and wherever. Second notable thing from my Penn State experience was that I dated a nurse and that could have killed me, well almost. There was an interesting business in town and they wanted your blood! Actually, they just wanted your plasma. Twice a week my roommates and I would head down and bleed. A nurse would check your vitals, including your protein level, and give you the go ahead to participate. Back in the late '70s they'd pay you something like $6 for the first pint and $9 when you came back later in the week to give the second. Simply, they'd take out a pint, separate the RBC (red blood cells) from the plasma, and then put them back into the donor. It was beer money for the weekend and you could study while lying there if you were so inclined. Most of us just flirted with the nurses.

We'd have loaded up on free peanuts at a bar the night before going. The protein levels needed to be high to participate. So what's the issue with dating a nurse? Well this one lovely thought she was doing me a favor and allowed me to participate while I was running a pretty good fever. Between that and the partying I got sicker than sick. Before long, taking my behavior and my grades into account, I left Penn State and focused on my motorsports photography, plying whatever I had learned studying journalism by writing feature stories, and finding a full time job. I never really liked the classroom anyway. Since I was already selling my work I figured, "who needed school?"

Eventually I was able to put my journalism and writing skills really to work and produced race coverage, feature stories, and a monthly column titled "Afterthought." To date, some of my most memorable excursions were to Sanair International, the dragstrip, about a fifty-five minute drive to the east from Montreal.

I had spent many summers in Quebec visiting my aunt, a cloistered nun, and was very familiar with the French-Canadian environment. Race fans north of the border are some of the most enthusiastic on the planet and flock to the tracks to be part of it all. In addition, many of the region's most beautiful women showed up in thongs. There must be something in the poutine up there! Aside from the skin show and the high octane Molson Brador, what sticks in my memory banks the most was Don Garlits. There he was sitting with us in the grandstands, enjoying a plum. He was amazed that the track vendors sold fresh fruit while back in the U.S. we were usually offered artery-cloggers like churros and French fries. It wasn't all fun and games though. One thing that occurred that weekend was unsettling and I still remember it like it happened yesterday.

I had already seen the ultimate price so many young men had paid in Vietnam. My cousin Stephen, serving as a medevac helicopter pilot, was killed in action during that damn war. His viewing, held at our funeral home, and burial wasn't the first or sadly the last we would be involved in as a result of the nightmare that was Vietnam but it most certainly was the toughest. My Aunt Jane, Stephen's mom, stayed with us in the residence above the funeral home. Just five months before that, Stephen and Jane and the rest of the family had been there to bury her husband Charlie, Stephen's dad. I was a junior in high school back then in 1972 and had learned to hold in the emotions and be as helpful and compassionate as possible for the people the business brought to our door. But that was a numbing week that finally ended as I watched my dad, Stephen's godfather, say goodbye graveside at West Point. Then, and in years to come, participating in the funerals of America's military veterans killed in action or at rest after a long life, was always a moving experience. Whether they were buried at a local cemetery, West Point, or Arlington National Cemetery, it was a privilege to have participated in honoring them.

A few years later, back at Sanair, I watched as Vietnam came back to haunt one of our friends who had fought in the war. As we stood near the finish line at the quarter mile mark, just as one of the nitro funny cars made it past us, the engine exploded in a very loud, fiery display. There were two distinctive sounds at big time drag races that spectators had to experience. One was the big vibration and roar of a race engine that was fueled with nitro as it launched from a standing start. If you have never been to a race and felt this firsthand you have to consider it a bucket list item. The other sound that nobody really wanted to hear was the concussive blast let loose when one of those 2,000 horsepower race engines suffered a catastrophic failure at 275 miles per hour. Engine parts of all shapes and sizes would fly from the race car and land pretty much wherever they wanted. In the stands, inside the driver's seat of an open pickup truck window, wherever. When the engines erupt they go off like a bomb and that's exactly what our Vietnam vet reacted to. We were all saying "wow" and looking around to see if anyone got hit and there was our friend, lying on the ground. Just as quickly as he'd dropped he jumped up, back on his feet. He was clearly shaken by what had happened and embarrassed by the look he got from the Canadian fans standing nearby. That was a sobering moment for those of us who had never experienced what he and so many others had. As fast as the incident occurred he put it behind him and went back to admiring the many thongs and race cars. It was the first time I had witnessed what's now called PTSD. It was unbelievable.

Now, in present time, those engines rarely let go but when they do there are a number of safety devices required by the NHRA and other sanctioning bodies to keep damage, oil leaks, and the shrapnel, to a minimum. I pray that all of our servicemen and women, regardless of where or when they served, always get the support and attention they need to help cope with what they've been through. Their service and sacrifices, and those of their families, should never be forgotten or taken for granted. That of course goes for our friends in law enforcement and fire and rescue as well.

CHAPTER TWO

MEANWHILE IN TEXAS

WHILE I WAS finding *my* way, Steve Burns was pursuing his passion down south. He grew up in San Antonio and his father had served in the U.S. Army, a veteran who came ashore at Utah Beach in Normandy during World War II. It was a patriotic household and that continues to pulse through "ASB" as we call him still today. Steve had done some drag racing in Texas but wasn't satisfied with the race gas products that were on the market there. If you knew Steve you'd know his natural curiosity won out and when his parents took him to Washington D.C. for an annual vacation his father mentioned that anything and everything you might want to learn about is within the building they were driving by. It was the Library of Congress and Steve immersed himself in what he found there. This of course was long before the Internet and Google searches and I suggest that he didn't keep going back just for the research. I knew damn well there had to be at least one particularly helpful attractive young librarian there and his boyish grin confirmed it the last time we spoke about those early days in D.C. Steve read everything he could get his hands on and his father may have helped point him in a specific direction. During World War II, there was a huge need for fuel development in Europe, particularly in Germany. The scientists in that country needed to get the highest octane out of the fuels they put in their military aircraft. They also needed to generate fuel products from any and every source available to them. When you're fighting a war with motorcycles, autos, trucks, tanks, aircraft, submarines, destroyers and everything motorized in between you need reliable fuels that you can source and that will perform. He learned what he could and went back to Texas in search of chemical supply. He'd knock on every door, visit every refinery, pester the foreman, and eventually get the small amount of chemicals he needed to make a batch of race fuel. For those of us lucky enough to have been to Steve's earliest "facilities" you'd see he'd have collected what he needed in used drums with Saudi writing on them. He'd clean them up, label them, make the fuel, and sell a drum to a buddy. Before long, he had a local dealer network. A buddy would buy six drums at a dealer price and the profits he'd make selling five would pay for his own fuel and then some. The products would outperform what was available and Steve was on the move. This got the first VP products into some drag cars but Steve had a good friend, Kent Howerton, who was a champion MX motocross rider. Before long he had a partner and more importantly, an advocate for VP in not just motocross bikes but in road race bikes. Amateur and professional riders, and their engine tuners, began to take notice. The fuels made more horsepower and torque, ran cooler and cleaner, and in a two-stroke (two cycle) motorcycle the products created a much crisper throttle response. Anyone in racing reading this knows these are the things you look for. For the non-racer, consider that a race engine is much like an athlete's body. The better the fuel you feed it, the better care you take of it, the better it will perform but that comes with a price. VP needed to charge more than the other brands not because they could but because they needed to. Things weren't cheap but business was really starting to take off.

If you think back to the opening paragraph you'll be reminded of the atmosphere that existed in Elmendorf, Texas back then, truly "back in the day." Steve's company, VP, was pretty much a one-man band and he was traveling the country getting his handmade products into as many race engines as possible. Steve would get a one-way rental truck. He'd load it up with drums of fuel and head for a racetrack, headed for Bakersfield, Indy or Gainesville, wherever the big car counts and best of the best using race gas were racing. The more he sold, the bigger the truck and eventual trailer rental. He'd talk with every racer and engine builder who would give him a minute and those minutes turned to hours. It was at one of those tracks that Bobby Thompson and Fred Morrison met Steve. By the end of the weekend, the truck would be empty, Steve's pockets filled with much needed cash, written orders for more, and very importantly, appointments made with the engine builders.

When BT used this Texan's fuel he made more power and went faster. Thanks to the formulations, using the best chemicals available, just like in the bikes, VP fuels burned cleaner, ran cooler, and flat out made more power. BT and Fred soon became dealers for Steve, and were very much hands on in everything from wrestling with the big blue drums to convincing local racers to try the new stuff. Thanks to their efforts and hundreds of others across the country, VP kept growing and growing. Steve liked what he saw in Fred and offered him a job in Texas. It took little time for him to accept and then it was *adios, amigos*. I wasn't doing anything special at the time, so I went along with him on the trip. A small suitcase, two cameras, a ton of film, and a portable typewriter aboard that was all I needed.

We passed the Sunoco refinery just south of Philadelphia in Marcus Hook right at the start and drove the 1,776 miles nearly non-stop to arrive at the site of the original VP "facility". I'm into numbers and I found it funny that this American success story, the young Texan taking on the competition including Sunoco, the big brand from the birthplace of our nation, had a somewhat patriotic touch to it. Some of the Texans I know think it's a separate country, or should be. There's an attitude, a bravado, that emanates from many of the heroes that came from the Lone Star State and I get it but the rest of the U.S. has plenty of heroes too. Dating back to the writing of the Declaration of Independence and the Constitution at Independence Hall and the fighting out the Revolutionary War when the original 13 colonies took on the massive British Army and Navy.

The drive to San Antonio took place in January and the weather alone made me wonder why anyone lived up north. The "warehouse" was nothing more than a small garage in a little racer community of garages much like what we had left behind in PA. One of the other businesses operating there was Lozano Brothers Porting & Race Engines. They were just getting started out too but in time would go on to be a part of big wins in the Indy 500, IMSA, Trans Am, Sebring, CanAm and the AHDRA.

A few days later, we loaded drums into the back of VP's only pickup truck and headed non-stop across I-10 west to Pomona, California. The NHRA Winternationals, the first race of the season, where in a few days one of VP's biggest customers—Pro Stock drag racer Warren Johnson—was waiting for his fuel. We drove all day and all night. The moon was so bright out in the New Mexican desert that we shut off the headlights and drove without them for a while just so we could see the blanket of stars that surrounded us on all horizons. Okay, better to keep the lights on though. They helped light up the deer or antelope or whatever the hell we almost ran into.

We got to Pomona safe and sound and made our delivery. It was the first time I learned how to lay down a 350-pound drum of flammable liquid in the back of a pickup, drop it onto an old tire, and pop it upright. Pretty cool. At the time, I had no idea how many times I'd wind up doing that over the next four decades. WJ was happy, Fred went off to work the pits, and my cameras, one with color film and the other with black and white, were ready to capture some action. The only problem was it snowed. Yep, in January 1978 it snowed in Los Angeles, California. The race was rescheduled for the following weekend, and I couldn't stay for it. I was very disappointed I didn't get many pictures and that I would miss my first West Coast race but was happy to be out of the $19.99 economy hotel room we had shared near the track. I had been accustomed to at least Holiday Inns on my trips to Canada. That night I was on my red-eye flight home to Philly to continue my freelance writing and photography career and hope for a full time gig in racing.

I'm supposed to be pretty creative and my cover photo of Slammin' Sammy Miller's rocket car staged on the grounds at Cape Kennedy in Florida was something I am still very proud of. The folks at the Cape couldn't have been more cooperative and even supplied us with a staffer dressed up in an astronaut suit like they wear on spacewalks. It was really cool. The shoot with Pat Musi, where we hired a bikini model to stand alongside Pat's Monza Pro Stocker in frigid cold until I got what I needed, was a trip. I took some shop photos first and then took the car to a public park. We knew the police would be along at some point to chase us away so we moved quickly and before long the hit and run was done. Pat's still one of the most interesting and entertaining guys from Jersey I've ever known.

The Bruce Larson shoot that took place just up the river from the infamous Three Mile Island near Harrisburg, Pennsylvania. In addition to winning the NHRA Funny Car Championship and dozens of their national events, Bruce is in just about every drag racing hall of fame there is. The vibrant white color of his USA-1 funny car contrasted perfectly against the dark and dreary clouds and surroundings where we captured the moment. The interview I did with TV Tommy Ivo, the famous drag racer who started out in show business as a Mickey Mouse Club Mouseketeer, were also a lot of fun. Heck, Britney Spears, Justin Timberlake, and Christina Aguilera wore the big ears too at one point in their careers. I also wrote a feature story on sportsman racer George Cureton and his "Tokyo Rose" drag car. All those appeared in *Super Stock* but I also did work for other magazines. A feature, with photos on our own Bobby Thompson, appeared in *Car Craft*. Soon after, *Hot Rod Magazine* dispatched me to the Jersey Shore to photograph a very special four-wheel drive car. It was a Corvette and it was wild! I loved what I was doing but freelance money wasn't enough and I needed a full time job. I drove down to Alexandria, Virginia for an interview with Dick Berggren. He was the editor of *Stock Car Racing Magazine* and my hope was that I could work for *SCR* and *Super Stock*, sister magazines, full time. As luck would have it, Dick was a no-show. He raced midgets or something similar in New England and had crashed out that weekend. He needed to mend rather than drive down to Alexandria to meet me. The interview never happened and in hindsight, things happen for a reason. Something better would come.

A few months after that, I hit it big. I had called Charlotte Motor Speedway looking for a job and, while they said they didn't have any openings, they did say that a race team might have an opening. Days later, I flew down for an interview and got the job. I moved to Charlotte to work for the #88 Gatorade-DiGard Racing Team and driver Darrell Waltrip. They needed a PR guy and they wanted a Northerner like the car owners who were from Connecticut. It's funny now, but back then I was that "damn Yankee" to the locals. I was learning everything I could about NASCAR racing, which was commonly referred to as Winston Cup Racing before cigarette advertising bans went into effect. Learned all about sweet tea, grits, the difference between supper and dinner, and a whole bunch more. I got to work with names like DW, the late Robert Yates, Gary Nelson, Buddy Parrott, and Butch Stevens while Fred was getting to meet every big name in drag racing. VP was beginning to leave a big imprint in the racing fuel business.

It wasn't long after our respective moves to Texas and to North Carolina that one of the first VP tractor-trailers was headed northeast on a delivery run with Fred and Steve driving as a team. They rolled into the parking lot at the #88 race shop at 9201 Garrison Road. After a brief tour, they were exchanging samples of race fuel for our dyno room with cases of Union 76 oils and lubricants. 76 was NASCAR's fuel and lubricant company back then and if you ran the circuit, you had to fuel with Union 76. It wasn't that big of a deal for the racers at that point. The fuel and lubricants were given to all the teams for free in return for running the familiar red ball Union 76 decals on the front fenders of each race car and affixing an embroidered Union 76 patch on the driver's fire-resistant suit. At Daytona, Union 76 had constructed two large red balls to resemble their logo, each probably eight feet tall, that served as viewing towers for safety officials. It was pretty creative marketing back in the day. Years later, I was so happy to see those same big red balls lying on the ground, weeds growing around and into them, behind a NASCAR building a few blocks from the speedway.

"You guys only make drag racing fuels, what the heck do you know about oval track racing?" was the question Steve and Fred often got from the engine builders and teams who knew how to race in circles. It was much of the same from automotive road racers. "Never heard of you. All we know is CAM2," came from drag racers coast to coast. CAM2 was a product made by Sunoco and it was the only race gas with any real domestic market share north of the Mason Dixon, at least for now.

Years before that VP truck rolled into their yard, DiGard owner Bill Gardner had been smart enough to listen to his crew chief when he told them he knew a race engine builder who could make a big difference. Before long, they were working with The Grump. One of the fastest racers in the U.S., Bill "Grumpy" Jenkins was contracted to help make their NASCAR stock car entries go faster. Jenkins was a legend in NHRA drag racing and people paid attention to what he did. The short answer from Jenkins after he got to work on the car was simple. "Donnie Allison won the pole at the 1975 Daytona 500 with my stuff." Jenkins was from Malvern, Pennsylvania, perhaps a thirty-minute ride from the Liberty Bell in Philadelphia.

Jenkins knew how to make power and figured out differences between drag racing and circle track. He realized the few things that needed to be addressed for a race engine that was traveling 200mph for three hours on 30 degree banking at tracks like Daytona and Talladega, compared to one that needed to launch from a standing start on a hopefully tacky drag race surface, travel a quarter mile in less than eight seconds, and reach a speed of 200mph. The fact that Jenkins had studied mechanical engineering at Cornell helped too. When Jenkins got to meet Steve Burns the two made quite the combination. Jenkins was short and "grumpy", while Burns was tall and charismatic. They would learn together, with Jenkins able to improve his engine performance and Steve developing his fuels. For someone unfamiliar with racing perhaps you could envision Bill Gates and Steve Jobs working together day and night at a workbench in a garage developing something new and exciting.

Burns would spend days on end in Malvern with

Jenkins. He'd have big drums and little pails of chemicals in a horse trailer that he'd be towing across the country going from engine shop to engine shop. He'd make up a concoction, an educated one, and Jenkins would do a series of dynamometer pulls to measure power output on one of his high-end race engines. Jenkins pushed Burns as hard as anyone could. Steve would think he had done well but Jenkins would counter with, "You can do better." He pushed and pushed for more. By the time Burns packed up and headed for his next stop, Jenkins had something special for his racing team and Burns had crammed everything new he learned about engines and fuel into his memory banks.

Jenkins would rely on VP to help win races and championships, while Burns would be able to name-drop when he was pitching his fuel to amateur and professional racers at the track and at their shops. "Grumpy knows we make more power. You can too." It made sense. Racers would follow the fast guys and things started to catch on. In Texas, Burns had relied heavily on his friends David Reher and Buddy Morrison of Reher & Morrison Racing Engines in Arlington. They had known each other for years and together also developed very powerful fuels and race winning engines. But it was a big country with so many dynos to play on so that horse trailer logged one hell of a lot of miles. At every stop Burns would try to learn more and more about chemicals and the diverse range of racing engines they'd be fueling. Considering he was self-taught in chemistry, what he did back then and over all these years is really impressive.

Acceptance and sales growth on the oval track side was slow but progressing. Racers are finicky and sometimes superstitious. I actually encountered a few who wouldn't use one of VP's products because it was green. Green anywhere other than as the color of the go-go-go flag, or the money you'd win, was supposed to be bad luck. Here's something you should know before going any further. For the most part, all race fuels are clear in color when they are blended. Petroleum dye colors are added to identify and differentiate each product. It's pretty easy to do. A ten thousand gallon batch of fuel might only need a cupful of dye to bring it to spec. So what's the big deal about color? Remember the Union 76 race fuel for NASCAR? It was dyed a distinctive orange-red. Once the DiGard engine builders got to see how much power VP made over Union 76, the next question was, how do we make it look the same and then how do we get it in the car for a race without getting caught? It was simple. Dye it! Back in grade school did you ever wonder, "Why the heck do I need to know this?" Well, knowing how colors mixed to yield another, and which ones wouldn't, definitely came in handy later in life. Making fuels *look* alike to the naked eye was pretty easy.

Now they had to get it in the car. Back then that was relatively simple. Just play a shell game with the fuel dispensing cans used during pit stops. The race cars fly down pit road, screech to a stop, tires are changed, fuel is "dumped" into the fuel cell and off the car goes back into the race. During pre-race pit set-up, dump cans already filled with VP would be staged in the pits. Nobody would notice what was going on. Within no time, VP was being blended in with Union 76 during race events and those cars were making a lot more power. "Makin' Power" would eventually become VP's slogan. Making more power than everyone else, both on the dyno and in race conditions at the tracks, drove its success. That and the passionate, dedicated people that worked there.

We can take that part of the story full circle pretty quickly though. It wasn't long before more and more race teams heard VP was good stuff. Many didn't want to let anyone know, including VP, they were "cheating" with it. They'd buy fuel locally, dyno with it, develop their own concoctions and mixtures to try to get the color as close as possible and pour it in. In some cases, perhaps outside of NASCAR, some racers ran a second fuel tank that contained the "good stuff." Some ran a second fuel line. Some filled their fuel lines from the cell to the engine with VP and topped off the tank with what they were supposed to be running. They figured the VP would be long gone by the time a tech inspector pulled a sample after they came in off the track. I'll never forget hearing about the poor team that didn't even try to blend their VP in with Union 76 to get at least close to the legal color. They wanted the pole position and rolled the dice, opting to run VP straight. At the post-qualifying technical inspection a fuel sample was taken, as was the tech inspector's discretion. *Oops* – wrong color. That episode, especially fueled by Union 76's protests, resulted in all sorts of pre and post qualifying and race fuel checks for proper color. In time, a portable gas-chromatograph (G.C.) machine was installed in NASCAR's technical inspection trailer. It was a test that told the operator pretty quickly if the sample was pure Union 76 or not. Simply, when chemicals are identified in a sample they appear on a graph much like a seismograph during an earthquake or a polygraph lie detector test. The Union 76 should have the same peaks and valleys, in the same spots, every time. Throw some cheater additive in the fuel and it will change the spikes and most probably identify the name of the chemical that was added. It's tough to make your fuel look exactly like the other guys when a GC is in place. Color was easy but this shut down our playing in their NASCAR sandbox pretty quickly. It was okay for VP though. Overall, sales were really starting to boom so losing those drum sales was a disappointment, but wasn't too painful.

Spec fuel – now that sounds interesting. That's short for specified or in reality, mandated fuel. It's where race fuel companies "bid" on obtaining exclusive sales and use rights to a track or a race series and that concept will be a very big part of our David versus Goliaths saga as the story evolves. At the end of the day though, it's an easy way that a track or a series can make more money that some would pocket or use for track improvements or championship point fund payouts.

While I was in Charlotte and working the NASCAR circuit I got to interact with all my heroes; the King, Richard Petty, Bobby Allison, A.J. Foyt, a rookie named Dale Earnhardt, and so many more. Tons of people have gotten to speak with Richard so my brief moments with him aren't anything remarkable to others but he is a true American legend and each time I did was a thrill.

Thanks to a great driver and great team, I got to stand in the Victory Lanes, also known as Winner's Circles or Podiums, of most of the top tracks on the circuit. It was a very exciting time in my life and a great time to be with NASCAR, just as it began to explode in national popularity. I also got to work with some very good people and some very colorful characters. Series Champion-turned broadcaster Ned Jarrett, CBS-TV's Ken Squier, and Union 76's Bill Broderick to name a few. Broderick was the self-appointed director of victory lane activities. Actually, nobody else wanted to do it. He'd flip one branded hat for another again and again for the cameras, but always made sure his company's Union 76 logo was in every shot. It was THE hat the winner wore first, then the series sponsor, the car sponsor, then Goodyear tire, and so on. Physically, Broderick was a big man and the fact that he was the front man for Union 76, one of the biggest sponsors NASCAR had at the time, fed his ego pretty well. Regardless of what hat the race winner was wearing, you could count on Bill, his shirt prominently displaying the Union 76 logos, to be right alongside the driver. I'd struggle to get the Gatorade hat back on DW as much as my bosses and our sponsor would have liked me to. Hey, try keeping a Gatorade hat on a race-winning driver who's being interviewed on live TV when the race sponsor is Pepsi-Cola. Frisbees, that's what I turned those damned Pepsi hats into, and in turn, the soda guy repaid the favor. It was "fun."

For the DiGard crewmembers though, most of whom were locals born and raised in North or South Carolina, I was still a "Yankee." This is back in 1978, long before Douglas Airport and the city of Charlotte grew to what they are today. The Charlotte I moved to was small. Heck, they had to roll a stairway up to the jet to let us off. Anyway, I did what I could to convince the crew that I was just like them, only from the north. One night during the cup race at Nashville Speedway, Waltrip blew an engine. It seemed like Buddy Parrott and Gary Nelson made the decision in less than a minute that they should change the engine. Buddy was the crew chief and Gary was the engineer, if I remember the title correctly. Gary had moved to Charlotte from the West Coast. He'd done a lot of racing with off-road ace Ivan Baldwin and brought a lot of "outside oval track racing" knowledge to the team. There was nothing in the rulebook against changing engines, so let's have at it. Everyone was under the car or under the hood disconnecting things and it was obvious they'd deal with the new engine when they could get to it. I asked a simple question; "Where do you want the new one?"

For the most part the crew thought all I knew about was getting the driver and the sponsor on TV and in magazines and dealing with the press, but I knew a bit about engines and certainly how to assemble an engine hoist. That was easy. I had done it at drag races and at Bobby Thompson's shop, so no biggie. I found the compartment where the hoist was kept; they showed me which engine they wanted, and *voilà*. When they were ready for it, I had the new piece sitting right where they directed. I slid the hoist under the car when Buddy waved me in. I got some cred that night. From then on, I was okay with them and the "Yankee" references seemed to fade. I continued to bust on them about why they seemed confused about which meal was served as "dinner" and "supper" but as long as there was food it didn't matter to me.

As is always the case, boys will be boys and one time at Dover they sure were. I had picked up the Sunday crew just north of the track at Summit Airport and got them to the garage area just fine. I don't remember how DW did in the race but it had been a long hot day and by the time everyone had climbed back into the big passenger van I had rented, everyone had just about enough of that Gatorade. I stopped and got them a few six packs of beer and continued in the slow moving post-race traffic up Route 13 toward Summit. It wasn't long before one guy then another and then another requested a pit stop. There just wasn't anywhere along that stretch and finally a crewman said, "You have ten seconds and then it's going out the window." Just imagine a family headed to Grandma's house for Sunday dinner, creeping along at 5mph thanks to the race traffic letting out, and you see about ten men wearing Gatorade 88 Racing Team uniforms, their backs to the traffic, standing in a row pissing on the side of the road. Thank God that day was long ago and far before social media and cell phones videos had evolved. It was a funny sight but as their PR guy I was more afraid something negative would come of it. Luckily, nothing ever did.

When I was growing up I learned you needed to show appreciation for people, especially employees, and I came across an interesting exchange late one Sunday afternoon. After winning the Cup race at Richmond, Virginia the team members all climbed into another rental van for the five-hour ride down I-95/85 to their cars parked at the DiGard shop on Garrison Road near the Charlotte airport. I can't remember who drove on up on their own or rode with us but I had an idea. As we were fueling up the ride I called one of the Gardner brothers, congratulated them on the win, and asked if I could put the dinner bill for the team on my company credit card. "Why would you want to do that?" surprised the hell out of me. We had just won a big race and had a five-hour ride ahead of us. Every member of the team had worked their butts off and all I was asking that the company pick up their $10 dinner. It wasn't like I was driving around looking for a Ruth Chris. It was more like a Cracker Barrel night if you have the feel for the long highway drives across Virginia and North Carolina.

We actually debated the issue for a while but by the time the guys had hit the head and had settled the fuel bill we were on our way. I announced that DiGard was picking up the tab for their dinner whenever they wanted to stop. The news went over pretty well and I didn't let on that I had to beg to get it done. We all enjoyed the meal and got home late but well fed.

Darrell and I got along well. He was this impressive, personable, self-confident young man maybe eight years older than me. He was from just outside of Nashville and could drive the wheels off of a race car. He was going places and I was very happy to be supporting him and the team. He had a wife, Stevie, and she had a big heart and a sweet smile. Back then, DiGard wanted me to get the Gatorade name in front of as many media people and general consumers as possible. "DW," on the other side, might have wanted me to be sure his name was on everything I touched, and hoped I was looking for endorsement deals. This guy was an athlete and he knew this was the direction a driver could and should go. I might have been in awe of not just our driver but also the stars I got to interact with, but I got over that pretty quickly and fit in as best I could. I thought I was doing okay until this one pit stop made me think I was a goner.

They told me to place two paper Gatorade cups in the cup holder that sat at the far end of a six-foot long aluminum pole. One cup had Gatorade and the other water.

"When the car stops just slide the cups through the opening between the windshield post and the safety net. He'll take what he wants and then pull it back." Sounded easy. Let's go.

It was hot as hell that day, wherever that race was, and the 88 came flying down pit road and screeched to a stop right in front of me. Butch and the front and rear tire guys jumped the wall to change the left side (driver's side) tires and I stretched to get the drinks over to Darrell. Almost there, almost there, oops! The jack man hit the pole, or I hit the jack man, and both drinks wound up in our driver's lap. You could just see the seething anger in his face as he mouthed something special at me. The car dropped and he sped off to finish the race. The guys in the pits all patted me on the back and laughed. They didn't think much of it and probably got a kick out of giving DW a cold splash. Once the race ended and I was there in the garage to help Darrell out of the car I handed him a towel, a bottle of Gatorade, and his hat. He patted me on the shoulder and laughed about the bath I'd given him.

Up north, my parents both began to deal with what would become their long and painful battles that would take them way too soon. I had married in the winter off-season and moved my wife and her belongings from Philly to Charlotte. She'd never been away from her family and missed them terribly. My being on the road so much made matters much worse. She'd go to some of the races but sitting on a pit box in the heat for 400 laps grew old pretty quickly. On one particular afternoon at Atlanta, she got to witness an accident on pit road that took a crewman's life and that put an end to her trips to the races. As seems to be the case with any racing tragedy, rules were *then* changed to slow the speed of the cars while on pit road. As an aside, I remember a race day morning once when I spent a few minutes with Neil Bonnett. He was a great guy and it was really sad when he was killed in a racing accident at Daytona. It wasn't until years later when Dale Earnhardt – that's Dale Sr. – died on national television at the same track as a result of the same type of injury that everyone stepped up and developed new safety gear and mandated its use in NASCAR and everywhere it made sense. It's like the armor turrets that now are standard issue on the military Humvees that are sent into harm's way. Those poor guys, the very vulnerable ones operating the incredibly powerful .50 caliber machine guns. They were exposed from the waist up as they stood through the hole in the Humvee's roof, easy targets for enemy snipers and IED explosions. I don't know how many of our brave warriors were wounded or killed as they served from that very vulnerable position, but thank God a light bulb finally went off somewhere and they got the money and the design to better protect our servicemen and women. I'm not accusing anyone of anything. Just encouraging people to anticipate what could happen and defend against it beforehand, think of the unimaginable and then imagine a fix.

At the DiGard shop, tensions between the team owners and Waltrip began to simmer. DW wanted out of his contract. He had been happy to secure the ride in the #88 car but over time felt he should be making more money and have more control over his future. The infighting was something I wasn't accustomed to being around, and if you picked sides with the driver or the car owner you were going to become collateral damage regardless. The day I saw Bobby and Judy Allison walk into the shop for a meeting with Jim Gardner I knew things were going to change. When I added everything up though, my parent's health, my wife's homesickness, and the uncertainty at work, before long, I resigned and moved back to Philly to make the new bride happy again and to help my parents. Now they needed help with the business, and between my sister and me we did whatever was needed.

I usually go with what seems to be the right thing to do so despite my disinterest in the family business I committed to becoming a funeral director. I rode the train each day from Philly to New York and back to study at the McAllister Institute in Manhattan where after a year I earned my Associates degree. During final exam week my mother fell into a coma. She had wanted to be home and so that's where we all took turns staying with her night and day. Within a few nights she didn't have to suffer anymore and went on to heaven. Months later I passed the national exams held in Cincinnati, got my state license so I could fully function in the funeral service in Pennsylvania, and continued to support my father any way I could.

Saying goodbye to a full time gig like I had in Charlotte stunk but it clearly was the right thing to do for my family. Traveling, dealing with the media, making sure all the race teams on pit road had lots of Gatorade, and slapping a hat on the race winner in Victory Lane at Daytona, Riverside, Darlington, and many other tracks had been awesome. Hanging out with the millionaires who owned the race team, and their friends and contacts, had some benefits too. "Keep quiet and your ears open and you will learn a lot." So I did. To this day, I prefer to listen and soak in every bit of intel or knowledge that I can, formulate a plan of action, and then execute. It's a continuation of how I looked at things and operated when I wanted to be in law enforcement and then in journalism. Just because the mouth's shut it doesn't mean the other senses aren't fully engaged. Plus for anyone involved in selling, that is one of the biggest lessons: listen. A lot of the time the customer will come right out and say, directly or otherwise, what they want or need to make the deal happen. If you aren't listening then you might miss it. Now back in suburban Philly, it was a sad time for me, both personally and professionally, and I thought my days at the races were gone forever.

CHAPTER THREE

TURNING POINT

AT VP, FRED and Steve had a falling out and he also moved back to Pennsylvania. These things happen. The guys eventually kissed and made up and since it made perfect sense to have a satellite office in the Northeast, why not do it where Fred grew up. They rented warehouse space along the Delaware River in the city of Chester and set up shop. Within five minutes of the location was I-95 and that provided connections to anywhere we'd need to go. It was a great location and looking ahead to the future, far into the future, it had rail. Delaware County had an Economic Redevelopment Authority and they did just about anything they could to entice businesses to come to Chester to help it grow. I think the rent for three acres of land was maybe $500 per month back then. When I had the free time Fred would pay me to unload drums from the supply trucks coming in from Texas. At the time I had no idea I'd wind up wrestling with those big blue babies for nearly forty years.

While VP was evolving so was I. The wife was back

where she wanted to be, very close to her family, and we had a newborn at home. David was awesome and other than colic, and the extreme shell shock every set of new parents experiences, his coming was a very special time in my life. My first-born. I remember sitting at the kitchen table holding this little bundle and feeding him his morning bottle. Those moments were so special. It was on one of those days that I mentioned earlier, the day I had to carry a dead baby and help his family say goodbye to him, that really impacted my heart and mind. That night I held David close and couldn't conceive of how painful that mother's loss had to be. That was the last straw and no matter what, I wanted out of that business.

I've always liked to help people and felt I was doing good by comforting and consoling them at their time of need, and helping to guide them through the arrangements, services, and final goodbyes, but enough was enough. I needed to get away from the sounds of people crying and the smell of funeral flowers. I wanted to get back to the sound of race engines and the smell of race gas and nitro. I hoped to return to motorsports. It wasn't long afterward that cancer finally claimed my father too. I think his broken heart did him in more than the damn cancer that ravaged him. With both parents now gone from our lives and from the business they had started from scratch, and with the neighborhood in decline, the decision was made to sell the funeral business to a competitor and move forward. I wouldn't miss any part of the funeral service but it was sad to say goodbye to the home I grew up in. But all things change, that's life, and we all have to move on. For me, the luck I had from the start and everything I had done up to this point would soon align with opportunity. I started looking for a better job and told Fred what I was trying to do. Despite the huge number of tracks and racers in the region, there wasn't anything of the same caliber as what I had been doing in Charlotte. Remember what I wrote about timing being everything? Business at VP was booming and Steve needed Fred's help in Texas. He talked him into moving back to their new location in Elmendorf and this is where everything came together.

As I began my career at VP, as far away from the funeral business as I could get, I really started to come alive. I was back in racing and operating with the freedom and the challenge that seemed to fit me to the core. Life is way too short to not live it to the fullest, to live it the way you want to, and there are two young men whose deaths really reinforced that point. Tommy Sewell was a great guy. He worked as a police officer for SEPTA, Southeastern Pennsylvania's transportation authority. He had married Glen Side's sister Jeannie and to make a few extra bucks he donned a suit and tie quite a few times to help me at the funeral home with the stretcher runs, removals as they were called, or driving a limo. He had a great sense of humor, a laugh I can't forget, and quite often made the funeral work easier. Sadly, very sadly, Tommy was stabbed and killed while on patrol but he was able to shoot and kill the bastard that got him. Then, another friend, a young man named Billy, was killed in a car accident. I had met him years before at the funeral home. His father had died of brain cancer and my father had handled the arrangements. To help their family my dad hired Billy to do some work around the place and put some money in his pocket. Billy was a great kid and he liked to go to the kart races with me in Maryland a couple Sundays each month. Karting was a blast and an inexpensive way to go racing. The only frustration for Billy was he was a big boy and couldn't fit the ride, but it was really cool to celebrate with him the day I won my first race. He was working for the funeral home, chauffeuring the priest to the cemetery for final prayers, when the accident happened. Losing Tommy and Billy, especially in such a short period of time, reinforced for me that life is what happens while you're making other plans and that you never know when God is going to call you home. I was determined to make the most of the time I had here.

Years later, listening to the employee retell his "shooting at stray dogs" story confirmed the kind of ride I was in for when I got involved with VP. It would an adventure, not a job. Forty years of dealing with drums and twenty-eight years on the payroll would teach me things and take me to places I had never imagined. Yes, there would be sex, drugs, rock and roll, fire, and an occasional gun. Combine that with the excitement of the sights, sounds, smells, speed, and competitiveness of motorsports and winning.

Eventually I'd be working within all forms of racing from the motocross novice on his first mx bike in New Jersey to some very big names in Formula 1 racing. I'd be back in the action. Being ever so close to what Jim McKay would describe every week on ABC's Wide World of Sports as "the thrill of victory and the agony of defeat." If that was before your time, look that quote up on YouTube and you'll understand. I was now part of the team and we were all hungry. We wanted to win whatever we were involved in. There was a ton of racing fuel being consumed and we wanted more than our fair share of it. Sales would be what fed our kids and financed our fun so it was serious business. I have to admit the motivation was also the excitement of the challenge and the environment that really drove me. VP was just starting to get going and now I would be a part of it. Little did I know at the time that this opportunity would be the greatest ride of my life. I was now back in motorsports and tasked with going after the much larger, well-established competition in my region. In the history of VP's very successful climb and its many challenges and challengers, the wannabes would come and go. While we were trying to take over the world, they'd be nipping at us from behind. Quite often they'd employ the only option or advantage available to them; they'd low-ball their prices to steal market share in an attempt to get a foot in the lucrative door. There was one particularly entertaining entrepreneur, a real wannabe, who wound up being sentenced to serve 14 years in a federal prison for tax fraud. According to news articles covering the case, the government charged that his company filed documents that reported their sale of very large quantities of tax-exempt fuel for off-road purposes. His company would then file the false records with the IRS to request refunds for fuel taxes that he had supposedly paid. The government refunded the money, up to $110 million, and he used it to sponsor race teams and acquire a private jet. The money also enabled him to sell race fuel at below market prices because profits didn't matter. Now that's an example of a paper Goliath. Eventually the law caught up with him, they followed the paper trail he left, and defunded his house of cards, but it got interesting for a while. Imagine a salesman trying to convince a customer, one who perceives he's buying a commodity fuel, that he should buy VP. Why should he pay $100 more for a drum of it? Over the years the pesky wannabe race fuel companies did rock the boat a bit but we handled them. Let me shed some light on a real Goliath, a tough competitor, that's still in the fight today.

Back in the early 1980s, Sunoco was a gasoline and chemical company that from a general consumer's viewpoint simply had gas stations in the Northeast. They sponsored two of the most familiar names in racing, Mark Donohue and Roger Penske. Donohue was from NJ and Penske from Ohio. Penske Racing, which prepared the Indy car effort, was based in Reading, Pennsylvania. In 1972 they won the Indianapolis 500 and in 1973 they won the pole for that event. But Sunoco also dealt in racing gasoline. For whatever reason they branded it as CAM2. They started blending higher-octane products, with tetraethyl lead among other things, in 1956. When I was researching the company I found it funny how they featured a photo on their website of one of the early Sunoco gas stations. I believe it was located in Ardmore, Pennsylvania right down the road from Villanova University and Bryn Mawr. Behind the station the photo revealed the signage of a monument company that made burial markers for cemeteries. Coming from the funeral business I thought it tied it all together nicely. Even though I was no longer burying people I wanted to help etch a new name on a gravestone. For me, once I became part of the crusade, I dedicated myself to VP's red, white, and blue and to defeat all enemies, foreign and domestic. But I didn't realize at the time that I would have to face my own personal struggles along the way.

I took over the Regional Manager gig in Chester and Fred headed south to the Lone Star State again. This time I was smart enough, and had a good excuse, to stay home and avoid that long ride. Chester was a bit rough and not too many companies followed VP there. Driving through town to get to the new job was usually uneventful. Don't stop too close to the car stopped in front of you at a sign or a red light. Never allow yourself to get boxed in. Always leave enough room to get out of there if shots rang out or someone approached your car. Be aware of your surroundings. These days they call it situational awareness. It could be said that the lesson of *The Art of War*, the one that states you must "know your enemy," applied here. It would apply to business all day long but this time it applied to safety. Many of the row homes and businesses had fallen apart or been burned out. The graffiti, pregnant hookers, police, and fire sirens added to the city's ambience. There were also the hard working people who were trying their best, holding down multiple jobs, to feed their families. We can't forget the 'wanderers. They were just looking to take something that wasn't theirs. I remember the first time Brad Horton, my VP drinking buddy, practical joker, and Regional Manager for Texas came to the Pennsylvania office to visit. He had grown up in a small town in North Texas and his family, his upbringing, instilled a strong set of values and work ethic that made him a very tough competitor. That was good for VP but very bad for its enemies. To add to his resume, Brad had a great personality and often seemed quiet and humble. Now he's a very capable pilot and when he's not flying, selling race fuel, or pulling a prank on someone, he climbs down into caves back home to collect snakes for the rattler round up in Sweetwater each year. I don't think much scares him but his first words to me in Chester were, "I'd rather jump down into those caves with the damn snakes than have to drive through here again."

Consequently, back then it was very tough to get good help. People didn't want to *drive* through the city, let alone work there. Those we did hire quite often shared the same passion for motorsports that everyone at VP shared and that made the drive, the rough neighborhood, the average wages, and the long hours worthwhile. For me, it was the start of an incredible professional and personal journey that would eventually take me to faraway places like Moscow, Sydney, and Tokyo. My kids were happy to see me home as much as possible but when I was away they'd pull at my heart pretty good with, "Daddy, when are you coming back?" There were more than a few nights that I had tears running down my face after I said goodnight over the phone. I hoped that at some point in their futures we would discuss the road I had chosen. I wanted them to understand that whatever the hell this bug was that was in me, it was a part of me and I had to go with it. At home, David was growing and then my daughters Melissa and Kristen came along, all two years apart. They brought so much joy to my life. No matter how tough the days were, or how dirty I'd have gotten at work, there they'd be jumping all over me the minute I'd get home. I tried to be the best dad I knew how and the best husband too but not everything turns out as planned. I remember one of my friends busting on me. "Stop treating her so good. My wife keeps bitching that I should treat her the way you treat yours." That's a true story. Unfortunately, my journey, the choice I made on how and where I wanted to live my life – in motorsports – put significant strain on my marriage and it eventually ended. We had grown in different directions. Once that happened the world changed drastically for me. I'd have my set two nights with the kids and sleepovers every Friday night that I wasn't away at a race. It actually seemed at that point that I was seeing more of the kids than before. Nothing would get in the way of that if at all possible but my ex was frustrated seeing me at the house that often and suggested, "Why aren't you like the rest of the divorced dads and only see the kids every other weekend?" Screw that. I divorced her, not my three children. Once they became old enough to understand, they needed to know my leaving was not their fault. Work was busier than ever and it was tough trying to be a good, present dad and at the same time trying to make as much money as possible. I now had two mortgages to cover. Despite being on the road in hotels so much I had never cheated on my wife but in all honesty I was in love with my job. Motivated to succeed and provide for my kids, I've heard it said that you have to follow your passion, and boy did I ever. Whatever it is about racing, about motorsports and travel and the challenge of taking on the Goliaths, I wanted and needed to be in it. Just as I had in racing, I liked the pursuit. I'd rather chase down and pass everyone in karting and take the win on the last lap than lead every one of them. I found it more gratifying – it's more fun. I'd rather be a predator as Steve Burns once referred to his team. Years later, for a feature story on me in a drag racing publication, I was quoted as saying, "My biological parents must have been a traveling salesman and a flight attendant. I think I was made in the air because I am driven to travel, to roam. It's in my blood. Dating back to the '70s, my nickname was "Ramblin' Man" as sung by the Allman Brothers Band. All things considered, I was perfect for the job and it was for me."

CHAPTER FOUR
CULTURE SHOCK

THERE I WAS, finally back in blue jeans. All of my suits, dress shirts, and ties were put away and hopefully for good. I had already told the family that when my time came they were to put me in my Wranglers and stuff my passport in my pocket. On further review, they may wish to toss a fire resistant suit and some sunblock in there too since I have a sneaking suspicion I may get sent to a hot spot for a while.

There I was, happily leaving behind the beautiful black Cadillac limousines and sedans I had been around since I was a kid. I'd been caught racing around in the hearse a few times but luckily it was usually by a local cop who might even had done some removals or limo work for my father. At the funeral home, if something was broken beyond repair we'd buy a new one. If something needed fixing, our handyman would come to the rescue. At VP's little operation in Chester, things would be completely different.

The once thriving city that grew strong through its manufacturing during the First and Second World Wars had fallen far from grace. For anyone paying their respects at the U.S.S. Arizona Memorial in Hawaii, take note of the propeller they rescued from under the water. It was built in Chester. Regarded as the oldest city in Pennsylvania, sadly, it now looked it. There, inside the gates of the River Bridge Industrial Center at Front and Lloyd Streets, was my new home. The sound of relatives crying for their departed loved ones was replaced by the constant ping and pop of the steel race fuel drums contracting and expanding with the changes in temperature. The smell of funeral flowers, although pleasant, was replaced by the scent of expensive petroleum distillates. Race fuel, VP Race Fuel, would never smell sweeter.

The original setup at the facility involved a very small office space in the main building just inside the guarded gate entrance. More than a quarter mile north of the office, across the vacant stretch of concrete and asphalt, sat four, 15,000-gallon above ground fuel storage tanks. Just another thirty yards or so further away sat a small warehouse. The structure had been found resting in another abandoned facility somewhere in the area, dismantled, transported to VP-Chester, and reassembled. Drag racer Mike Cannon was a contractor by trade and had laid the concrete tank pads and retention walls. He also framed out and poured the dock that over time would see thousands and thousands of drums of high-octane race fuel roll across it.

When I arrived there was one warehouse worker, John Davis, and he was one of the hardest, old school working men I had ever met. He was sincere and had little time for bullshit but did anything and everything he was called on to do. Tony Feld, a very likable and easygoing guy, was the one and only truck driver. John and Tony worked the warehouse, dock, tanks and the one tractor-trailer while Fred put as much time into the office as he could. The guys needed help loading and unloading drums but Fred needed to be in the office making sales calls, taking orders, plotting strategies, and keeping the "books".

I used the term "books" lightly because in actuality there were about three bookkeeping items in the office. There was an order pad to record them, a black and white composition book used to record invoice numbers and track receivables, a Rolodex for contact info, and that was about it. The typewriter used to generate invoices and write correspondence was a used but workable piece of office equipment that had been salvaged from a dumpster in the complex. Things were tight in the early days. I mean *really* tight. The entire focus was to make the best fuels by blending together the best chemicals and getting them to market. Obviously any time the word "best" is used that means expensive. That's where all the profits would go – right back into making more product and growing the sales.

Over the first week I got to work with John, Tony, and Fred. I was there to learn as much as I could as fast as I could. Tankers would bring bulk chemicals. I had to learn all the safety procedures regarding static, sparks, fumes, and flame. We'd ground the rig, hook and unhook the 4" chemical grade hoses from the tanker's manifold to our tanks, and so on. A pump that would move 200 gallons of fuel per minute could empty or load an 8,500-gallon fuel tanker in no time. It would also be used to stir up a batch of fuel inside one of the blend tanks. We would blend A and B together to make C, the finished product. Samples would be taken from the top and the bottom of the tank and I learned how to check to make sure the product was on spec and ready for racing. We'd load other tankers for deliveries to customers like regional oil jobbers, racetracks, speed shops, etc. Some customers would have a bunch of empty VP drums at the ready and the tanker would use a much smaller line to fill their drums to the 54-gallon mark. I was taught what I needed to know about spill prevention and what to do in case something went wrong. Common sense and paying attention to what you were doing, along with some luck, allowed my record to stay somewhat intact. The only thing I ever spilled there in Chester might have been coffee or some extraordinarily colorful language. I did manage to give myself a chemical bath one time when a drum hose developed an impressive leak but my clothes seemed to have captured 99% of the hazardous material so other than what looked like a bad case of sunburn it's all good.

One of my first experiences with loading a tanker wound up showing people that no matter what I manage to maintain a sense of humor. There we were toiling away and up to the tanker loading area rolls a big rig from Buffalo, New York. Normally customers would phone in their orders to confirm availability and schedule the loading time. This guy wanted to pick up a full load of race fuel and we were out. Most truck drivers are nice guys and this one, I was told, usually was too but he wanted to get back to Buffalo. I'm not sure if he was just devoted to his customers or had a really hot date but he became somewhat "animated" when we said, "Sorry, Charlie."

"Why the hell aren't you bastards ready for me?" he yelled. We went back and forth on the matter. "We never got the order." We were assured his dispatcher left the order on our answering machine but it just wasn't there. It would take twenty-four hours to make everything right, which put the driver and his customers in a pinch for race fuel for the weekend. I'm not sure about his hot date but she'd have to simmer, I guess. To help diffuse things I brought the answering machine out to the parking lot. I told him it must have failed so I wanted him to run it over. He looked at me like I was nuts but I assured him it would make him feel better. So he did. And then I did. Then I had to replace the old machine with a brand new one. I didn't tell Fred what we had done to the POS machine. I just said it stopped working. Within a day the new machine was in place, the tanker was loaded, and the driver was headed home. I say it was one of the worst experiences because any time the pipeline to our customers was threatened or interrupted it drove me crazy. The last thing I had ever wanted to do in any job I had ever had was let someone down. Eventually I would learn you can't do it all but I would try. By the way, that day I picked up the new answering machine for the office I also came across a sign that I bought and would hang in every office I would occupy for the next thirty years. It has nothing to do with lessons from *The Art of War*. It's common sense. ASSUME NOTHING. It wasn't until years later that someone told me that was short for if you assume something you "might just make an ass out of u and me" but I prefer my way of thinking. I just don't assume things. Meanwhile down in Texas one day, they had a big problem and assumed something. Lady Luck was on site that day otherwise it could have been really bad.

First, if you don't know what static is, go walk across

your carpeted living room or office. Do it in your socks and rub the carpet real good. Then touch something for fun. What I find entertaining is kissing my unsuspecting wife. Do it with the lights off for effect. Crack! Now imagine doing that with gas or chemical vapors and liquids right there with you. Ever seen a video of someone filling a fuel can in the plastic bed of their pickup truck at a gas station? Little bit of static and now it's the 4th of July. Whenever dealing with flammable liquids you have to eliminate static by grounding tankers. At the plant in Texas, the guys working the tank farm way back when had a big issue. As I recall the story, one of the employees stated he heard the crackle as the static charge engaged with a plastic bucket that was there to catch any fuel as they connected or disconnected a heavy 4" hose line full of flammable race fuel. In seconds, the fire was raging. As one quick thinker shut down the valves to cut off the flow from the huge race fuel tanks, the other employee started hitting the fire with the extinguishers at the slab. Luckily someone at the plant saw what was happening and yelled. Before long there were thirteen fire extinguishers working the blaze. The truck driver, wherever the heck he was from, had disconnected his air and light lines, pulled his fifth wheel release lever, and drove his tractor out from under the tanker and left the premises. I don't think they ever saw that guy again. Someone had called the local volunteer fire department but they never showed up. To make matters worse, at the small plant – very small way back when – the thirteenth fire extinguisher killed the fire just as the powder ran out. If it had kept flaming, who knows what would have happened. So don't assume anything, especially when people's lives are at stake. Spend the money, have more than enough fire extinguishers on hand at work and at the house. I had been involved with fire victims in the funeral business and never wanted anyone to get hurt at work or at a race. Happy to say we never had a fire on my watch at either plant in the Northeast but it could have happened to us. Shit does happen to us all, so better to be safe than sorry.

When not working the phones or helping a customer I was up on the dock drumming gas, getting Tony's rig loaded for a run, or replenishing inventory as it came in from Texas. Drums of products that could not be transported in bulk would arrive from Texas, be offloaded, and pretty soon reloaded and be out the gate.

That first tractor-trailer that poor Tony had to work with was painted worn out white and tired. The tractor was a cab-over design. That meant the engine pretty much sat under and somewhat behind the driver. It was noisy and hot, and only had one set of drive tires that simply put meant it could haul less weight down the highway. Look at the tractor pulling a trailer out on the interstates today and you'll usually count eight drive tires and the two steering ones. The trailer was also had limited capacity. It only had four rear tires. Most of today's big rigs have at least eight trailer tires. So we were trying to run full loads on ten tires where modern rigs can haul significantly more weight on their eighteen. What does that have to do with anything? It meant Tony, remember I called him poor Tony, would have to go out twice each week. He'd load up first thing Monday and drive up into New England. He'd be back Wednesday late, reload at whatever hour we needed to, and head back out to finish his week's deliveries. Quite often, actually as often as possible, he'd wind up at or near a racetrack by the weekend. There he'd make contact with existing dealers and customers and work the racers and engine builders to try to swing them to the VP products that were coming in from faraway Texas.

I caught on to things in the office and at the plant pretty quickly but there was trouble brewing that took me by surprise. A racer friend of Tony's first related it to me and eventually it blew up and had to be dealt with. Apparently Tony had the expectation that when it was time for Fred to move to Texas that he'd be Fred's replacement. Suddenly this new guy, yours truly, is on board and telling Tony and John what to do. His feelings were hurt and I understood that. He was very well liked and it was obvious he had shared his expectations and now his disappointment with our customers.

Initially I was "the guy who stole Tony's job" but with some discussion and bar time both Tony and the people who were up in arms got it. I had a decent amount of business experience whereas Tony had none. A simple example made my point one afternoon. Even though nobody had ordered them, I insisted he take a dozen cases of 5-gallon plastic race fuel jugs with him on each run. He argued it was a waste of time. "You can't sell it if you don't have it," was my mantra and before long he was coming home empty and loading twice as many on his subsequent trips. Case closed.

Eventually Tony grabbed an opportunity to make significantly more money working for a tanker company hauling street fuel to gas stations. I believe we parted ways as friends and the last time I ran into him we laughed and reminisced and had a good old time. He worked his ass off for VP and for Fred and then me.

Looking back, it's hard to imagine this is true, but in my first off-season, my first winter at VP Chester, the damn phones didn't ring. From mid-fall to early spring the orders for fuel were almost nil. Sure, samples for engine builders came and went and an occasional snowmobile racer might want to try something but otherwise it was very quiet in Chester.

After checking in and looking busy for a bit, Fred and I were free to do whatever we wanted and that usually meant screwing off. With the exception of engine builders, not too many racers wanted to talk about buying a drum they wouldn't use until the spring. So many of them counted on money from snow plowing and so they weren't sure what sort of shape their wallets would be in until then anyway.

I was into racing karts so Fred, and our friend Glen, all got them. There was this little asphalt kart track just south of the Conowingo Dam in Maryland. For $1 you could practice on the track. The old man who owned it would just wander out of the woods, usually his old donkey accompanying him, collect his fee and wander off. Regardless of the temperatures, if it was dry we would run laps. We might have suggested to our boss, Steve Burns, that we were doing fuel testing. That was true but secondary. We'd play with some of VP's products and some additives to see just what worked best. It amazed me how much power my little 100 cc Yamaha engine would pick up by adding nitro to the race fuel I was running. We also played with tire softeners that were designed to make the tire softer, stick better, and hopefully give an advantage. I was racing against people that were fifty pounds lighter than me so I figured all is fair in love and war.

When Conowingo wasn't an option we'd go to the Malibu Grand Prix across the river from Chester in New Jersey. We'd run laps until they'd throw us out of there, usually because someone would have broken the rules a time or two for that final ejection to be invoked. The off-season back then helped make up for being away from family and friends so much. It was time to relax and reconnect. The race season in the Northeast ran from about mid-April to mid-October. That's six months of nights and many weekends doing whatever it took to succeed. Back then in the Northeast a few trade shows populated the off-season calendar. Events like November's Parts Peddler in Syracuse, January's Area Auto Racing News in Valley Forge, and March's Racearama in Springfield, Massachusetts. Two things amazed me about these events. There was this thing called Lake Effect Snow that anyone from Buffalo to Syracuse can relate to. Before going to work for VP I had never heard of the phenomenon. We're talking feet of snow, not inches. What amazed me the most though was the incredible number of devoted race fans and racers who turned up at these shows regardless of the weather. Many days and nights would be standing room only and be capped off with beer and BS-ing with the racers and dealers afterward. I was very surprised to find that there weren't events like this in every city in the U.S.

I wound up making it through my first summer, fall, and winter at VP. Steve Burns was really pushing for Fred to finish up my training and head south. Down in Texas, Steve had set up a respectable tank farm and warehouse just off

I-37 near the 1604 loop on Lamm Road in Elmendorf. The doublewide office trailer was a big step up from the single-wide the receptionist had fallen to the floor in. Progress was being made on all fronts.

I knew enough about the job to turn me loose now. That last day in Chester, before he moved down to Texas, he shared his forecast, his prediction, that since he had done such a great job working the Northeast that he would be surprised if I grew the sales any more than 15% or so per year. That was his way of challenging me to beat his projection and so the stage was set. Fred's last words to me were pretty simple; "Don't screw it up!" Before heading south though there was one more thing I just had to have and it would mean spending some money. We were working in a crammed office and running or driving a quarter mile back and forth to the warehouse to deliver a message or escort a customer to the dock to fulfill their order. It was always fun to confront an agitated customer who wasn't comfortable driving through Chester. For new customers typically they'd drive to the dock only to be told they had to first go find the office, pay, and then come back to the dock for their order.

Aside from the convenience factor, and safety, it became clear that I needed to be closer to the team. Some boys will always be boys – and girls can be guilty of that too – if the boss isn't nearby in some cases, one or more of the guys might have a tendency to slow down or even stop working altogether. That's the downside to hourly employees. In some cases, slower is better – for them. Tony had moved on, Fred was in Texas, and John was pretty much the dock lead. If you wanted to screw off he didn't have any time for you. Finding good help, especially asking people to travel through and work in a depressed environment like Chester, was tough. Asking them to work overtime and then have to navigate the city in the dark of night was tougher.

Sales did continue to grow and it was clear with all the added activity on the dock and with customer pickups that I just had to get an office of some sort adjacent to the warehouse. Before long we made a deal to secure a used office trailer. Found it, hooked it up, and drug it across the Commodore Barry Bridge from New Jersey late one night. We made it. The bridge police weren't around and neither were the fine men and women of the New Jersey State Police. Thank God. The trailer tires were junk and I think we even drug it over without a tag on it. We got it home and spotted it very close to the warehouse's customer service area, wired it for power, moved the office furniture and meager office equipment and supplies into it, and we were set. Functional, yeah, that's the word, functional. We were set, or at least I thought so.

In Texas, the reality was that Steve was an ideas man who had zero interest in the day-to-day operation or managing the books or the people. As he would express from the early days until the most recent ones, "I didn't want to run some big operation. I just wanted to make some really good race fuel and some money." We are all very thankful he put Fred into play down there. It let Steve be Steve, Fred be President and the doer of all the things Steve resisted or ignored, and the rest of us to move forward with confidence in the leadership team. I'd be the captain of my regional ship and as this story evolves you'll see why that rank, that position, is regarded as one of the loneliest.

For anyone wondering when the hell we're going to

address the big David versus Goliath battles I've mentioned, I can assure you they are coming. Way back then, VP wasn't the well-oiled machine it is today. I thought it best to first set the stage that existed back in the day. There we were, dragging office space over a river in the middle of the night while just over three miles downstream in Marcus Hook the massive Sunoco tanks and their decent sized multi-level office building sat churning race gas and making money.

Chapter Five

NEVER A DULL MOMENT

From Philadelphia, if you travel south down I-95 for a half hour and you hit Chester, travel another ten minutes down the road and you're in Marcus Hook, Pennsylvania. VP had now set up shop in a location that sat physically between the corporate HQ and the production facilities for Sunoco. Can the world get any smaller at this point? It sure can. I was tired of pouring money into an apartment and I wound up buying a house that would put me close to my kids and work. I didn't know it at the time but Jim Meisner, one of the top dogs at Sunoco's race fuel division at the time, lived right down the street. I loved that property. It was the first ranch style house I had ever lived in. I'd never have to go up four flights of stairs to find my bed ever again. There was plenty of land out back to play ball with the kids or ride VP's quads when I'd sneak one home. The fall sunsets over the sprawling Linvilla Orchard behind me were breathtaking. They were almost as impressive as those out at Lake

Havasu in Arizona during the annual World Finals for personal watercraft – almost.

From the plant it was an easy drive over to the Jersey Turnpike and within a few hours you could be in Connecticut to find John Holland and New England Race Fuels. NERF is the distributor for Sunoco branded race gas and they have a pretty solid footprint on the region. John's partner, Mike Joy of FOX's NASCAR broadcasts, grew up in the region like John, and he is very well known and liked in the industry.

John wasn't always a Sunoco man though. I may actually have helped make him one. When I started with VP, John sold our products and did pretty well with them. I was having marital issues in my early years at VP. On one occasion, when I had a particularly rough week and I needed very badly to connect with my kids, things came to a head with John and me. He needed fuel and the truck that was carrying it to him broke down. "I might have to jump in a rental and drive up 95 and get it to Connecticut," I told my ex-wife. I think if she'd had a gun she might have used it. She was taking care of our three kids all week and due to my schedule hadn't had a weekend relief for nearly a month. "You go tell them you can't take them tonight. I'm not going to. I'm not the bad guy on this, you are!" I just sat there in that office trailer, wanting to see the kids, wanting to take care of the dealer and the racers that needed fuel. One thing I learned a long time ago. If you give someone a reason to try another brand and they do like it, you might not ever see them again. That applies to fuel, restaurants, and girlfriends, whatever. I looked at the picture of my kids sitting on the desk and that was it. "John, I'm really sorry but I just can't help you." That call went over about as well as the one to my ex. An hour later the kids and I were having pizza and milkshakes while John drove his truck down to retrieve his fuel. In hindsight, I should have done more, I should have come up with something better, but at the time I'd had enough of racing fuel, broken down trucks, and not enough quality time with my kids. I may have loved my job but I loved them one thousand times more.

Before long, I got the news that John had accepted an offer from a man by the name of Bob Regis. Regis was the Sunoco distributor of record and reportedly offered John the use of a small tanker truck and the race fuel concession contracts at two local tracks if John agreed to switch brands. My bet is that they had been trying to get him to switch, and his having to go and retrieve his fuel that night was the last little push he needed to switch teams. Well, John's a smart guy and he made the move. I was pissed, but in the back of my mind at the time I wondered how much my unwillingness to help him that one night might have played in his decision. Oh well, you lick your wounds, get pissed off, learn your lesson, and get back at it. Still sorry I let you down, John, but all things considered I think you believe you made out better with the new brand.

Within a week, Norman Turnberg from Hampden Fuels in Massachusetts called and asked, "Since I can't get VP from Holland anymore, can I buy direct?" Years later Norman has grown his business exponentially, partially because he has the warrior mentality and loves to work hard. He was also a racer and could relate very well to them. He also had a really good product line to sell. To recognize his accomplishment and thank him for his tireless efforts, I took him along on sales trips to events in France, Germany, and Japan. To this day, he's one of the hardest working people I know. In the history of VP's more recent successes in New England, Norman was a part of them. There are only other two people, people who promoted and sold VP, I can think of that had larger roles in VP's history and rise in that region. Andy Costello from Colchester, Vermont is one of them. He built race engines, ran AC Performance, and had a parts truck for many years at tracks in the area. He knew his stuff and he knew VP. Steve Cultrera from Steve's Auto Body in Eliot, Maine. Steve was and is so passionate about what he does, whether it's drag racing, running his business, or selling VP. He would load six pails in his car and drive an hour each way after dinner to make sure someone got their fuel. He worked his butt off and did more than his fair share to grow the business up there and to establish VP as a major force in New England motorsports. Strategically, and with pulling budget from whatever rabbit hole I could find, we managed to wage a pretty good regional war in that beautiful part of the country. The fact that we, and so many racers and engine builders agreed, had better performing products always made the job a little easier. But when you have guys who go above and beyond for the cause, you're usually going to be successful.

These three men, and so many other dealers and distributors, contributed to laying the foundation but they went on to build it further and further to the point that it is today. They were strategic, knowledgeable, and were willing to work 24/7 if that's what it took to secure a customer and keep them for life.

Jumping back to geography for a moment, if you were

in the Philadelphia area and opted to stay on I-95, south-bound around or through the Baltimore and D.C. beltways, you'd eventually run through Richmond. But be wary of those damn beltways!

Years ago when Fred and I were headed south for either Daytona or Gainesville we had left very early in the morning. We were all coffee-d up and laughing our butts off as we told stories and made up some along the way. At some point one of us said to the other, "Are we still in Maryland?" Turns out we'd been laughing so much that neither of us paid any attention to the damn road. We'd gotten on one of those beltways and drove around it a few times until we realized we should have crossed the Potomac and seen the Washington Monument by then. We opted to keep this story to ourselves but I guess I've let the cat out of the bag at this point.

Travel about an hour's drive to the west of Richmond, among the many monuments and historic locations of the Civil War, and there was another element of this modern day David versus Goliath, VP versus Sunoco, saga. A man named Frank Lesueur from New Canton was heavily involved in motorsports. He promoted special drag racing events, what we call "booked-in" shows. He'd represent drivers who raced what were called Funny Cars and those cars ran on nitro fuel. Funny cars had bodies that resembled street cars like Chevy Vegas and Monzas and they would be mounted on a race car chassis and powered by incredible engines that made 2,000 horsepower back in the 1970s. With technology, that increased to 4,000 HP in the 80s and now in 2017 the NHRA reports a staggering 10,000 horsepower from those wild rides. If you haven't seen one in action look for them with the volume turned up full throttle on YouTube or better yet, support the sport and attend an NHRA national event next time they come to town. It's sensory overload for sure.

Some of Lesueur's customers were crowd pleasers like "Jungle Jim" Liberman and the very popular sidekick "Jungle Pam." He liked catchy, memorable names and "Jungle Jim" stuck. He was quite the showman and always put on a great display with his car. Pam, always clad in a halter-top, daisy dukes, and some sort of heels was a real crowd pleaser too. She'd stand in front of the race car and would use hand signals to direct Jim as he backed up from a very smokey burn out. She was a photographer's dream and when I was shooting for *Super Stock Magazine* I always made a point of bringing her into focus. Heck, everyone else did too.

To assure the show would go on, his clients needed a reliable source for quality nitro at a good price. Frank took care of that. He was handling their bookings and before long selling them their fuel. Smart man. Fuel and tires are the two things that racers, track owners, and series promoters must have to put on an event. The NHRA took note and asked Lesueur to provide that supply reliability at their events, ensuring "the show would go on."

Soon after that the people at Sunoco were introduced to Lesueur. Within a short time he had CAM2 race gas on the truck along with his nitro. Frank's young son Stevie had helped his father with the bookings for the Funny Car circuit and worked at the shop moving drums and selling fuel. They were given the region by Sunoco and became their distributor. That, in turn, made them part of Sunoco's big team and for anyone who likes to compete and to win, we all know what that means. The Lesueurs had sold VP products at one point early on but according to Stevie a dispute arose when they received a batch of fuel mistakenly dyed the wrong color. Without a satisfactory resolution, Stevie said that was the end of their relationship with VP and Steve Burns. One can only guess at this point if Frank and Stevie would have broken off with VP at one point regardless. Their eggs were in the Sunoco basket at that point and just another adversary we'd have to contend with.

Years later, after competing for business side by side with our trucks at many of the tracks, Lesueur passed away and eventually the business was bought up by a businessman from Richmond. Stevie remained in racing and got into other things, which included working as the nitromethane safety advisor at NHRA National Events. In recent years I hired Stevie to work with us as a consultant at VP for a time. These days, he's back selling race fuel on the same property his father had owned and that Stevie had grown up on. Recently we got together to have lunch and then tour the historic Appomattox Court House where Lee and the South surrendered to Grant and the North. Forget any symbolism though, because there wasn't any. It was just former foes that appreciate a good laugh, good food, and American history. Okay, maybe there was a little symbolism. I'd been regarded as a "Yankee," a "damn Yankee," and a few others things down south over the years but as Jason Kelce of the Philadelphia Eagles would boast after eventually winning a Super Bowl, "We're from Philly!" and I'm proud of it.

Outside of the Northeast region, the only one that seemed to have motorsports fan trade shows, we'd also participate in high profile national events like the dear departed Circle Track Trade Show in Daytona, Florida. The February trip to Daytona was a big deal for me as I looked back to a few years and saw myself standing in Victory Lane with Waltrip and the 88 crew after he won a Thursday Twin 125 Qualifier and the Saturday 300. That was a dream come true and it was the closest I'd come to being a part of a Daytona 500 winning team.

Craig Von Dohren is a very popular dirt racer from Pennsylvania. He raced on VP and became a dealer of ours. I can't thank him enough for helping to put us on the map with so many of those racers. More importantly, he introduced me to two very special people who would become friends for life. Craig was in Florida just like every other racer from the Northeast and he walked into the VP booth and introduced me to his good friend Freddie Turza. This former U.S. Marine was an engine builder, a very good one, and built engines for Craig and other race winners and area track champions like Billy Pauch. His wife Kim was a travel agent and from that first meeting we all hit it off.

In addition to the Daytona show the managers would all work the other big off-season trade shows. SEMA took place in Vegas each year but PRI had been a bit of a nomad before finally settling down. It might have started in Louisville, Kentucky and then moved around to Nashville, Columbus, Indy, Orlando and then back to Indy where it resides today. Louisville was coincidental because I had been there just a few years before taking my national boards to get a step closer to my funeral director's license in Pennsylvania. Nashville was cool even though we didn't get to see the Grand Ole Opry or anything memorable other than the hotel and one night in particular, somewhere intriguing that scarred me forever. Fuelin' Around was to say the least.

One of our distributors was very familiar with the hot spots and talked me and another manager into checking out one in particular. So there we were, three guys sitting innocently in the lobby of a mid- to low-end massage parlor somewhere in Tennessee. Out walked this amazing woman in her underwear and heels and before either of us VP guys could move our host jumped up and was escorted into Shangri-La with a twang. Okay, this is looking promising. I'd been a good boy down in Nuevo but I was single now and happy to be sitting there. Out came #2 and she was equally as impressive. My bud jumped up and off they went. Now at this point, I'm thinking they've saved the best for last and couldn't wait to see what #3 looked like. Well, guess what you get when you mix #1 with #2?

Now I've always been respectful of women. In most cases they are indeed God's gift to us men, but come on. My #3 was a bit bigger than I am and whatever the hell she was wearing came right from the irregular lot pile. I think she could tell from my expression that she had a better chance of winning the Powerball than seeing mine that night but she was a gamer and hell, "when in Rome." To close out the story, it was pretty simple. I had no interest in any part of her but I will confess that she did give a pretty damn good backrub. When I rejoined the two who were now finished and waiting for me with shit eating grins on their faces I knew what had happened. They got me, those bastards, and we laughed all the way back to the hotel.

In the early years trade shows were great because not only did we get to visit with our dealers and racer customers but we got to talk with all the people who had heard VP was good stuff and wanted to know more about selling it and fueling their racing with it. One sure thing at the end of every trade show day I'd get back to the hotel room to call my kids and get changed and then the nonsense would begin. Soon we'd all be at a happy hour and then the morning hangover would be just twelve or so hours away. Typically we'd start doing tequila shots and at one point at one of the many PRIs I lost the ability to speak. I could only laugh. Try explaining that to the new Mrs. when you call home at 2am to try to say goodnight. If you know Al Wilcox from Trackside Products in New York he can attest to my impressive performance.

This one morning, after a particularly brutal evening, Brad and I wandered into the VP booth to sit quietly and try to gather our senses a half hour before the show would open. Wouldn't you know some attendee had gotten into the show early and stopped by the booth to ask a few questions. Normally that would be great, that's why we were there, but in the shape we were in we just looked at him with disdain. Before long we had to apologize and ask the man to come back a bit later. He was as relentless as the throbbing in my head and neither showed signs of quitting. The questions kept coming. I think "Dude, I hate to be rude but if you don't leave the booth and let us get our acts together one or both of us are probably going to puke on you" finally got the point across. He left and luckily, he came back later.

Guess you can tell that booze and life on the road go hand in hand, at least for many of the road warriors. The smartest thing we tried to do with that in mind was stay in hotels that had a bar and that were within walking distance of whatever show we were working. In one spectacular case, the booze really set us back. I had worked with Leeann Tweeden on our 2000 and 2001 VP calendar posters and with her great personality and appeal we asked her to spend some time with us signing them during the Dealer Expo at the Indiana Convention Center in downtown Indy. As I said before this lady was an angel and I looked forward to seeing her again.

I flew into town and the Midwest office boys were responsible for setting up the booth and stocking it with posters, brochures, decals, etc. The booth façade was in place but that was it and nobody else was around. Not answering their phones either. I like to have everything set and in place, ready to go, but this was out of my hands and for the moment I figured it would fix itself somehow. Later into the evening still no answer on their phones. I confirmed they were there, some of the other vendors had seen them leave the building. Okay, they'll be here in the am with all the stuff. This was before Kim Turza did the hotel bookings. We weren't staying in the same building and I had no idea where they hell these boys might be.

Next morning I went over to the booth to finish the set-up and get ready. The show drew a very big crowd and our booth location was close to an entrance and that meant we'd get slammed hard early. But there was still nothing to hand out. People started flooding in and all I could say was that the airlines lost the boxes but more were coming. This went on for hours and eventually one of my colleagues showed up, white as a ghost, and dropped off a few boxes of whatever he had managed to carry in. He looked like death warmed over and ready to barf if you looked at him funny.

He apologized but then had to go back to whatever hole he had crawled out of. He was hurt but I was happy to have my supplies and that he was accounted for. We got through the day without any help and I eventually tracked them down. Turns out they had gotten involved in some sort of a whiskey drinking contest the day before and passed out in the room they were sharing. The one guy remembers watching the maid come in and step over his legs as he sat on the floor, propped up against the wall. The other guy had been face down and barely moved the entire night and day. So much so that he pissed the bed. Now, boys and girls, this is not the best way to spend your day. The next morning they made it to the booth and started to resemble the human beings I knew them to be.

I don't think I ever got as smashed as those two but perhaps my drinking was due in part to boredom. In hindsight it was more likely due to a sense of loss and frustration for having to bury a marriage and do emotional damage to my kids. All things need time to heal and in time I cut back on the booze and focused much more on being the best part-time dad I thought I could be and totally focused on succeeding in my career. If I couldn't be with them as much as I wanted, I would do my best to provide them with everything else that I could.

The trade shows were a lot of fun, at least in the beginning. Getting to connect with so many people, everyone from the counter guy at a NAPA store that loves racing to world champion drivers and riders was pretty cool. Perhaps one encounter really got me excited more than most. I had spent years and years listening to Howard Stern on the radio. He'd fill my mornings with outrageous entertainment and incredible interviews when he was broadcast on WYSP in Philadelphia. Around the time we moved from Chester to the new plant we built in Newark, Delaware, Stern moved to SIRIUS satellite radio. That gave me forty-five uninterrupted minutes of drive time every morning to enjoy the ride and fill my brain with oxygen from all the laughter. I always wanted to get on that show and one morning at PRI in Orlando I thought I'd get my chance. There he was, larger than life; Bubba the Love Sponge! Bubba was a radio personality with great ratings and a huge following who had also moved to SIRIUS from conventional FM radio and at the time was broadcasting on Howard 101. It was on satellite radio that everyone was able to say what they wanted, however they wanted, and man, did Bubba deliver. He and Howard would call in to each other's shows on occasion and that made the drive time even more interesting. Better yet, Bubba was a race car driver. He knew racing, knew the business, and knew the logo on my shirt.

He and I exchanged introductions and within minutes we were making a deal to put our fuel in his race car and VP would be getting radio plugs to his massive audience. His followers weren't all race fans but I can guarantee you that they all drove cars, pickups, bikes, and boats. They loved racing and having a good time. Bubba was someone who could put the VP name in front of an audience that didn't necessarily watch auto racing. But they did fuel up their street rides and boats at convenience stores and gas stations and walked into NAPA stores to buy everything from motor oil to octane boosters. The cost of buying ad time on SIRIUS would not have been cheap but the cost of a fuel sponsorship, all things considered, was minimal. The ROI, the return on investment, should be, or I at least hoped would be, great. The deal made perfect sense to me, trying to get us national airtime for cheap, developing a relationship with a very interesting character, and possibly an opportunity to get to meet Stern. Even though I had met so many of my heroes like Richard Petty and Mario Andretti and been blessed by Popes at least six times, meeting Howard was still a goal. Mark Klein from VP Southeast had referred to me as VP's Howard Stern a few times and Fred Morrison nicknamed me "Wild Man" a few times. Okay, guilty as charged. Actually, I didn't want to just meet the guy I wanted to sit in on his show and lob a one-liner from time to time. He was an incredible interviewer and the journalist in me learned so much from listening to him but he was also funny as hell. I also related to him in a lot of ways. The fact that he got to interview the top players in the music and movie industry and that he had hot bikini girls in the studio playing all sorts of games had nothing to do with my interest in him. Nobody ever called me Pinocchio but with that last line they will now. Bubba's sponsorship worked out great for VP and I believe he enjoyed it too. So many people acknowledged hearing him mention us on the radio that I took things a step further.

"Hey, Bubba, can I fly you up to Atlantic City so you can sign autographs in the VP booth in January?" First-class tickets from Tampa to AC were all it took for him to make the trip and he brought his beautiful, but now former wife, Heather with him. We had a line wrapped around our massive stand at the Area Auto Racing News show at the convention center. It was awesome. Again, as I may have mentioned already, the move was probably premature. Finally I had someone with massive appeal to a large national audience of riders and drivers and the only thing we had to tout was racing fuel. Products for general consumers, like SEF, had been developed but any connections to national pipelines that could make this and other products readily available to them didn't exist yet. Nonetheless, VP was regarded as a cool brand and the corporate Goliaths were anything but that. People would often complain, to our hearts' delight, that they could call Brand X or Brand Y and never get a call back. The surest way to lose someone is to ignore or take them for granted. That applies to anything and everything in life. Eventually Bubba left SIRIUS but broadcasts on the internet to a global audience and remains a fixture on many of the popular FM stations in the U.S. He bought a dirt race track in Florida and appropriately renamed it Bubba Raceway. His son Tyler can drive the wheels off anything he climbs into and with the help of his friend and mentor NASCAR Champion Tony Stewart, the sky is the limit for Tyler. Eventually and for a variety of reasons outside of my control, Sunoco became Bubba and his speedway's fuel supplier. I never did get to sit and watch Stern work his magic in the studio but I still recognize and appreciate everything Bubba did for us while I was at VP.

Riding the high of making the VP booth the place to be to meet a non-racing celebrity, I figured okay, let's try it again. The Area Auto show had moved from AC to the Philadelphia Expo Center near Valley Forge. They advertised the show dates in the Philly radio market. Danny Bonaduce, originally from the area, had been on television, movies and radio since he started out on *Bewitched* and then *The Partridge Family* in 1970. He was now a fixture on WYSP radio in Philadelphia and that's who I wanted in our booth. He called me when he arrived and I greeted him at the frigid smoking area outside the building. There he was in his black leather jacket, standing amidst the frozen breath and cigarette smoke of a dozen other guys just doing their thing. A few minutes later he was in the VP booth and his incredible personality took over as I hoped it would. He was signing photo cards and conducted an impromptu marriage counseling session for my office manager and her boyfriend. "You're doomed," is all I remember him telling her and everyone laughed and continued to enjoy the event. An hour or so later, he was gone as quickly as he had arrived but the VP booth was again the place to be. That was the last time I booked a celebrity. I did try to step it up by another notch by getting professional ball players into our booths and perhaps some print ads. It's amazing how much money they command though. I reached out to the then Philadelphia Phillies baseball legend Chase Utley. This is the all-star player that President George W. Bush said he would select if he were an MLB team owner. Chase was BIG and I wanted him to represent VP in some fashion. Then reality set in. "How much?" is all I could ask his agent. "Thanks but tell Chase that's a bit more than we can spend." That was the extent of the conversation and my idea. Nothing against Chase, he deserved to command big prices and he probably wasn't even aware of my pitch. I had been forced to sit at Citizens Bank Park to stare at the familiar Gulf logo that occupied a space and had envisioned at some point, if I ever got full control of the advertising budget at VP, that damn sign would be replaced with a familiar red, white and blue one. But again, that thought was before its time. The experiments had worked well. Who knows, in time, as consumer products are developed and VP gas stations pop up from coast to coast perhaps someone like Fletcher Cox, the Eagles football player and VP customer, could wind up helping to introduce the VP brand to a national, non-racing, consumer audience.

A few years after Von Dohren introduced us in Daytona, Freddie Turza got a job offer to work with NASCAR teams. His wife Kim had taken on orchestrating my extensive travel plans and started to help out a lot of VP's managers too. She was already supporting tons of race teams and racers so she was happy to add us to her list. Only thing was they had to move to North Carolina and that made us all long distance friends like so many that I've made around the country and around the world.

Once they moved away we didn't get to hang out very often but when the economy took a bad turn and Childress Racing laid off a bunch of employees, including Freddie, I seized an opportunity. As an admirer of President Ronald Reagan I followed his mantra of surrounding yourself with good people and did so whenever I could. I liked to load my bench, to identify a weak spot in my armor, and fill that void with someone very capable. Sometimes I refer to it as acquiring a DH, a Designated Hitter. I understood engines and how our fuels worked. I knew how to do basic tuning and what to adjust when switching from one fuel to another. But I was spending a lot of time on the phone talking tech and felt like a dumbass when I couldn't answer a tough, highly technical question. I thought Freddie might be just what I needed.

Fred knew Freddie and so convincing the boss to

approve the hire and free me up to focus on growing the business was easy. It added not only a significant, experienced technical person to the staff but also one that was very well known, liked, and respected in circle track and drag racing. If David needed a big hitter, I just got him one. To this day, Freddie has remained a very valuable part of the VP team and kind-hearted Kim continues to bail out the lost whenever someone goes astray in their travels.

The PRI event may have begun in Louisville but it made stops in Nashville, Columbus, Indy and Orlando before finding what's supposed to be its permanent home in Indianapolis. My buddy and fellow manager Brad Horton was usually fun to room with but that often depended on where the TV was in the room. It's no secret that he's hard of hearing in one ear so if the bad side was aimed at the TV you could rest assured the volume would be sky high. He was also quite the practical jokester. To this day, I swear that bad ear changed from one side to the other just to screw with me. I think when he was growing up in Roby he probably tortured his friends and anyone he knew in that little town. You just never knew what he had in store for you.

Remember those little bottles of shampoo and body lotion they leave for guests in those hotel bathrooms? Well this guy would wait until you were down in the bar or not watching and he'd put that crap all over whatever he could think of. He'd moisturize the damn TV remote, the phone, your briefcase handle, and the doorknobs; whatever he could think of! I did finally did get to pay him back though. Not sure what year it was but it was for sure in Indy for the PRI show. That cold winter night we all went out to dinner and while we waited for our food to come he left the table to use the men's room. The other guests watched in amazement as I removed the tops off not just the peppershaker on our table but I borrowed a few from our neighbors at the next tables. Actually it wasn't a few, I think Indy had a pepper shortage after that. I quickly dumped them all into the coat pockets of Brad's jacket and we all went about our business of chowing down and having some laughs.

An hour later, as we all walked toward our hotel, he pulled one of his hands out of his pocket to scratch something and before long his eyes, nose and mouth had a pretty good pepper dusting. Gotcha — finally! Years later, again at PRI, Brad told me he had just gotten rid of that old coat and believe it or not it still had some remnants left in the pockets. I feel sorry for the next guy who wears it.

Back to life on the road, there was another guy I roomed with and he had an issue with using the bathroom. In a nutshell, he couldn't go to the bathroom with the door closed and so unless you wanted to enjoy the full glory of his post-Taco Bell meltdown you'd get dressed and move to the lobby and wait for the smoke to clear. This might be at any hour of the day or night. The positive was, it helped build camaraderie. The negative, especially if you didn't share the same interests or were a little tired of one another's jokes from your ten-hour day together, sucked. In modern times, as I'm writing this, I get a kick out of all the options that exist today that would have made life easier back then. Cellphones with music, movies, social media, sporting events, eBooks, and ear buds! Eventually as the years passed and we could afford it, everyone would finally get to have their own rooms. In the beginning it might have been a hassle, dealing with the sights, sounds, and smells of the person in the next bunk but persistence and effort got us the reward we all wanted.

Getting to Florida in February for the trade show and away from the winter's cold was heaven. It gave us a chance to hang out with the rest of the VP managers, meet up with our racer and dealer buds, and look for new business. The Daytona event was a blast for a multitude of reasons. It took place at the Convention Center during what is called Speed Weeks. In that part of Florida during a two- to three-week period there was the trade show, the Rolex 24 Hour race, nightly asphalt oval track racing at New Smyrna, nightly dirt track racing at Volusia Speedway, and all the NASCAR events taking place at "the big track". We were down there to connect with everyone but also to sell some fuel wherever possible.

If I were to tell you that a trip to Alaska got me out of a speeding ticket on the way to Volusia you'd say no way, right? Well it did. I had been out at the big track for one reason or another and was hauling ass west across State Highway 40 when without warning the Florida trooper's lights lit up the inside of my rent car. Damn. I hate being late for anything! We went through the usual "where's the fire?" and all that, and my telling him I needed to get to the track to open the truck up and start selling fuel so they could start practicing that didn't faze him one bit. I tried. As he took my license and headed back to his cruiser I said, "Man, I haven't had a ticket since Alaska!"

In no time we were friends. Turns out the ole boy loved the 49th state despite never having been there. Hell, it's only a 4,300 mile drive so what's the excuse? He told me he got *Alaska* magazine every month and watched every television show that was set in it. I related how I had been up there one summer by myself after working the Indy Light event in Vancouver. I told him that I had been hauling ass, again, and somewhere between Anchorage and Valdez an Alaskan trooper got me. That northern trooper had no sense of humor and thought my excuse for missing the speed limit signs "because I was paying more attention to the 'Watch for Elk' signs" was lame. It was lame but I had to try something. If you haven't been there, get going. I've been lucky enough to make it up there at least three times now and the cruise I took my three kids on was spectacular. Go for it! The Florida trooper sent me on my way, license back in my pocket, ticket not issued. I don't know if you ever made your way up, trooper, but watch out for those damn elk! I got to the track just fine and life went on.

From a business standpoint it was great to have a presence and personnel there during those events. We got the fuel trucks in pretty much everywhere. If we couldn't make a deal with the track then we'd make a deal with the guy who owned the parking lot across the street. We got the fuel trucks in everywhere except for the big track. That was originally Union 76 country and was now Sunoco's exclusive territory. Or at least they felt that way at the time. It was the center of the motorsports racing universe and the start of the big thaw each year.

For me, it got me back to Daytona International Speedway. It was the site of many very good memories from my first days in racing with Waltrip and the rest of the gang. But it was different now. I wasn't trying to get the Gatorade logo in front of every lens. I was trying to get VP fuel in anything that raced. I was on a mission. I was part of a campaign. There would be no more in fighting like DW and the Gardners or issues between people on the team. Okay, people are people so yes there would eventually be some infighting but that happens everywhere except in a one-man circus. Once all the action around the trade show and the three tracks came to a close it was time to head north and get ready for what was to come.

Once the sun came out and the temperatures started to climb up in our region we were rocking. We busted our butts to make everything happen. We continued to visit the engine builders. They were the ones who recommended, and many times dictated, that VP was to be in their engine. The fuels had proven they not only made more power than the other brands but our products burned cleaner and cooler. Those were huge selling points that made my life somewhat easier. The tough part was the pricing. In some racers' minds, "I've used CAM2 for twenty years and never had a problem." Then there was my favorite quote, "I've won two track championships without you and your stuff is $100 per drum more expensive." That's where the engine builders came in very handy. When CAM2 was the "only fuel in town" they may or may not have supported the engine builders with discounted or free fuel programs. Many engine builders have dynamometers, "dynos" akin to the one Bill "Grumpy" Jenkins used to break in his engines and test their performance. Make a tuning change, use a different part, try a new fuel and then take what you learned to the race track. For every racer that swore by his CAM2 we quite often found an engine builder who felt the same way. For some change is an issue. What we needed to do was convince both to give us a try.

First, engine builders would get free samples and then discounts on fuel for their dynos. All we wanted in return was feedback and a recommendation to their customers if they liked the performance. Some engine builders were open to trying new things. Some would say they'd give the samples a try and then when we'd stop in to visit, the dusty sample pails would be buried under all sorts of other pails and empty parts boxes. In some cases the testing delays were legit while in other cases we found that the builder was just being kind and was happy to say yes to accepting samples if we'd just stop calling him. People are people, regardless of their profession. For the ones that were open to change, many used our fuels to enhance the performance of their engines and further grow their customer base. In addition, many became VP fuel dealers. When a racer would stop to pick up his engine he'd also grab a drum or two of VP. Makin' money and making power is what it's all about.

Second, we needed to support the racers. Fred and Steve had already done a great job across the country making deals with racers who were willing to switch to VP. Some would get discounts and others would get free fuel. Whatever we could negotiate as long as confidentiality was promised. A problem that I don't think any of us even considered back then was what would happen over time. A racer can help build a following but what about when their best days are behind them and their performance falls off? Do you continue to support them in thanks for what they helped you accomplish? Do you reduce their deal or perhaps cut all altogether? What about the racer who leverages you against CAM2? For me, there were racers that helped put us on the map and they could get whatever they needed regardless of how their racing was going. Loyalty is everything.

Some racers who were forward thinking and not creatures of habit embraced VP and became fuel dealers. That only downside to that was this sort of comment from one of their on-track competitors. "I race against that guy. He stuffed me last week so there's no way I'm going to buy your fuel from him and put money in his pocket."

Back in Chester, I can remember one twenty-four-hour period in particular that exemplifies the dedication that was mirrored across the company. The phones in the office trailer were ringing off the hook. People wanted to come down and pick up fuel, wanted to find a fuel dealer in their area, or wanted to start selling VP. Trucks needed to be off-loaded and reloaded. A tanker was due in and to make the day really enjoyable it was raining. I think there was one warehouse guy left and he was hot and tired. Nobody wanted to work hard in the heat for the hourly rate we could afford to pay. We could hook people on "working in racing" and "you get to go to Englishtown to see the national event for free" but that only went so far. By 5pm the VP truck had been loaded and headed out for deliveries. The driver would have stayed to help if he could but he needed to be sitting at Steve Cultrera's in Eliot, Maine early the next morning. He had a long ride ahead of him. Steve's customers needed fuel before they headed out to their tracks and the driver would have a full day of deliveries left to do after pulling out of Maine.

The tanker finally arrived and our warehouse guy agreed to take care of the load and unload but he was done after that. The tanker would need to be at Summit Point

Raceway in West Virginia the next morning for the start of a big race weekend. The area where the tank pumps were located had a corrugated aluminum roof overtop but the sides were all open for ventilation and access. The office girl took care of greeting customers and answering the phones. She also prepared the invoices and transportation paperwork for the shipments. She'd take care of the mail and make the bank deposits of cash and courier the checks overnight to Elmendorf. It was a very busy job and took a real "get it done" personality and mentality to survive there. I appreciated everything the driver, warehouse worker, and office girl did for their effort but on that day she couldn't work past quitting time either. I remember running between the warehouse and the office, waving goodbye to her as she drove away. I was drenched and so were the warehouse man and the tanker driver when they walked in behind me. "All we need is a bill of loading and I'm outta here," the driver volunteered. "See ya tomorrow, oh that's right, see ya on Monday," was the last thing I heard the warehouse worker say as he clocked out and closed the door behind him. "Now where the hell is that paperwork?" I kept saying aloud. I still had a lot of work to do. My kids were expecting me and I was dripping rainwater on everything on the receptionist's desk. Couldn't find it. She must have forgotten to prepare it. Oh well. Five minutes later the driver had signed for his load and we exchanged, "See ya down there."

I retrieved my phone messages and checked the new answering machine for any that hadn't been picked up. I quickly called anyone that seemed important but it was past five and most offices had closed by then. Many times I'd use my drive time home to catch up on calls but this night I needed the time to decompress. Those other calls would have to wait until morning. I always kept a fresh change of clothes and shoes at the office in case I got a chemical bath or was just dirty and needed to get cleaned up before leaving work. I changed and then hauled ass to see the kids.

The twenty-minute ride to my old house was easy. Rush hour traffic had died down but it was still raining heavy, I was late, and my ex and I agreed that it would be better for me to feed them there while she ran out for a bit. I picked up some McDonalds along the way. As they always did, my three jumped all over me when I opened the door to the kitchen. An hour later I was wrestling with the midgets and before long they were being tucked into bed. "You can't stay any longer, Daddy?" tore at me as it always did. I'd give the usual reason, explaining that I had to work late just like both of their grandfathers used to. On the way back to the plant I swung by my house, packed a bag, and got back to work.

The rain was still coming down pretty hard but you do what you have to. I needed to drum off fifty drums of race fuel so they were ready to be picked up the next morning. I also needed to load four of them, and all the gear needed to work a race event, into the company van and drive to Summit Point that night. This is nothing more than what men and women do all over the world on their jobs. Well, some of us. I at least took a dinner break. Racers will work 24/7 to repair, rebuild whatever they need to.

So I rearranged the lines at the pump slab, switching off the 4" tanker lines and 200 gallon per minute tanker pump to the easier to handle 2" drumming line and the smaller, 60 gallon per minute drumming pump. There was an underground line that ran from the tank farm pumps to the loading dock at the warehouse. I finished with the pump hook up and then rolled fifty empty 54-gallon steel VP drums from the drum company's storage trailer into the small warehouse. I think it measured 20' x 80' and there were already 100 or so drums full of other type products, taking up some of the valuable floor space inside. I attached the 2" drum line at the dock and ran it into the warehouse and started drumming. By now it was 9pm or so. Between filling the drums, tightening the 2" and ¾" bung openings and affixing the VP factory seals on both closures it probably took about two hours. Ventilation in the small space was bad and I got a pretty good dose of fumes that night. I put the drumming line away, loaded the four drums of product that were special ordered for Summit Point into the van, threw in everything else I thought I might need and then went inside the trailer to do the paperwork. Any time you're transporting 1,000 pounds or more of hazardous material you needed to have the proper paperwork in the vehicle and the proper markings on the outside of it.

Instead of affixing stationary placard mounts to the four sides of the van we would use temporary placards that would peel off when you were finished with them. The only downside of using the temporary placards was they didn't like being applied in the rain. It took a while but they were finally in place. Now they just needed to withstand the 70mph, four-hour ride to the track.

You've probably noticed the diamond-shaped red 12" placards on gasoline tankers and on the sides of transport trailers going down the highway. Those markings are there to alert authorities of the hazardous contents on board the vehicle. Quite often the numbers, like UN1268, are displayed with the placard and the numbers are also listed on the driver's paperwork. That specific intel, the UN1268, will tell HAZMAT or fire and rescue crews what's on board so they can determine the inhalation risk, fire risk, how to fight the fire (water, foam, etc.), and how to contain any spilled material. To be licensed to be at the wheel on a vehicle transporting hazardous material you need to have a Commercial Driver's License (CDL) and the HAZMAT endorsement on the license.

I remember hearing about a truck driver who had just left the VP facility. A dealer coming to pick up an order reported he saw the truck driver climb down out of his cab and peel the red placards off his truck and trailer. He might have wanted to avoid detection heading south and through the Baltimore Harbor tunnels but if he had gotten caught it would have been *really* bad for him. What a knucklehead, to put it mildly. Can you imagine if that rig had been involved in an accident, and anyone trying to assist or the first responders who rolled in to help had been unaware of the dramatically flammable load he was carrying, and was probably leaking fumes or liquid inside the trailer? All you need is a spark. It could come from a dislodged drum giving way to gravity and sliding inside the trailer. Maybe something as simple as a state trooper's flare or a tossed cigarette. On the paperwork, we always required that anyone transporting a load requiring placards sign for the placards we would voluntarily supply and that they acknowledged that placards were indeed required. In hindsight I should have called the state police. The next time that happened, I did, and I made it a policy in the office.

So there I was at 11pm. Even the clothes I had changed into were wet. Fired up the diesel Ford Van, and headed out. Between coffee and pee stops I think I arrived at the motel around 4am. Three hours later I was headed to the track. Tired but excited to be there. A few days later, thanks to the monsoon that had struck the region for days, we loaded up and headed home with nearly all of the fuel we had brought there. Roads were flooded. Track time had been drastically limited. And we had to get ready for whatever Monday morning would bring.

The office worker wound up quitting at some point. Her story was that her husband had seen where she worked and didn't want her anywhere near there. I put an ad in the local paper and we had a quite a few calls but once they heard exactly where we were located we only saw an interview or two. One afternoon, I watched from my office window as an attractive blonde pulled up and climbed out of her car. She had on this great dress and I got a kick out of watching her stumble as she made her way through the gravel parking lot, stiletto heels and all, to the door. *If she can type and speak English, she's in*, I thought. I'll affectionately refer to her as "Blondie" and not only did she pass the interview I found out pretty quickly that she too had a "whatever it takes" attitude. As an example, some time later when a former VP dealer, Bruce Insigner, needed some drums of fuel for a race that night she came to the rescue. Nobody else could make the six-hour round trip from Chester up to Dushore, Pennsylvania that Friday afternoon but Blondie did. She did the paperwork while the van was loaded and off she went. That is the type of winning behavior that I needed for my team. As the weeks went by and the late nights at work continued, things between "Blondie" and I evolved. She often needed to work late too. In my mind it was okay, my wife and I were no longer together and since we were such a small company at that point, policies against office romances hadn't been established. One thing led to another and before long we were in a relationship. We had a lot of fun and at that time I needed some in my personal life. Eventually we parted ways and she moved on to another job much closer to where she lived. A few years later, I remember getting an "OMG" from one of my sales reps when I remarked with a big grin just how fond I was of the desk they were now using.

Winning teams can happen by accident but also most times by design. As the years passed I would analyze what the region had done, recognize what was needed to improve, and add it to the program. It might take begging, borrowing, or bartering but I usually got the assets needed for the plant or the personnel needed to fight the war we were in and for the next initiative or assault I was planning.

Chapter Six

TRUCK DRIVERS

THEY MAY BE rarely appreciated or even thought of but from my vantage point, and from VP's, we couldn't have done it without some very special ones.

Back in 1978 when I drove from Texas to California with Fred Morrison we spent a good bit of time on Interstate 10, maybe thirteen hundred miles or so, and got to see quite a lot. I mentioned the blanket of stars that covered up as we drove through the night but at the time I neglected to mention the many westbound "bat out of hell" truckers who passed us at 100 miles per hour.

I love going fast but the reality was, some of these guys were living on caffeine and who knows what to get the job done. There were regulations, logbooks to be kept, that would track driving time and down time but those were easily manipulated. The more miles a driver could run and the quicker he could do it meant more money. I can think of one driver I knew who drove from Jacksonville, Florida to LA without sleeping, and all of us should have a problem with that. Those rigs can legally weigh 80,000 pounds so imagine one going 100 miles per hour with an exhausted, sleepy driver at the wheel in the middle of the night coming up on a family trying to get home from vacation. Not good. Don't get me wrong, I've driven way too fast way too many times and probably manipulated a few rules and regulations myself to make something happen but I don't believe I ever put someone's life in danger other than my own. The point I am getting to is that thankfully some regulations were put into place to slow these guys down and make sure they were forced to stop and get some rest and some nourishment other than speed and whatever else they could buy from the lot lizards in the truck stop parking lots. Lot lizards are kind of like lounge lizards. The biggest difference is they will knock on the driver's door or cab of his tractor no matter what time of the day or night it is. At least that's what I'm told. So since the late '70s the Federal DOT, Department of Transportation, added some regulations to make our roads a bit safer. Drivers had to be more aware of their cargo, especially if it was hazardous. They also needed to check their rigs before and after stops to make sure everything was working properly. For those of you who have noticed the "weigh stations" on the country's interstates, that's partially what's going on. The driver's paperwork is being checked for everything I just listed and whether for cause or randomly they will wave a truck to the side and give the driver, his rig, or his cargo a closer look.

The states added some more regulations and then of course the counties and towns and cities jumped on board to make things even safer. Or perhaps it was to generate revenue from fines as the poor trucker was just trying to find his delivery and didn't know the local regulations, especially if they weren't posted.

Tony Feld had been the first real truck driver that I had worked with at VP's Chester location and it wasn't long before I began to encounter some of the company's other road warriors. Encounter is the best word at this point because some of them were "doozies." Remember, VP was still an infant and was suffering growing pains. Money was spent on buying chemicals and making everything else happen. Truck drivers who were attracted by the thought of working race events quite often were willing to work for a bit less money but with the promise of being around motorsports and its celebrities. There was the guy who loved working the NHRA races back when Kenny Bernstein's Budweiser King was on the tour. This guy would see all the cases of Bud cans stacked inside the rear of one of Bernstein's trailers and hit the crew up not once an event but every day for his share of the beer. He was a funny guy and told a good story but we had to shut down his behavior. It put undue pressure on the Bud guys who didn't want to say no but also wanted to make sure they always got their fuel at a moment's notice. Even though VP was working its way to the top I had always believed that we should look and act as professionally as possible. That would be a struggle for some. Why someone can't find a trash can for their burger wrapper is beyond me.

Sometimes our regional and national race schedules would make things tough and managers would lend their driver and truck to another, and at times travel to the races to help out the short staff. It amazed me how many drivers would behave like their VP rig was their own. That's a good thing when they're taking good care of the equipment, which they were already being paid to do, but when they started putting reflective decals and all sorts of crappy, tacky sayings on the rigs we had to crack down. One knucklehead had placed "Hauling Radioactive Material" in 6" reflective letters across the back bumper of the tanker we had. That might be cute but it was way before anyone was trying to get social media attention on Facebook or Instagram. Those didn't exist back then. If anything, he could be ticketed for improper markings. Anything pertaining to HAZMAT had specific rules for identifying what the truck was carrying. The driver was pissed off at me but so be it. Most assuredly he gave his manger an earful once he got back to his base but the reality is the manager should have known better. Putting the right people in positions of responsibility and authority is critical. Fines are expensive. Sometimes finding the right person, whether it is a dockworker, truck driver, or regional manager was tough. For me though, I had a job to do and part of that was to protect the interests of the two men who gave me this dream job, Fred and Steve.

So having met some of the characters who drove for VP I kept reminding myself, "it's not a job, it's an adventure," and kept going. Some drivers in the Northeast came and went. What we did find was that because the cost of living was so much less in South Texas than it was in the Greater Philadelphia area, getting Texas-based drivers to work in the north made financial sense. Many of these drivers loved the road and were okay with being away from home, if there was one. Either it was not a big deal or was accepted as the price of doing what you loved, driving the open roads and working races. They'd be okay sleeping in their rigs during the week but at the races, they'd get a hotel room and that seemed to work for them just fine.

Texas had made a deal with a driver leasing service. Drivers would be paid by the mile, which I had issues with, and would also have a "per drop" charge. Imagine getting paid .18/per mile to drive from Philly to Montreal and back, making 10 stops along the way. Running 1,000 miles over three days would get you $180. Making $20 per stop adds on another $380 before taxes. If you left out Tuesday morning and got back to the plant Friday morning there wasn't much you could do that day. So what did some drivers do to make more money? Take the long way around or just lie about your trip! Yep, I couldn't believe it when I saw it for myself. This one dipstick in particular turned in a toll receipt from the George Washington Bridge. For the stops he had to make there was no reason to cross the Hudson. It padded his miles and also cost VP a lot more thanks to the big toll charge. Nice guy. You're fired. So the service sent me another driver and this is where it gets really interesting.

The guy's credentials were sparking. Military career teaching truck driving and truck maintenance. Great personality so he'd be good with the customers and appeared fit enough to wrestle the heavy drums with the rest of us. He did the job pretty well for a few weeks and then I got the call. "The engine let go in the Freightliner," is the message he left on the new answering machine. "I checked the oil in Harrisburg and it was fine." This was before cell phones were in every pocket.

Eventually the driver called in from a truck stop off Route 322 near State College, Pennsylvania. I knew the area very well since I had driven it dozens of times when I studied and partied at Penn State's main campus. There was that long, winding hill that rigs lumbered to climb while others grabbed lower gears and engaged the "Jake brake" that essentially retards the engine and keeps the speed down. In many small towns these devices aren't allowed because they do make quite a bit of noise. But in a heavy rig headed downhill, they're a huge help and have been lifesavers.

So we had a catastrophic engine failure in the only truck my office had. It came as a surprise since it had always been well maintained. That meant we needed to arrange to have the 80,000 pound fully loaded rig towed further up the hill. We needed to rent a replacement tractor so the driver could continue on his delivery schedule. His stops needed to be called so they could waive off their customers who were expecting to pick up their fuel later that day and so on. Since I knew a thing or two about oil pans from motorsports I knew that when a race car is running on high banking there needed to be baffles and pickups and design changes to allow for the oil to continue flowing through the engine.

The same could hold true for a truck going up a steep hill. Most oil pans and oil pick-ups are designed to accommodate this sort of thing, going up and down hills, in street cars and trucks. Not many rigs take the 33° high-banked turns at Talladega and have to worry about maintaining engine lubrication. The law enforcement/investigator in me took over and before long the case was solved.

The customers had been taken care of and the junk engine was being fixed by way of an in-line overhaul at a repair shop in central Pennsylvania. The driver rolled back into the Chester parking lot, turned in the cash and checks he collected for the fuel, his expense receipts, and whatever was left of his trip money. Hmm, there it was. "Hey so-and-so," I asked, "if you checked the oil in Harrisburg before heading up that hill and it was okay and then the engine seized half way up that hill, why did you buy four gallons of motor oil two hours later at the truck stop where they towed you to?" It was clear the guy had bought the oil to cover his tracks. He actually poured it into the hurt engine so in the event anyone checked they could say there was oil in the engine. WTF!

So this guy's days at VP were growing to a quick end but I was in a pinch and needed help that weekend working a drag race at Maple Grove. I think it was the Super Stock Nationals back in the day where nitro cars would put on a show along with the running of an NHRA Divisional Race. Bernstein got his fuel, the professional and sportsman drivers all got theirs and I had a fun night ahead of me trying to talk this truck driver into not walking prematurely. He knew that he was going to get canned by his boss. He just wasn't sure how it was coming. He was demoralized that he'd made such an embarrassing and costly mistake. He also really liked working the races. It was a dream gig and he blew it. In reality, he screwed up bad and looked like a POS for lying about it. "Look, let's get cleaned up and head over to the Red Lobster. I'll buy," seemed to get his mind off his future and let him focus on some food. After calling home to talk to each of the kids and make sure they knew I was still alive and loved them more than anything, I left my hotel room and headed down the hall to see if the driver was ready. The door was ajar but I knocked just the same and called out his name. No answer. I slowly pushed the door open, hoping to not find him dropping a deuce with the bathroom door wide open. Nothing. He wasn't in the room. And then I saw it. The hotel room window was wide open and the curtain was moving around as the summer heat blew in.

I'd been around suicides back in the funeral home days and wondered to myself if the police were going to delay my trip to the Red Lobster. Hey, I was hungry. I'm not dismissing the seriousness of those fatal acts. They're devastating to those left behind and such a horrible place to be in life, where ending it seems better than sticking around. I slowly walked to the open window and looked out, expecting to see a body and a bunch of horrified onlookers. Nothing. There was just a car trying to park and a few people unloading some luggage. Relief set in. Surely they couldn't have cleaned up the mess that quickly. Okay, what gives?

As the elevator door opened into the lobby there he was, all cleaned up and ready to eat. We exchanged a few laughs about what had just occurred and then during dinner I got to deliver the news. "That's what I said. They told me to take you to the nearest bus terminal in the morning. Your replacement will be here tonight."

He was devastated and despite the fact that he was a nice guy, he had to go. I dropped him off at Greyhound on the way to the track the next morning and set out to teach the new guy how to fill race fuel jugs and swap out drum pumps. Weeks later, after this guy didn't work out, I got a call about this man named Frank and it was one of the best things to ever happen to me back then.

Chapter Seven

YOU ALWAYS REMEMBER YOUR FIRST

To PUT THINGS into perspective, we were setting ourselves up to make a good living and take on the giants of our chosen industry. Money was tight – why else would someone climb into a dumpster to retrieve an old typewriter? That said, the first official annual meeting at VP took place at the old doublewide in Elmendorf. The single wide where BAM-girl's orientation took place in was being used elsewhere or perhaps was left behind.

I flew down to San Antonio from Philly and found their airport back in the late '80s much like the one I found in Charlotte in the late '70s: small, and far from the international status both fields would achieve as their economies and the populations grew dramatically over the coming years.

Today, VP is one of the biggest race fuel companies and is recognized and used around the world. At that first meeting, however, some of us felt like we were back in grade school. Apparently, and to my great surprise, some of the staffers needed help filling out a work order. You'd think it was simple but for whatever reason people left off dates, neglected to write down the color of the jugs desired, and so on. As I looked around the room it scared me that a few were actually taking notes. Clearly we had a ways to go before we would be able to accomplish what we had set out to do.

Steve Burns wandered into the office trailer at some point during that first annual meeting. After he sat through it for about five minutes, maybe ten, he was gone. I don't have a tenth of his brainpower, knowledge, or experience but we do share one thing and that is we both bore very easily. I'm sure he was as impressed as I was that we were being shown how to take an order. We thought that might be the last we'd see of him.

During our lunch break, Bubba Corder, one of *the* main guys back in the growth days at VP, shared his plan for the afternoon. "Everyone put in twenty dollars and I'll run up to the gun store and buy some ammo." That was all I needed to hear. Back in the '80s, six guys kicking in twenty dollars apiece for bullets might have bought just enough for some real fun.

To get a better sense of Bubba, here are two quick tales about him. First, he was known to catch scorpions or rattle-snakes for fun. One time he followed something into the warehouse and came out with a dead snake in one hand and a bad snakebite on his forearm. An hour later at the hospital they literally fileted his arm so the tissue could ooze the poison and heal up. The second story about him is much more important and significant to VP. One afternoon I called Bubba at the close of business and told him I desperately needed a special order made, packaged, and shipped for a customer. Without questioning, he made it happen. That scenario happened time and time again. Bubba would work 24/7 if needed to get the job done. He would do anything and everything asked of him and then look for more things to do. He was one of the key elements to VP's success, and without his dedication and abilities I am not sure what the company would look like today. He's retired now, just like me, and down there Darryl—Big D— as I'd call him, continues to make things rock.

Late that afternoon, once the meeting concluded, it was on. Cold beer and bullets sounded like a pretty good Texas Happy Hour to me so let's roll. The old plant on Lamm Road sat on probably thirty acres or so. Since many of the guys, including Burns, liked to ride MX bikes they had acquired a front-end loader at some point and laid out a decent small motocross course behind the warehouse. Typically they'd ride at the end of work so the very recognizable sound of two-stroke MX bikes running the property was commonplace. Soon, there'd be even more noise.

Bubba, yours truly, and perhaps three others loaded into the full size rent car one of us had grabbed on arrival at the airport. Beers were handed out and we drove as best we could along whatever parts of the property weren't littered with discarded pickups or appliances. Without warning, with the muzzle inside the car, Bubba pointed one of his pistols and blasted an old washing machine. Now BAM-girl might have experienced an out of body experience on her first day on the job down there at VP but if you haven't been in a car when someone shoots off a gun, don't be. They say, "when in Rome" so I assumed "when in Texas."

More beer was passed round, the rent car was driven faster, and a few guns were handed out amongst what at this point we might want to call the "wild bunch." All of a sudden though, Bubba waved his hands for us to stop. "Here they come," is what I think my destroyed eardrums picked up. Second later, Burns and another rider flew past the front of the rent car and disappeared again. "Okay," Bubba shouted as he fired at something in the field. Between the piss breaks and everything else it was quite an interesting safari that I'll never forget. We managed to do something similar year after year until someone finally came to their senses or got tired of paying the rental car repair bill. I neglected to tell you that we managed to blow at least three tires off their rims late that day. I knew this would be an adventure and man, was it. What I didn't know was that we were far from finished.

The next day they introduced VP's first computer system to us. By today's standards it was stone-age caveman stuff but it was the best VP could afford and we were happy to have it. After a few hours of more nonsense, I mean "training," it turned out there were even bigger and better plans for that second night in the Lone Star State.

San Antonio sits about 150 miles north of the border with Mexico. On the U.S. side sits the city of Laredo. On the Mexican side, there's the town of Nuevo Laredo and within its limits is a quaint little walled village known as "Boys Town." We all piled into another rent car and headed south with the promise of a fun-filled evening in another country. It's pretty cool that just north of where I lived in Pennsylvania was a country where they spoke French and you could feel as if you were in Paris or Marseilles if you wanted to. Now, to our extreme south, was a polar opposite.

The ride was relatively quick and we laughed the entire time. Got across the border without any issues and headed for what we were assured was a hot spot.

It was way past sunset now. Sitting in traffic watching a few locals take a mouthful of flammable liquid and then spit it to flame to the amusement of the tourists was different. After the thrill show the performers would approach each car and ask for money. We obliged and I can still see the wasted expression on the badly scarred man's face. We clearly were in another world. I was used to the big cities of the Northeast and the good, bad, and the ugly they had to offer but this was just sad.

Before long we rolled through the front gate of Boys Town and slowly drove to the big bar at the end of the road. As we passed the many adobe type one-room huts we got a sense of what we were in for. There, inside each hut, was a woman waiting for another customer. As we rode past every open door, the lighting inside their rooms showed us quite a variety. There was very young girls, old ladies, skinny ones, and very large ones. The constant was they were perched on the side of a broken down bed, legs apart, lips pursed, and eyes beckoning. Actually not all the lips were pursed. Some were beckoning. It was time for a quick reality check.

We're in a foreign country, actually an area akin to a Third World country, with bordellos all around us. Oh man. This isn't fair. As we parked in front of the bar and climbed out the reactions were mixed. The two single guys were like, "Oh wow, WTF," while the married guys, me included, were like "Okay, WTF?"

Our tour guide laid it out for us. We'd just go into the bar and have some beers. If anyone didn't want to partake there were two hand signals to give the girls and they'd leave you alone. The first was to hold out your hand and bend your index finger down at the knuckle. That would mean, "Your unit doesn't work." The other signal was hands empty, meaning, "I have no money." Regardless, the married guys all agreed that we'd behave ourselves and have fun experiencing the environment and watching the single guys go crazy. I *was* a good boy that night but one thing I always lived by and professed to others is, "If you're going to do something you shouldn't be, at least be smart enough not to let anyone see you do it!"

We sat down at an open table and quicker than gasoline can catch fire, there was a stunningly beautiful Mexican prostitute sitting on my leg. "Oh F—k!" was the first thing that came to mind. Actually, that was the second thing. She was angelic and man, did she smell really good. Anyone who has been to certain tourist traps has dealt with beggars, street vendors, children bugging you for money, etc. But this was different. This gift from above was right out of *Playboy* magazine. Her tan complexion against her skimpy white whatever the hell she was barely wearing knocked her rating up to maybe 11.5 out of 10. "Want to buy me champagne?" Sure. It was $10 per glass but who cares. She proceeded to whisper the menu in my ear. The sexy time one, not the nachos and guacamole version. Once I told her I was out of money, as quickly as she had landed on mine, she hopped onto another guy's lap.

As the night wore on, it was like watching musical laps. These ladies would bounce from one to the next to the next without hesitation. Some would stay and party and eventually guide some lucky customer up the stairs and into seclusion. For us married guys, the entertainment was in just watching it all happen. I'm proud we behaved and did the right thing. What about the single guys? Well they could barely walk. It's amazing how cheap the girls were and how $50 could get you three lays, including the condoms. What a deal. Hours later we were back across the border and headed for the hotel back in San Antonio. Back in the U.S.A. after a very memorable night "abroad." We did have to pull over once at a random checkpoint. The border patrol simply looked at all of us, opened the empty trunk, and waved us on our way.

It was on that first trip to Texas that I met Keith Simmons, VP's first salesmen. He rode competitive MX all across the country living in the back of his truck and trying to make ends meet as he followed his dream. When he wasn't riding or working out he was selling VP. I'm not sure how he and Steve Burns met but they were like brothers. They were a couple of smart, good-looking single Texans who did well at anything they were involved in and that included the ladies. Yes I know you want to read more about that but we'll save it for a Netflix mini-series if we can ever make that happen. I got to know Keith very well and in years to come he would leave VP and become one of their largest racing fuel distributors in the world. He, like Burns, is an American success story.

At the NHRA events, the primary and most high-profile series we would follow back then, there had been too much transition with truck drivers and people working the races. That led to confusion and frustration between the fuel truck and our customers. We had four offices dividing up the country and servicing the traveling circus when it came into their region. While he was still employed by VP, Keith became the recurring face at the NHRA national events attending every event from coast to coast, February to November.

For the first event we would work together, Keith flew into Philly and was supposed to spend the night at my house before we headed off the Englishtown the next morning. While we were driving to dinner we saw a young woman who was stranded alongside the road with a flat tire. My kids were with us and they were known to get "hangry" if dinner wasn't served pretty close to feeding time so Keith and I decided to help this lady in distress but do it like a pit stop so the kids wouldn't start to chew on each other's arms. We had the spare out, the car jacked, her tires swapped, and back on our way to dinner in no time. Later that night, this young playboy from Texas got to fall asleep in one of the kids' rooms. All he remembers was staring at the Mickey Mouse wallpaper and the stuffed animals and decorations that made him think he was in Disney that night. Next morning I said bye to the kids and Keith and I hauled ass to the races and whatever adventure would come next.

With the first annual sales meeting concluded we all flew back to our regions and prepared for whatever the New Year and new racing season would bring. In years to come, as the company grew in sales and staff, we'd continue the annual trek to San Antonio. Gone would be the days of sharing hotel rooms and jamming into office trailer meeting rooms. There are way too many good times at the Embassy Suites at the SAT airport to recall here. They had a free happy hour, free breakfast, and each room was like a mini suite so there was a living room big enough for a six-person meeting. Okay, here's just one tale that would demonstrate my lack of patience, hatred for monotony and boredom, and appreciation for shock value.

The Midwest office had gone through a handful of managers for one reason or another. When they hired this new guy, he and I really hit it off. We liked to have a good time but we also shared similar responsibilities. We both operated the only two remote blending facilities for VP. I ran the one in Chester, Pennsylvania and VP also rented a facility in Terre Haute, Indiana.

Since the new manager and I became buds and like to screw with each other, it wasn't long before we broke things up. He could see I was bored by all this talk about accounting and molecules and DOT regulations. I was looking at the window wondering if they'd open far enough for me to jump and then I looked at him. Without saying a word his lips read "F – you!" In an instant I jumped up from the sofa and headed for him. He quickly got up too, just in time for me to tackle him like an Eagle defensive end on a Cowboy quarterback and up and over we went, landing between the back of his sofa and the wall.

Nobody in the room understood what had just happened. They didn't know if this was a fight or just what. As our laughter from behind the furniture got louder it made it clear we were just doing what a team does. The camaraderie amongst us was very good and Fred Morrison, our leader, knew when we'd had enough. It was time to break early and head down for the free beer. Before leaving the Embassy

Suites for good and moving on to bigger and better things, I have to tell you about a moment that scared all of us.

As the company continued to grow it was clear that we needed a marketing department. Heck, even a marketing intern borrowed from a local college would help. Fred met someone that had taken an early retirement or some sort of package from a company down in Texas and was looking for work. Before long, we had our guy. Nice guy, actually a very nice man with a good sense of humor and a very smart head on his shoulders. Only problem was he might not be the "wild and crazy guy" that some of us thought would be a better cultural fit. At that point in time I'm not sure anyone had a vocabulary developed enough to define or properly describe our culture. We worked hard, loved what we did, and loved the competition amongst ourselves. We also shared the same passion for clobbering the Goliaths we sought to overtake. And we liked to party rather hard. While beer and shots might be the order of the night for most of us, the new guy preferred wine and boat drinks. He didn't have much time for our brand of humor either because it was blue. Turned out that he was a churchgoer. We might have been all Christians but didn't necessarily attend church other than for the occasional wedding or family funeral. Our jokes were raunchy, as if we had learned them all at truck stops and at Boys Town. Marketing had expressed their frustration but relentless knuckleheads that we were, we kept going and going until late one day he'd had enough.

We were close to concluding the annual meeting. If the agenda ran long or the discussion was engaging it was easy for all of us to remain in place and simply order room service so we could continue the brainstorming without interruption. Fred and the others had an expectation of just how long I could go before saying something completely off the wall or outrageous. I bored easily and would try to derail the topic if I wanted no part of it. To this day I think Steve Burns kept me on board partially for my passion and dedication but mostly for my random ability to make him piss his pants laughing. I liked to say things to get a reaction. So when I had my chance I said a one-liner and in an instant, to everyone's surprise, the marketing guy jumped up and ran out of the hotel room. What the hell just happened? "Dude, I think you just pushed him over the edge," someone said. Oh crap. If he just quit because of me then I'd have to help find a replacement and Fred wouldn't have been too happy at having to break in a whole new guy either. A few of us got up and walked out into the hallway that overlooked the huge atrium. I think we were up on the 7th floor. We looked to my left and to the right and the guy wasn't in sight. Now I'm thinking, *okay, he must have jumped*. I looked over the railing and it was clear down below. Maybe he'd just had enough of my nonsense and decided to get away from it. I'd seen some of the girls I used to date behave this same way so it was nothing new but he was a nice guy and I hoped he'd come back. "He didn't jump so we didn't kill him," I suggested. We went on with the meeting. About ten minutes later he walked back into the room, smiling, margarita in hand. "When I realized happy hour was almost over I jumped up and ran for one more." Okay. He did fit in.

In the years to come we'd manage to convince Fred to take us to new places. In my life, I've always said timing is everything and I think that's true for Bruce Hendel. Bruce grew up in New England but eventually moved to Terre Haute, Indiana. He owned a printing company if I remember correctly but he also rode MX bikes and was involved in a powersports shop in the area. One day, when Steve and Fred were visiting VP's Indiana location they met Bruce. He was there picking up race fuel and they struck up a conversation. Months later, when it was determined that VP needed to open an office on the West Coast, Bruce got the call. He was interviewed and hired on the spot. He and his wife Kelley moved out to Southern California and began an onslaught on the race fuel competition that rocked sales. Bruce was a natural. He loved motorsports, bikes in particular, and was very smart businessman.

For years, as the Dallas Cowboys and the Philadelphia Eagles loved to compete on the field and try to bury each other, Bruce and I would do the same in our sales contests and in our vision for the future. Off the field we got along but to many it looked like we wanted to destroy each other. The benefactor of the rough waters between us was VP. We both wanted to be the best, to win at everything, and the yardstick was sales and the sales contest. The only thing is, nobody told Brad Horton. He might not have ever expressed an interest in running the company as Bruce and I had but he loved competition and he liked to win.

Chapter Eight
LAY DOWN SALLY

SOME PEOPLE ARE self-motivated while others might need occasional encouragement, incentives, or a cattle prod to get things done. In a sales environment where what you earn is based on how much you sell, I've always felt that bonuses and incentives, structured properly, can reap huge benefits to the salesperson and their employer. Case in point, if you've made enough money for the day but as you're walking out the door to go home the phone rings. Do you keep going or answer it? The owner would want you to answer it regardless of what you made that day or how tired you were.

Not everything is perfect and to illustrate that I once asked for an increase in base pay after a very long time – years – without one. I was told, "If you want to make more money, sell more gas." It made me think of something my father had related years before. He had a job selling ties at a specialty store in Philadelphia and apparently was pretty good at it. He told me about the day he asked the owner for a .25 per week raise and was turned down. That was the day he decided to go into business for himself. He always said be your own boss. Well I wasn't going to go off and start my own racing fuel company or go back into the damn funeral business so like the Marine slogan, Improvise, Adapt, Overcome, I chose to follow those noble words. So what the heck does all this have to do with Eric Clapton's song from back in the '70s?

I talked with the other disgruntled managers and we agreed that pitching the idea of a sales contest would be great. We were all very competitive and if we could get the idea across a few hurdles we'd be in business. Since I have a tendency to be persuasive, relentless, and so on, convincing ownership that a small investment in some contest money would reap big dividends for all. It worked.

I've tried my best to rely on a pretty decent memory. Some say mine's like an elephant's – they never forget and that works well with one of my mantras, "forgive but never forget." I like to think that the contest idea was mine and selling it was my very convincing push. The goal was simple. Grow your regional sales per month more than the other offices and you get a bonus. If someone was having an exceptional month then you didn't want anyone to give up so we also posted a second place bonus. We also had quarterly bonuses. Success was purely based on a manager's sales increase by percentage on product sales and did not include freight or taxes. The sales numbers from the previous twelve months were laid out on an Excel spreadsheet and it was off to the races. Man, did it pay off!

Everyone wanted to win. Second place sucked but it was better than third or worse. According to Vince Lombardi, "It is and has always been an American zeal to be first in everything we do, and to win..." There's also his, "Show me a good loser, and I'll show you a loser." Finally, "Winning isn't everything, it's the only thing," and "second place is meaningless. You can't always be first, but you have to believe that you should have been – that you were never beaten – that time just ran out on you."

Everyone tracked their sales performance. We were all watching the scoreboard to know where we stood. There were reasons and justifications for everything though and they had to be considered. Bad weather might have affected the sales numbers from the base month or quarter. If it had rained then with little effort in a dry period, sales would look as though they'd increased. With no extra sales effort at all you could do well that month. In the Northeast, for example, there might still be snow on April 1st at Thunder in Vermont and New England Dragway in New Hampshire. Mild winter meant no snow and vice versa so you could have a late or early start. Sometimes customers had fuel left over from the previous season due to bad weather and delayed their spring orders. Some had run out and ordered early. Hopefully the weather or other factors would only delay a sale. In VP's younger days we might not have had the product needed to fulfill all the orders that were sent down to the main production facility in Texas. So who would get the fuel that *was* there? Was it decided by the date the order was received, by relationships, or by other considerations?

All these things influenced sales and consequently the sales contest. It also didn't take too long for people to start playing games either. The internet was just starting to evolve and consequently our regional offices weren't yet tied together by an accounting system. The managers you were competing with couldn't see your sales numbers. Poker and a touch of chess became the game.

"How's your month going, JK?" one of the guys would ask with three to four days left in it. I'd lie. I'd tell them I was way off due to weather and would have to hope for a better month next time. Then there was the "We are kicking ass – already at 31% growth for the month! I'm actually thinking of delaying some sales to ship on the first and get next month off to a good start." I'm sure this happens in a lot of sales organizations but since the majority of you readers might not be selling anything I figured you could at least get a glimpse into this world.

A week after the month's books would close, the sales contest information would come out and there'd be a happy guy, one or two frustrated guys, and at least one guy who was pissed. Hopefully not too pissed. We all fibbed about our numbers. It became standard and that added element contributed to the intrigue and the camaraderie and the competitiveness of the sales contest. Sales were booming, partially in thanks to the bonus money. Unfortunately, it came at a cost.

In all fairness to the team, we weren't necessarily playing on a level playing field as far as earnings potential or responsibilities. In the early days, some of the people who held the title Regional Manager might not have had the same amount of business or sales experience as others. In a few cases, men and at least one woman who expressed enthusiasm for motorsports and race fuels were handed the keys. Some were truck drivers, some were racers, and one came from a machine shop. Sure there were better, more qualified candidates out there but VP, at least in the early days, wasn't in a position to spend a lot of time recruiting or for that matter training. Moreover, they weren't in a position to pay the high dollars some of the very experienced, professional salespeople commanded. That was okay. Passion is key and plenty of people find success without a college degree. Burns and I are living proof of that.

So to a degree, at times, some of us might have had an advantage. Some knew how to build and tune race engines while others had limited technical experience. There was also the size of the territory to be considered. For me, I was responsible for thirteen states in the Northeast United States. Many of the other regions had similar numbers of states but not necessarily the dense populations and high number of race tracks. I also had Eastern Canada, from Ontario and Quebec all the way to the Atlantic Maritime Provinces. In addition, I had Puerto Rico and everything on the other side of the Atlantic Ocean. The Texas region had parts of Mexico and South America while the West Coast office was responsible for everything that went across the Pacific. When I measured a line of demarcation out one time, our "38th parallel" was somewhere around India/Pakistan. I know I may have been anxious to fly across the sea to work England, Germany, France and so on but I'm not sure my California colleague was all that interested in jetting off to Islamabad.

"Damn, I wish I had twenty-three countries and the domestic stuff too," was thrown out there a few too many times by a jealous counterpart. Yes, I had greater income potential with such a massive territory but I also had the responsibility of trying to sell fuel in all of those states and countries. One guy with a handful of states matched up against a guy with a large part of the globe. What the others needed to remember was that we all had varying levels of responsibility outside of sales. I had a chemical plant to run along with all the other responsibilities of a regional manager. Remember now, I did love my kids and wanted to see them as much as possible. Trying to balance never missing a birthday, which I never did, with attending races, trade shows, and meetings wherever the job would take me was tough. For me, the travel at the beginning of my career was a thrill. I loved seeing all those cool places and meeting people from all the different cultures. Trying to understand what the hell they were saying half the time was difficult. I hired translators whenever necessary but that was often problematic. It doubled the length of the meeting as everything had to be retold and not many translators knew how to say things like "compression ratios" or "exhaust gas temperatures" in their native tongue. What would have been a mid-morning meeting with a Brit in the lobby at the Heathrow Hilton would be an all-day affair with the Russians at the Sheraton Palace in Moscow.

Getting to know people you want to do business with can be an interesting and rewarding endeavor but not being able to understand them can be a problem. To negotiate most times you need to be able to read their faces, their inflections or understand their mannerisms. Business is business but sometimes a bluff or bullshit doesn't translate properly.

I may have stolen this trick from the movies but sometimes we had to pull a stunt on a potential or existing distributor to find something out. In Montreal one time we had been struggling to replace a distributor we'd had "difficulties" with. My experience up north was that most people in French-speaking Quebec Province actually understood and spoke English, they just chose not to. Maybe it was meant to frustrate the tourists or toy with them but when it comes to business I wasn't necessarily in the mood to screw around; at least not until happy hour.

A meeting had been scheduled through a long distance call that had featured a lot of broken English with a wannabe distributor near Montreal. There were supposed to be three or four French-speaking business people in the room and just little old me so I asked a female friend from Vermont to accompany me. "I'm taking her up to Quebec City to meet my aunt after this," I told them. We had our hourlong meeting, I found out what I needed to, and then we said our goodbyes and headed south, back to the border, instead of north to QC.

"They were dicking you around," my accomplice told me the minute we got into the car. "As they spoke to each other in French they said VP would never know what they were doing as far as other business ventures and if they wanted to sell one or two other race fuel brands VP would never know." We had been looking to secure someone very passionate, qualified, and capable to take on the responsibility of being an exclusive VP fuel distributor for the province. I had learned they couldn't be trusted so I'd keep looking.

I had something similar occur at a meeting in France once. It was alleged that the person I was meeting with was offering a financial incentive to the translator to actually work with them, suggesting if the translator could convince me to give the distributor more interesting pricing, the translator would get a percentage of the savings. Heck, there was another time that I had a meeting in New Jersey with someone I had done a lot of business with. He had introduced me to "a friend" who had come along for the ride. After we had spoken strategy, the "friend" outed himself and let me know he was a distributor for one of the Goliaths. He said he had wanted to get to know me in case we would ever do business. Oh yeah, I replaced that NJ account the next day. Lesson learned. Always know who the hell you're meeting with. Google wasn't around back then but it is now.

Back to the size of our territories and responsibilities, the income potential for me was great but the reality was once you work a part of the territory and you get the initial sales growth established, you might have had an edge as you got the first orders but after that, they all needed to grow. In the end, it's all relative. So for anyone who felt the deck was stacked against them, or who knew the rules and decided to take advantage of them, the contest's real game playing began.

I find myself reliving it as I write this, and I am laughing at how it all played out. If you were smart, I mean shortsighted, you could game the program to your benefit. If your July was doing okay but you heard the rest of the offices were doing good, you could let a bunch of sales fall into August. Then, you would have a big edge on winning the following July since your numbers had looked so pitiful. It was easy to find out what was really going on if you were friendly with the girls at those offices who did the accounting. Generally I was friendly with all of them. I may have already said that I had often found girls liked guys with a sense of humor. If I had them all laughing whenever I called, then I was doing good. It got to the point where Fred began to ask, "Are you talking to JK?" Their snorts and belly laughs gave it away. Jason Rueckert had that same effect on people.

Guys would take the sure thing, the monthly win money, and look bad in another month just to come back a year later and "steal" a win. It affected the quarterly bonuses and made Steve and Fred start to wonder if the team was spending more time on scheming and less time on selling. When I was asked about it my response was simple. "If you've got guys on the squad that want to win that way then perhaps you need to trade them to Cleveland." Now in all honesty, I might have been guilty of encouraging a few knuckleheads to "punt" sales into the next month. Hey, all is fair in love and war right? It's like *Survivor*. Do you want to win the million or get the Nice Guy Award? Last time I looked you can't buy groceries or plane tickets to Tahiti with trophies. What's their slogan? Outplay, Outwit, Outlast?

At this one meeting, to address the issue of the game-playing I found a great prop in a Halloween store. Remember that Fred Morrison, VP's President, and I were long-time friends going all the way back to high school. I was very grateful for the opportunity he and Steve Burns had given me and I was loyal to them first and foremost over and above the loyalty to my peers. We discussed the possibility of the game playing and its serious ramifications and so after really looking at each manager's behavior during the past year we rolled out the Halloween costume. "Since it's clear one individual more than the rest may have manipulated the contest this year and logged a lackluster sales year just to look good next year we are awarding the first annual 'Lay Down Sally Award' to whoever the hell won it the first time." Man, she was a beauty. The apron was of a female hottie, torso only, all rubber and plastic, in a full bustier with black leather girdle and no bra. The oversized boobs were eye catchers themselves but the plastic ring that pierced an equally interesting nipple topped off the outfit. The winner had to stand up and put it on for pictures and then keep it on at least until the next break. We all laughed our butts off at the presentation and in years to come we would award it again and again, with each winner autographing the inside of the outfit and noting the year they had won it.

I'm not sure whatever happened to poor Sally but if I know that bunch, some lonely guy took her out on a date, got drunk, and lost her forever.

When it came to finding new places to have our meetings, Bruce Hendel, as the West Coast Regional Manager, knew just what we needed. He was totally dialed in to off-road racing and set up extraordinary trips to race along parts of the Baja 1000 course in Mexico. His wife Kelley, who also worked for VP, was a tremendous business asset but also showed us she had a fun side too by smuggling a Spencer's Fart Machine into one of our conference rooms. There's nothing like a well-placed squeak, squeal, or exclamation point at just the right moment to break things up. So the plan was to have the meeting in San Diego then start at Ensenada and wind up in Cabo? Sounds like a great time, right, but just watch out for random cows wandering the course. Running off-road you get to run wide open at times through the open desert but also have to maneuver twists and turns, avoid 14' cactus, and follow specific directions just like a rally car navigator calls out or you're not just catching air, you're falling 500 feet. I've driven around oval tracks and run down drag strips but *this* form of motor-sports is the shit! Nothing like the time I hung the left rear off the high cliff-side, grabbed a gear, and powered on. Each turn and winding bend is different and if the ever-changing course isn't enough there's always the guy in front of you who isn't going fast enough or the guy behind you lets you know he's back there every now and then. Watch out for the same big rock I nailed with the left front. That was the first time anyone at Wide Open Baja had ever seen a wheel split in half. They shipped the souvenir back to me in Pennsylvania but sadly I think it became someone else's souvenir. We'd drive down out of the high mountainsides onto the beautiful beaches and then dive back into who knows where for more fun. Satellite phones were the only things that worked out there but it was great to disconnect and get away from it all. At the end of the day, the Wide Open crew would have ice-cold Pacifico beer in our hands the instant the helmets came off. Great for team building and great for putting the thrill back in your pants. We all did the Richard Petty thing at Las Vegas one year and that was really cool but this takes it to a whole new level. By the way, my friends in Moscow still owe me a ride in a Russian Army tank. They got Freddie Turza and me genuine army uniforms as souvenirs and we were all set to do it until the base commandant decided to show up that day. Our distributor and his army buddies thought it best they not sneak the American visitors in for a test drive. The tank wasn't part of a corporate outing, just our good friends wanting to show us a good time.

I had always wanted to see Yellowstone so I was able to convince Fred to give Jackson Hole a try. We'd meet all day at the Wort Hotel, drink at the Silver Dollar Saloon, and once the business part of the trip was behind us we'd spend a day snowmobiling through Yellowstone where we'd have to pass within five feet of slow moving bison or follow a frustrated moose down a small road until she decided to disappear into the woods. I think the coldest it got that day out there was -27 F. One of the coolest things I can remember was checking out the many hot spots that exist in the park. It's where boiling hot water percolates in ponds and steam escapes through natural vents, with the smell of sulfur there to top it off. There in the brush we saw a massive bison quietly watching us as it stood as close as it could to the warmth of the hot vapors, bits of snow and ice caked on various parts of its fur and face.

Many of the VP team liked to snow ski but that just never interested me. I had tried it in the Poconos once and didn't enjoy it at all. I dealt with crazy New Yorkers during the week so the last thing I wanted to do was deal with gridlock at the damn lifts. I did enjoy the beauty and serenity of the trips to Jackson Hole and its surroundings but I, like just about everyone else, really did prefer the sun and fun of the more southern spots. Going back to Yellowstone in the spring or fall, with the crowds gone but the vibrant colors of the seasons in full bloom, would eventually become my ideal vacation.

The meetings weren't all fun and games though. At one meeting Fred suggested to all of his regional managers that we identify, or find, someone who could fill our shoes. Succession plans are commonplace with big companies. If you retire, get fired, or die prematurely the company has to have a go-to guy or girl to assume your responsibilities and keep the ship moving forward without a glitch. With this small company of only five RMs and perhaps ninety employees total most of us felt somewhat threatened by the suggestion.

"Yeah, sure, we'll start thinking about that," was most of our responses to Fred but in our own minds and at the bar that night after our meeting ended, most of us shared sentiments along the lines of," NFW – no *friggin'* way," and so on. We were growing sales, increasing profitability and our paychecks were finally at rewarding levels. The last thing anyone was willing to do was groom their replacement and be taken out as part of a reorganization. I had seen that move a dozen times at other companies I had knowledge of and that was not going to happen to me if I had anything to do with it. To us, we had fought the fight. Most, if not all, of us had our marriages that ended in divorce, or would, and whether it was partly or fully to blame on our love for motorsports and for our jobs, we had bled for VP and felt threatened by this. In reality, yes we *had* all worked out butts off doing our jobs and growing the business but we had *all* been paid for it and got to do some pretty cool things along the way. It was Fred and Steve's company and they could do with it as they wished. We just didn't want to make it easy for anyone to burst our bubbles and have to make us get real jobs. Remember, this was an adventure, not a job, and most of us hoped to work there until we chose to retire. Some time later, at another get together, Fred and Steve mentioned they might want to sell VP. At that meeting, everyone sat there stunned. Life was good and we didn't want anyone to mess with it but we all knew all good things must come to an end at some point. Now it all began to make sense. Succession plans and such. Eventually Fred and

Steve parted ways and Fred, who was lucky enough to go on to pursue another of his many passions, never looked back.

Once Steve named me Corporate Director of Sales & Marketing, long after Fred had left the company, one of the many things on my long list was – you guessed it - succession. I did not have anyone in place or groomed to replace me as regional manager for the Northeast and Europe and there were some opinions that I needed someone in that role. I wasn't going to move to Texas as Steve had asked me to so many times. There is and was NO way I would ever take myself any farther away from my children. My passion, my love for racing and travel and for winning had kept me away from them physically and mentally way too much already. I intended to maintain the regional manager responsibility as well as assume the new corporate role. In actuality, I wanted to maintain the regional spot in case the corporate gig didn't work out. As Steve began to move ahead with his plans Bruce and I got to meet with potential buyers and I remember vividly one of them asking us, "Are either of you willing to move to San Antonio?" I remember Bruce and me both saying no. If Steve was going to sell, I needed to maintain the regional spot where I would be considered of greater value. My momma didn't raise no fool.

When it came to the sales contests, some thought there might be a conflict of interest but I stated very clearly that if anyone ever felt I tipped the scales in my favor they could protest and our company controller Rebecca Koen and in-house attorney Susan Gray would review and rule on that behavior and that I would abide by their decision. That never became an issue though. I might be a mad dog at times but I've always been a fair one.

For meetings we'd eventually travel to Vegas where we had a blast racing karts on a large road course. We'd go back to Mexico to take a stab at the Baja course again but this time starting and ending in Cabo. One January, while we were off-roading somewhere in the desert between the Pacific Ocean and the Gulf of California, my wife left me a message that would cut my trip short. "I've got two tickets to the NFC Championship Game at the Link. You want to go?" Yes, I was having fun but if you are an Eagles fan and you have this chance you take it so I told the boss I needed to get to the nearest airport and head east. It was Saturday in January 2005 and my flight took me from Mexico to California where I had a connection in Los Angeles that would get me home very late Saturday night. The weather in Mexico had been 85F all week but the weather at home was heavy snow and colder than a witch's – nose. "Not sure if the airport is going to stay open," was all they could tell me at LAX but they took my bag after I cleared customs and I was so excited to get home for the game.

"I don't think I can get out of the driveway," is all I heard from my Mrs. The snow had pretty much brought the Philadelphia region to a dead halt. Within ten minutes of boarding time, my flight was cancelled. I was able to get my bag back and check into a local hotel where I watched the weather and hoped for the best. But it was clear I wasn't going to make it. Worse yet, if my flight did take off in the morning I'd miss most of the game while I was in the air. To make it more interesting, my wife has some health issues and not being able to get out of the driveway in an emergency doesn't cut it. Knowing I wasn't going to make it home in time, and that the temperature at the kickoff was expected to be around 17F, her decision wasn't a happy one but a good one. She called out to the two teenagers that lived next to us. "Get my driveway clear and these tickets are yours." She felt relieved and they froze their asses off watching the Eagles beat the Falcons 27-0. When I landed in Philly I went right to the Marriott that connects to the terminals to watch whatever highlights there were of the game. The silver lining, if there was one, was I got to meet 6' 6" Tight End Chad Lewis there celebrating with friends and family in the bar. He had caught two touchdowns and despite hurting his foot in the game, he and his team were headed for the Super Bowl.

For those of us who spent an inordinate amount of time on the road and particularly on very many lengthy overseas excursions, Cabo was always nice but we were tired and the last thing we wanted to do in the off season was take another long trip. VP was now bigger and better than ever but if chemical costs skyrocketed or weather rained on our sales parade, or both, then profits fell and adjustments would need to be made. Since many of us attended the SEMA show in Vegas in November or the PRI show in Orlando or Indy, we would up flying in a day or two earlier and had the meeting in advance of the show. It saved money and in my case, it saved me needless additional days away from home. Over time Fred would move on and many of the meetings would return to San Antonio and then elsewhere. After our practical jokester, Brad Horton, brought a very special guest to the meeting room at the historic Crockett Hotel near the River Walk, I am not sure if the city of San Antonio suggested we never come back.

Whenever the management team got together for our

annual meeting, each day usually ended over laughs and drinks way into the night. Thankfully the morning hospitality staff was bright-eyed and had the coffee and sweets flowing as we all sat down to get started. We were all recovering from the night before and a few of us may even have been wearing sunglasses. Then in walks Brad. He's got a big shopping bag in his hand and a shit-eating grin on his face.

I'm not sure which one of us he asked to unwrap his "fragile" Christmas gift to us, but whoever it was laid the box on the meeting room table and proceeded to have at it. Off comes the bow and holiday paper and there sat a large plastic container with duct tape sealing it tight. Now I don't know about you but where I come from, Tupperware's pretty good stuff. If you have to duct tape it closed something's definitely not right and neither was Brad. Inside the damn box was a live rattlesnake! We wound up watching that damn thing, something that was so foreign to this Yankee and everyone else at the table, all day. Apparently the waiter who delivered our lunch caught himself staring at the package too so we put the Tupperware down on the floor in a corner for safekeeping. To make the day more special, Steve Burns popped in to listen to what we all had to discuss. He noticed the box and that led to him saying, "You guys just aren't right," a grin emerging, "But that's why I love you all like brothers."

Later that week Burns took me on my first feral pig hunt. See, meetings at VP can be a real blast. I think by that point in my life I had only shot a rabbit but had nailed some squirrels with my pickup. I get hunting but just didn't derive any enjoyment out of the thought of shooting a whitetail deer up back in Pennsylvania. From my photographer days

I much preferred shooting wildlife through my lens. If I ever do need to kill something to eat then I'll load something that's appropriate and have at it. Remember, I said my kids get "hangry" and you can guess which parent they get that from. When it comes to shooting animals for sport, deer might be safe with me but feral pigs are in trouble. They're dirty, deadly, and running like the plague through the South Central U.S. I have no trouble killing something that can harm a kid or knock down an old lady and have her for dinner. We got the gear we needed, all except the damn bug spray, and sat five feet off the ground on a perch waiting for something to come into view. The rifles were equipped with night vision so I was set. "Keep your legs up," Burns told me. "If they come in under us they can bite." Okay, now they're a threat so yes, let's kill 'em. It was fun to sit with Steve out there waiting for our prey but the bugs were killing me. Not sure how long we waited but some deer were feeding at the spot the guide had set up and all of a sudden they ran off. "They're coming," Burns whispered. A minute later a few pigs walked into scope's view and on the count of three we both squeezed off a shot. Mine was down but flopping around like a fish out of water so I nailed it again. It was a pregnant female with about six inside and I only know that because the ever-curious Steve Burns decided to conduct an autopsy. Considering they multiply like rabbits, technically, I eliminated dozens of the damn bastards. An hour later we were headed back to town and the bar that had a cold Bud with my name on it. Fun night, shot a pig, drank a beer. It sure beat watching television.

For the first meeting I got to plan in my new corporate role, especially under new ownership, I wanted to do something impactful. The destination would be Syracuse, New York for the World Racing Group's Super DIRT Week on the Mile. Every sport has its Super Bowl. In motorsports there are the Indy 500, Daytona 500, 24 Hours of Le Mans, U.S. Nationals and this one had become very special to me and my region. It was essentially the Speed Weeks of the Northeast. During the daylight hours teams would tow into the paddock area at the New York State Fairgrounds and participate in practice, qualifying and eventually if they made it into the show, race in the 200 lapper on Sunday. Each night many would load up and head out to one of the six or seven other dirt tracks in the area to race. There was action at Fulton, Brewerton, Rolling Wheels, Utica-Rome, Five Mile Point and so on. Fuel was being consumed day and night from Wednesday through the checkered flag of the 200 on Sunday and I wanted every drop of that business.

Aside from the massive racing at the fairgrounds there were all those nightly events for Big Block or Small Block DIRT Modifieds at the tracks that surrounded the area. I wanted to show the team not just the value of our partnership with WRG that included the Sprint Car and Late Model touring divisions, but also the amount of spec VP racing fuel sold in the area that week alone. Syracuse had been the first big race I had worked, although somewhat covertly at the time, with Fred when I started at VP and I hoped the rest would get a sense of just what's possible with some vision and hard work. I wanted everyone on the team to experience the happening but I also wanted them to understand what it had taken to get there.

When I started at VP it was the spring, perhaps April

1986, and we filled orders and worked races of all kinds in the Northeast region. Once the fall arrived, sales fell off as dramatically and the phones stopped ringing. It was as if someone pulled the plug on the season, much like when the driver pulls a parachute on their funny car as it crosses the finish line at 320mph. The leaves all began to change from green to orange, yellow and red, and that meant it was time to load up and work my first Super DIRT Week.

We checked into the same hotel off the 7th North Street exit of I-81 that Fred and Tony had stayed at the last few years. As I've indicated already, money was tight back in the early days so we had to share rooms, and working Super DIRT Weeks was no different. Sometimes that meant enjoying the same television show and having a few beers before bedtime. Other times it meant sleepless nights as the chainsaw snoring of your roommate caused you to consider sleeping out in the truck instead. We'd park the fuel truck behind the hotel and one of us would wait at the rig while the others used the white VP van to ferry loads of blue 55-gallon drums of VP fuel, filled to the 54-gallon mark, to the track. Throughout the day, whoever would man the truck would direct racers in pickup trucks as they backed up to the trailer's lift gate. We'd slide as many drums into their beds as the racer wanted to buy. It was October, the end of the season except for dyno testing and snowmobile racing, and we wanted to sell every drop of fuel we had on board. Our drag race friends in the area would come by and pick up a few drums and perhaps a case of fuel jugs they'd want to give a buddy for a Christmas present in a few months. Makin' money was what we needed to do. It didn't matter if the drums we sold in October there wouldn't be consumed until the spring and perhaps make the April sales look light. It cost us money to make the inventory and we wanted to make it back with some profit as quickly as we could. It didn't help us if drums were sitting in storage for six months. Later we'd of course manage inventory so you only had what you needed but, for example, a rainy September would have left us with way too much to sit and gather dust.

Finally it was my turn to run drums to the track and I can tell you that my first trip to the Fairgrounds left quite an impression. You'd sign in and get a car pass and then drive through the maze of RVs and camping trailers parked on the outside of the track. There were dirt race cars and trucks and trailers and quads and people *everywhere*! The pits were packed and so was the infield.

Hundreds of race cars in a handful of classes of competition would practice, time trial, and race on the mile and many would tow to the surrounding tracks for more. Even Oswego, the famed asphalt track that sat on the edge of Lake Ontario, might have had something going on for the NASCAR asphalt modifieds and Super Modifieds that champs like Jamie Tomaino and Bentley Warren raced respectively. We should have sold a ton of fuel and made a truckload of money up there that week, right? Fred had in the past. Not so fast. Sunoco and its distributor M&R had been around in that dirt oval track market forever and they had exclusive on-site supply agreements with DIRT and the area tracks. Okay, not a problem. It wasn't long before not only DIRT but also the Goliath's distributor noticed each year that there were more and more blue drums in the pits and race trailers, and sales of their on-site tanker were on a decline each year.

Glenn Donnelly was the owner of DIRT and controlled everything that went on at the Fairgrounds but to a very large degree, everything that happened on dirt in that region. Something I discovered very quickly in motorsports was that successful promoters and organizations/sanctioning bodies were forward-thinking visionaries. Glenn Donnelly, a brilliant businessman, was one of them. He convinced twenty-five or so dirt tracks within a five-hour drive of Syracuse to join his new organization. He named it DIRT and that stood for Drivers Independent Race Tracks. It was a win-win for the member tracks. In theory, they would work together on race schedules rather than fighting over fans from the same areas. Another member benefit to the tracks would be a good deal on very costly liability insurance. Volume purchases usually yield lower costs to the customer; in this case, the tracks and their racers.

Teams would race under one rulebook so everything was fair and balanced. The top drivers, the most popular ones with the largest fan followings, would participate in a tour. The tour would make race stops at a dozen or more tracks. The fans at each track would get to see their local hero and weekly race teams take on the best of the best, the touring professionals. It was sort of like when the traveling circus came to town once each year. Clearly some of the more successful teams could afford to spend more money on updating their cars and buying expensive, top performing race engines. But for the fans, seeing their local hero – who knew that track better than anyone – run with and sometimes beat the big name professionals was what they came for and kept coming back for year after year.

To encourage participation from as many cars as

possible, Donnelly put together a point fund that would be paid out to participating teams at the end of season banquet in November. To get the check you would have to follow the rules, run his races, and support DIRT. There were many channels that filled the point fund bank. Promoters would pay a fee to DIRT to get a tour date and Donnelly also owned or leased some of the tracks the teams ran on. Then Donnelly started to sell "Official" designations to the companies he had been dealing with. Sunoco was his Official Fuel. I can't remember who his Official Tire was but at this point you get the picture. So to collect the check, racers not only had to follow all the rules but they also had to run Sunoco decals on their race car and Sunoco patches on their driving suit. You didn't have to run Sunoco fuel but it was recommended and no other fuel company's decal or patches were to be displayed. Racers were allowed to run VP or other fuels, they were just encouraged to support the DIRT sponsor.

He probably tired of listening to M&R's complaints about VP and racers bringing VP drums onto the property. I understood that perfectly. I can just hear someone saying to him, "We pay DIRT all this sponsorship money but you're letting VP in and they're hurting our sales." Glenn reacted. One year, just prior to Syracuse and without much warning, a DIRT tech bulletin came out stating NO 55-GALLON DRUMS would be allowed on pit road or even into the fairgrounds. Fred Morrison was brilliant and came up with a fix in a flash. We rolled into the area with a truckload of 55 and 30-GALLON drums! Sold a ton of them but before long we were busted. We got caught sneaking fuel into the Fairgrounds. While all eyes were on VP some of our dealers, two superstars in particular, kept up the effort until they were caught too. Mike Litz from Albany and Al Wilcox from Vestal were a few of our original dirt racing dealers and when it came to "whatever it takes" and "get 'er done" you could count on them. Fred, whose father was a Marine who fought in Korea, improvised, adapted and overcame DIRT's ever-changing regulations. The size of our guys' hearts and their drive to succeed made the difference and would eventually help little David, little VP, grow into something well-armed with people, passion, and chemistry to take on and defeat any Goliath. People, and their passion, would be our David's slingshot.

That "whatever it takes" attitude ran through everyone's blood at VP. When the same pushback came at Volusia in Florida, Tommy Chapman made a deal with a property owner right across the street and set up a fuel truck. When Sunoco had the deal for a race at Sebring, Fred and Mark Klein from Florida would deliver drums to teams late at night. When Watkins Glen wouldn't let me make a delivery to the Archer Brothers for their Trans Am entry years back, later in the day I met the team and rolled the drums under the cyclone fencing. Sure, sometimes the police or a fire marshal would stop by but by the time they arrived we were usually met with, "What drums?" Sometimes it was the attitude of the gatekeepers or the arrogance of the Goliath dealer that fired us up even more.

We all know for every action there is a reaction and back at Syracuse, Donnelly finally decided to make a big move. Now, if a racer wanted to receive Sunoco's portion of the point fun money at the year-end banquet you needed to fuel exclusively with Sunoco. Not just that but you had to run their decals and patches and couldn't run any from a competing brand. Some racers followed suit while others might have forgotten about it or thought it was just an idle threat, but boy, were some people "surprised" at the banquet.

The top 10 or so racers from each class were presented with an envelope. Inside was a check or in some cases, a note that read to the effect: "Had you participated in the Official Fuel Program you would have been entitled to $25,000. As you did not, you will not receive any funds from the fuel portion of the point fund." Ouch. We had secured a bunch of customers, gotten around many of the roadblocks, and kept building momentum but the note in some of those envelopes was like a gun going off. I'm talking someone just shot our DIRT sales in the head, not the starter pistol kind. *Holy Shit* is all I could keep thinking. "Hang in there guys," is the best I could tell any of our customers who were out a bunch of point fund money. They liked VP. They knew it ran better that the other brand. They just couldn't afford to give up anywhere from $2,500 to $25,000. For the non-professional racer who operated without sponsorship support, which was many of them, they counted on those funds to make it through the winter. We needed to do something and do it fast.

Within a few days I had sent formal letters to the teams stating that going forward we would match the money they forfeited by running our fuel. If they couldn't run VP Racing Fuel decals on their cars then we gave teams VP racing lubricant ones to use. To help some teams out we gave them some drums of free fuel that they could sell to snowmobile racers up in New York and use the cash to help pay some winter bills. At the start of the next season, big names like Brett Hearn were on the VP program and flying our colors. The guy's smart, presents himself very well, wins a ton of races, and knew the value of making more power AND having an engine run at cooler operating temperatures on those hot July nights. I still have the photo of Brett posing in front of his pole winning DIRT Modified at Super DIRT Week. He won the pole on VP and a month or so later he got the envelope that said he missed out on $18,000 in fuel point fund money. It was expensive for us but if you're in it for the long haul then you dig in and keep going.

If there was a lesson to be learned that week by the team, it was that if you follow the thought of aligning tracks or promoters to put on good paying races with touring stars taking on the local champs you might have something that can grow big sales for your regions. I preached control the tracks, control what the cars burn, and you will help control your future. Make all the tracks VP tracks. This wasn't something I came up with, I had learned it from the best, watching Glen Donnelly and Howard Commander. Partner with a tire company and other companies to create a viable series with good payouts and point funds. With tracks closing and the stands looking leaner at times, a company that did what they could to help the tracks succeed could assure the future of both. Glen Donnelly had developed the model in the region and WRG continued to develop it, as has Brett Deyo with his very successful efforts. After I first met with Brett a few years back, before he really took off, I wanted him on the VP team either as an employee or a consultant. He could be the guy that could make what I had been professing happen not just in the Northeast but spearhead the efforts for the other regions. We had the same game plans, Brett and I. This all occurred during the ownership transition and I couldn't pull it off but I was able to sign Brett's series to a multi-year VP deal. After I moved on he continued his relationship with VP but as this is being written news is out that he's signed a very lucrative long-term contract with Sunoco. Bummer.

Meetings and conference calls can be very beneficial and productive. If they aren't, then make them so. Make the most of the time. Bring in speakers, experts in their fields, to teach and develop and fix problems and design solid sales strategies. Collaborate. You can never stop learning and despite what some people think, no, they do not know everything. To show how crazy this meeting nonsense is in some corporate cultures, I know of a few companies that have meetings to discuss when they want to have their next meeting. Seriously?

Meetings can also be fun but they are what you make them. They can build camaraderie and help dissolve hard feelings or disagreements that may have evolved and festered over time. But make the most of them. On another excursion, this one part pleasure the other part business, I was able to get a very close look at a former enemy and my current competition all in one trip.

I had always wanted to visit Japan. The culture intrigued me and it was the gateway, at least in my geography, to what I hoped would be eventual trips to China, Thailand and Malaysia. I'm not sure if I told the manager in charge of the region that I was going for fun and he should come and we try to do some business at the same time, or vice versa. Either way, it was a memorable experience. Fourteen hours or so in the air from Newark, New Jersey to Tokyo, Japan and I was finally in the country of geishas and samurai but also the one that attacked the United States at Pearl Harbor in 1941. We were now in what is known as the Land of the Rising Sun and for all of us we'd flown with the sun as we traveled all those hours and miles. Enough already, how about a sunset and some sleep!

Beer at the hotel bar is my cure for that sort of jet lag followed by some Tylenol PM and some shuteye. The next day we got moving early, finding it awkward how every hotel employee bowed to us as we found our way around the buffet. The train station was a trip in itself. No English signage whatsoever! In Europe at least, with most romance languages coming from Latin origin, you can sort of figure some things out. Not in Tokyo but luckily the people were super-friendly and supportive.

An hour later we were on a 198mph bullet train headed south toward Hiroshima. I'd been on banking at Daytona and Talladega. That's what allows the race cars to travel around at great speeds and the train tracks in Japan were banked in many places too. It became a somewhat surreal experience from there on. Walking into our hotel we passed a tree that survived the atomic bomb blast of August 6, 1945.

A short walk from there and we began a self-guided tour of the museum and various landmarks and memorials that are there so that none of us are ever allowed to forget what happened there and why. The photographer in me was having a field day but it didn't take long to put that enthusiasm aside and stop to consider where I was and what all of this meant. One of the most poignant spots near the

Genbaku Dome, the skeletal building that "survived" the blast if you can call it that, was what you can still see all these years later. Burned onto a concrete barrier overlooking the river was the silhouette of a person. Someone had been sitting there during the blast and the extreme brightness of the explosion burned their shadow onto the barrier and remains there today as a reminder of the intensity of that event. I left the others in the group and spent much of the day wandering around that area by myself. It was far away from the noise of racing and my three kids, and it gave me a lot of time to consider just how lucky so many of us are and how unlucky so many of those poor souls were.

From the business side, the manager I met there on my excursion had set up a few meetings and one of them started over lunch at a 100% authentic Japanese sushi restaurant. It was interesting but since I don't eat bait I played with the wasabi and hoped dinner would be better. Right after that the man we met with took us with him to attend the rehearsal for his daughter's wedding. That was exceptional. Kimonos and all sorts of different but beautiful things were part of their customs and ceremony. The evening ended at a hotel that was a real treat. It was the first and last time I ever used a toilet that had a remote control that included a free rinse cycle and a blow dryer! After another meeting or two we sat at an open air bar late into the night watching New Zealand's All Blacks take on an equally impressive team in a rugby match. The next morning we returned the custom of bowing to the staff in the hotel lobby and headed our separate ways. I loved the trip to Japan but there are only two other place on the planet that I've been to that had a greater impact on me. Katmandu, Nepal to see Everest is one. I had worked a trade show in Dubai and then took a few days off and burned some air miles to go even further east, flying over Afghanistan and India and stopping just short of China. My dear friend and distributor for the Middle East, Ameer Akhtarzadeh, was a great host in Dubai and took me first to a beachside hookah restaurant for lunch and then an incredible Italian restaurant downtown for dinner. I can tell you there's nothing like 90F at 10pm. He took me past the indoor snow skiing recreational facility and shuttled me to meetings with local motorsports contacts and the trade show. This guy is one of the most charming people I know and thinking back to another trade show I worked with him there's a story you just have to hear.

Milan, Italy might be known for its fashion and food but for motorsports it's close to the famous Formula 1 track at Monza and is also home to a motorcycle trade show every other year. Ameer came to work the show and to spend time with the VP team. Randy from Toronto came as a sales contest winner, Bruce from California came too and so did our marketing director. After a long day at the show we went to a great restaurant and over drinks I noticed a very famous face sitting at a table nearby.

"I think that's Jackson Browne," I told one of the guys at the table and everyone who knew the name looked over. Yes, it was the famous American singer. I had listened to this guy's music since way back in high school. Songs like 'Rock Me on the Water' and 'Doctor My Eyes' first caught my attention. Ameer caught on that I was impressed and when he saw Jackson head to the WC, the water closet, he saw his opportunity and followed him in. "I'm going to bring him over to meet you," was the last thing he said to us at the table.

Probably ten minutes passed and we were starting to wonder just what was going on. A few minutes later here come Ameer and Jackson, laughing as if they had grown up together. There were smiles and handshakes and introductions all around. God, I hope he washed his. I'm a bit of a germaphobe from back in the funeral home days. "So tell the story, Jackson, tell the story," Ameer begged.

The singer pulled up a chair and related how he had realized someone followed him into the toilet and so he went directly into a stall and locked the door. He took his leak but then realized the man who had followed him in was still standing outside of the stall by the sinks. Not sure if the man was a fan or a threat he opted to stand inside that stall and wait the guy out. "And I was determined to wait for him outside the stall. We never said a word, we both just stood there waiting for the other person to make a move," Ameer related while the rest of us all laughed hysterically. Eventually they exchanged a few thoughts, Ameer stating he wanted Jackson to come over and meet some of his American fans and with that, the stall door opened wide and they hit it off from there. There we were, with this rock star, talking about how we were in town for a trade show and that we sold racing fuel all over the world. He countered that he drove a Cadillac that had been retrofitted to run on used French fry oil and that the car smelled like McDonalds fries wherever he drove. Before long everyone returned to their business but it was a funny occurrence none of us will ever forget.

Returning to my adventure to Nepal, you know you aren't in Kansas anymore when there's a poolside Hawaiian themed Indian wedding going on at the hotel. I had flown in at night so I didn't get to experience the full wonder of their airport but the next day I did for sure. There were monkeys in the parking lot, just like in other parts of the world I hope to see some day. A quick flight on a small plane to check out that beautiful mountain range and especially the one that's as high as the jet stream at 27,000 feet. *People climb to the top of that sucker*, I kept saying to myself. It's an amazing feat but I also thought about those who didn't make it and the loved ones they left behind. I was back in town at the hotel by early afternoon and wanted to see what Katmandu was all about. I took a long ride downtown to the area the concierge had told me was THE place to go. There were dozens of tourist shops and just as many selling camping, hiking, and climbing gear. Jumping out of a perfectly good airplane, and returning to Nepal for a trek to base camp, are at the top of my bucket list. Hey, maybe I can kill two birds at once some day.

I have always counted on two things when traveling overseas. You can count on Hilton Hotels to give you the same fantastic cheeseburger and fries no matter where you are in the world. The other is the Hard Rock Café. You can count on the same menu and top quality so I figured I'd find the HRC for a beer and burger, buy some t-shirts, and head home. Ten minutes later, surrounded by a street full of Nepalese people, I watched as the only other white guy in the area was chased down the street by a small mob. All of a sudden I felt like I was on the moon.

Apparently the prick had been caught shoplifting and the local justice would involve him getting his ass kicked or worse. For me, just in case these typically peaceful people of Nepal got worked up in a shark-like feeding frenzy, I figured the bar back at the Hyatt would do me just fine and before long I was in a cab headed for the hotel. The next morning as scheduled, I headed west through Qatar, over Israel, over Europe and the Atlantic and finally home. Twenty-eight hours and 7,600 miles after leaving Nepal behind me I was back in the City of Brotherly Love.

Seeing Everest in person had been a bucket list item but also a quick exploratory trip as I like to do recon before I get more involved. The photographer in me went nuts at the opportunities but convincing the VP boys to trek with me to base camp was my ultimate goal. Things changed before I ever got the chance to pitch the idea. The other spot on earth that touched me the deepest? Well my wife is still pissed about it.

"You're not going," is what I kept hearing. She's never kept me from doing anything I wanted but she would strongly voice her concern. She had no interest in becoming a widow or having to sell the house to pay my ransom after hearing some of the ideas I'd come up with since we first met. I had envisioned seeing the Holy Land for some time but all she could think of were the scenes broadcast on the nightly news of burned out buses in Tel Aviv that had exploded at the hands of suicide bombers. "You can go but I REALLY don't want you to," she would say. Okay, don't worry.

I don't lie to my wife. Opting to not tell her something is another story and in this case, I opted not to share my full itinerary. I really wanted to see Jerusalem and so she wouldn't worry I just forgot to tell her where the last stop was on one of my European business trips.

My beer and Tylenol PMs combo were always my go-to

when jet lag would screw with my sleep cycles. One night, when buzzed and ready for bed I inadvertently emailed the Mrs. the full itinerary. I had flown from Philadelphia to meetings in the U.K. and then Frankfurt, and the story was to take an extra day or two to slow down and smell the German roses. In reality, I was flying from Frankfurt to Tel Aviv. Security checkpoints at the departure airport were impressive. I think I was screened three times. The night flight got me to Israel around midnight and things were going smoothly until I checked my voicemail. Needless to say, someone was pissed when they learned where I was really headed and we'll just say we didn't talk for a day or two. I waited in the typical long lines for customs clearance and the next roadblock to a peaceful and spiritual visit to the Holy Land came when the customs guy didn't believe my story. "There's no way you are stopping here for just twenty-four hours!" It took some convincing but I got through finally. I told him I had miles to burn and always wanted to visit so here I was, and within a short time I was in front of the massive Dan Panorama Hotel just a short walk from the center of my religious universe. It took twenty minutes for the hotel security to find my reservation before they unlocked the front doors and let me in. In that city it is clear things are a bit different from our tourist destinations.

Anyone that knows me might be surprised to read that I have anything to do with church. After all, most Sundays most of my friends, colleagues, and customers are at race-tracks getting ready to go. But I grew up in a Catholic household, dealing with priests and nuns throughout my parochial school days that included being around them at the funeral home. Remember too that I had an aunt that lived as a cloistered nun at a convent outside of Quebec City. For me, it is clear that Christ lived and died and despite what the Catholic Church may have evolved into, nothing can change my faith in Him. I never ask Him for anything. He's busy enough and I have been blessed many times already. I just thank Him every day for my life and the lives of those most dear to me. Now I was finally as close to the places where He walked this earth as I could ever get. I was excited to be where I was, cognizant of the fact that evildoers weren't necessarily that far away, and disappointed that I had upset my wife. After a decent night's sleep I got moving. Leaving the hotel room I noticed the small wooden case that was mounted on the doorway molding outside each room. I believe it's called a Mezuzah. I am told they contain a specific verse from the Torah, written on parchment. Jews kiss this before they enter their homes. I don't go to Communion since I am a sinner and am not worthy. I didn't kiss the little case since I am not Jewish and didn't want to offend anyone.

A quick buffet breakfast and walking directions to the Old City, and I was off. Fifteen minutes later, passing under the palm trees that stood outside the tan colored buildings that lined the streets, I walked through the Jaffa Gate and before long, after being "harassed" by rug and trinket merchants, the little map I had acquired got me to the Church of the Holy Sepulcher. Being able to stop at the various spots where so many of the most significant events in Christian history occurred was powerful. Standing in deep lines made up of fellow Christians from all around the world was easy. There were no complaints, no pushing, just people sharing in something extraordinary. I'm blessed to have been able to go there and see what I did, to pray before the spot where they say Christ was laid to rest after being taken down from the cross. Then as quickly as the monks controlling the flow through the innermost part of the Church, the Edicule, I was back outside and interested in exploring. My flight back to Philadelphia and to a seething and disappointed wife was scheduled to take off around 11pm. I had plenty of time. I had been told there were certain areas you could go through safely but there were others you should avoid and within twenty minutes of checking out the shops that lined the stone walkways through the Old City, I stopped dead in my tracks. There is a Christian and an Arab element there and the Arab man, standing under a different flag than I had been seeing throughout my walkabout, let me know I should not continue on. Not a word was said but the environment changed. The people past him were not smiling and happy. My gut and years of experience around people of all types said, "Turn left," and so I did. I was immediately back among friendly faces and outgoing merchants. Hours later I was back at the airport, heading home, mission accomplished.

The 14-hour long flight west to Philadelphia, over Europe and then the cold, dark Atlantic, went quickly enough. I had been able to fly business class and that meant a fully lay flat bed, big television, two meals, and an open bar. The flight landed on time around 530am and an hour later I was home and being hugged by a very happy soul mate. I shouldn't have hidden the trip from her but I wanted to do my own recon. I needed to see if I considered it safe enough to take her or any of my children there if I got the chance to go again. The media in one country can make things look totally different from what is actually going on. We've seen that for years as I watched coverage of the U.S. while overseas and vice versa. No, at the time, buses were not being blown up every day. Violence was rare and tourism seemed very safe. I will go back again some day, hopefully with at least my wife in tow. But a few years after this first trip, I found myself in Israel in the back seat of a taxi driven being driven by an Arab. The taxi quickly came to a stop and was surrounded by Israeli military forces holding automatic weapons. Earlier that week snipers had killed two uniformed Israeli personnel and tensions were on edge.

Having arrested most of my wife's fears, I scheduled a return trip to Tel Aviv and this time it was business. My job was to grow sales in every country that had any form of motorsports and it turned out there was plenty of off-roading and some drag racing in the country. We had been shipping pallets of pails of our race fuels to one shop but I needed to see just how big the market was there to determine if it was all we needed or if we could do much more.

Freddie Turza and I visited the U.K., Germany and I believe the Czech Republic before flying Lufthansa to Tel Aviv. Everything went as planned. We checked into the same hotel I had stayed at a few years before and even though the hotel bar and restaurant were closed at that late hour we walked a few blocks to essentially what was a 7-11 and sat outside under the warm star-filled sky and toasted how lucky we were to work in something as cool as racing and that gave us opportunities of a lifetime like the adventure we were on.

We had a meeting at the hotel with two great guys who were entrenched in aftermarket parts in the region and had a very good understanding of motorsports in their country. It was clear to me that there should be more sales and with their connections we intended to get them. Later that day I was able to act as Freddie's tour guide, retracing my walk beneath the palm trees and past the impressive King David Hotel until we reached and walked through the Jaffa Gate and entered the Old City. We prayed at the Wailing Wall and stopped at every significant site we came across until we knelt inside the Edicule, at the spot where Christ had laid after being taken down from the cross. Daytona and Indy might be a big deal in motorsports and Everest is the ultimate for mountain men and women. But this place, for all Christians, was the holiest and most significant spot known to man. For me being blessed like this, to have visited that very special place now a second time, is incredible. Hours later, we were back at the hotel, packed up and ready to head for the airport. "I'll grab a cab," I called out as Freddie finished up with his credit card at the front desk. We threw our bags into the trunk and I told the driver we wanted to go down the hill to the Garden of Gethsemane before heading to Ben Gurion International Airport. "No problem," the driver responded in English.

You could see the hillside where Christ is said to have given sermons and where he spent his last night with the Apostles before being dragged off by the Roman Guard to be tortured and crucified. Unfortunately, when we arrived at the entrance to the garden all we could see was the CLOSED sign. I've had that happen twice before when I was in Rome trying to see the Sistine Chapel. It turns out it's NOT open all the time. But not being able to go inside the garden was such a disappointment. I had been able to get in two trips to Israel and the way life is you never know if it's the last you'll ever see of something. "Okay, airport please," is all we could say at that point.

On my past trips between the airport and Jerusalem we had spent most of the time on the interstate before entering town, passing the U.S. Consulate, and arriving at the hotel. This time however, after leaving the garden area, it was a slow ride through a rundown area. I kept thinking to myself, "the airport's that way," but perhaps my sense of direction was thrown off which is extremely rare for me.

The knife I always travel with, the one I pack in my checked luggage, was out of reach locked behind me in the trunk. I always have a knife with me to cut the ends off zip ties when hanging VP banners, opening shipping boxes, getting ready to explore that strange noise I heard in the hallway outside my hotel room door at 4am, and so on. Freddie and I looked at each other and just wondered what was up. We didn't have a sense of danger, just that we were strangers now in an even stranger and often dangerous land. Remember the face of the Arab who gave me the look to go somewhere else? I didn't get a sense of impending danger, just a nervous curiosity. As we passed the high walls and guard towers the driver pointed out that was what separated Israel from the Arabs. Okay, keep driving.

Then we were waved to a stop. The Israeli army wanted to know who we were, why we were there, and why we were riding with an Arab driver. Okay, my bad. I thought a cab in Jerusalem that looked like the hundred others was just like the rest. Not so.

"We sell racing fuel made in the U.S. and we're here meeting with motorsports people to get more product into

Israel," I said. The soldier told me, "There's no racing here!" I laughed. "There is, you just don't know where, I guess." They checked out papers and we were waved on. I think we went through two more checks before arriving at the outskirts of the airport, only to be stopped again. This time we had to get out of the car and present our papers while they checked our luggage. We understood. We wanted everyone to be safe, including us. The one soldier's words, "Just don't ride with an Arab driver next time," still ring in my head. Can you imagine getting into a cab in Manhattan and asking someone's nationality first? Next time in Israel, I will.

CHAPTER NINE
JOKER

JOKER, TAKEN FROM the Batman comics character, was his nickname. We'd had enough issues with other drivers and finally a good one arrived. Frank Friske, from "San Antone" as he would proudly say. This guy would be another winning piece to my success puzzle and to VP's but more importantly, a very good friend. You might think he was another DH that I brought in. As I say over and over, timing is everything. Now that I was single after all those years it was an even stranger world. On some nights I'd be the great, loving, devoted dad. On the other nights, and on the road, I was party boy and there was Joker, right there alongside.

By now you've gotten a sense of what a typical day might look like in Southeastern Pennsylvania and this one wouldn't be any different. Having worked a race over the weekend, Monday was filled with offloading the race truck, offloading incoming shipments from Texas, working the phones to get outgoing orders, customer calls, sales prospecting, ordering product from suppliers, and so on. I hadn't seen the kids since Wednesday night so I was really looking forward to getting out of Chester and into their hugs. My ex had been taking care of them day and night since that last visit and she had her own life and things to do that night so I needed to get there at a decent time. No problem, it's race season and the phones are ringing off the hook. The new driver from the leasing company was flying into PHL (Philly International) late that afternoon. Knowing the back way, we could get to the airport in 11 minutes. I-95 would be flooded with rush hour traffic headed from the city south toward the PA suburbs and Delaware. The idea was to pick him up, get him back to the plant, give him his trip money and paperwork and strap him into the rig and send him north. First stop might have been Brooklyn and then on to Long Island.

Cell phones still weren't the rage back then for everyone. All I had been told was to be looking for a tall guy with a beard coming off a Delta flight through Atlanta. Everything so far that day had gone well so of course I was expecting an abortion of some sort but I was pleasantly surprised. The flight was on time and here comes this 6 foot 4-ish big fella in a three-piece gray suit and full beard something along the lines of a Grizzly Adams. Pleasantries exchanged, we were headed down 291 toward Chester. Thirty minutes later he was changing into jeans and doing a driver's pre-trip inspection on the truck. It was quick and I wish I'd had more time but the kids were waiting, the ex was pacing, and I needed to get going myself.

"Here's my home number and office number. If you have any problems or questions, just give me a call." With that, road atlas in hand, he was headed across the river to NJ and the turnpike north and I was pushing it to get to my kids. The deal I had worked out with the ex was I'd pay child support and a lot extra so that she could stay home and take care of the kids until the youngest was in grade school full time. For those of you who have never gone through a divorce, I can tell you it's a very strange thing. You're paying for the kids, paying the mortgage on the house, and you have to knock. Strange but fair, as it was my choosing to try to find happiness elsewhere and this, among all the really bad things that come in a divorce when there are children involved, was a consequence.

I got there late, got "the look", and the kids smothered me with hugs and kisses that always made me forget about the look and everything else. They were the center of attention, the center of my world. We'd pile into the extended cab pickup or whatever I was driving back then and head for the mall. They'd get to decide on Pizza Hut, Denny's or Roy Rodgers. After catching up and walking the mall for a bit we'd pile back into the ride and head home. I'd help get them changed into their pajamas and then spend some time with each of them individually as I tucked each one in and said goodnight. After that it was a quick check-in with their mom to make sure everything with them was good and then adios. I'd be back in the second house I was paying for, the one I was living in, within twenty minutes and would decide on one of three things. Get cleaned up and go out for a beer, relax in front of a ball game on television, or do some work. Monday night football might have won out that night after a quick trip to the beer store. One thing I did know, I loved my kids and missed them but I didn't miss the cigarette smoke and other things that helped to chase me from that house. The smoke was so bad there that when the kids would come out with me, people could smell the smoke on their clothes. Worse than that, some kids in the neighborhood weren't allowed to play with them because of the smell. Parents thought they were sneaking a smoke with one of my kids or just soaking in the bad air. I get it, smoking is an addiction but there are solutions. Heck, I've beaten all of my demons except one.

The next day at the office I got to hear all about Joker's first day on the road with us. "Some prick I asked for directions sent me down a dead end street." Okay, welcome to the Big Apple, Mr. Joker. Apparently they have a sense of humor there too. In all seriousness, that could have been an attempt to set up a robbery. Put the truck and the unknowing driver in a tough spot and take advantage of it. Luckily, he backed her the hell out of there and found his way onto and off of Long Island. Weeks went by and before long Joker and I were working a race. He'd learn how we did things, setting up pumps and back-up drums and pumps for as many as 12 different race fuels. We had quick-release male/female connections on the hose ends and drum openings so we could swap out a pump from an empty to a full drum in about six seconds. He also learned how to deliver drums to paddock and pit areas if needed, and so on. Joker caught on really quick and he also really seemed to be enjoying working with us. After a long day we'd head to a hotel, get cleaned up, and meet in the bar. I think I am still foggy all these years later but at some point, Mr. Joker introduced me to Mr. Cuervo; Jose Cuervo that is. I don't believe I've ever been the same.

Again, I liked to look at my operation as a football

team. I wanted a good facility for my players, the best player at every position, and a solid game plan on how to make max money and not just defeat but also eliminate the competition. You have to dream big, aim high to get there. The latter would never happen, it couldn't happen, but it was a goal and just like aiming at 25% growth each year, you can't get into space if you don't reach for the stars.

So the girl answering the phones, preparing the paperwork, and managing the office (second-hand, single-wide office trailer) was doing her job. The warehouse guys were doing what was needed of them and then some, and this new driver was getting it done. All we needed to complete the rosy picture was good weather. Remember how I drove from Philadelphia to Los Angeles via San Antonio in January 1978, only for the race to be postponed due to snow? For me, there is nothing worse than wasting time. If we worked our butts off all week, juggled family time, and loaded up and traveled for a day to get to a race only to sit there for three days watching the clouds take a leak on us, then I was pissed. Wasted effort, wasted expenses, wasted time away from family and then having to return to that same location a week later to service the rain date was a real nut punch for me.

Thankfully, the crazy racers we got to work with could be counted on for entertainment. One rainy afternoon after we had ingested a dozen donuts, a gallon of coffee, and one or two of those "guess what animal this crap came out of" cheeseburgers, Bob Kaiser saved the day. He's been around racing forever and I knew him personally since he ran an automotive garage in the town where I lived. He had heard my *Survivor* story and had something in mind just for me. Wait, you might not have heard about my casting call.

I love that CBS show *Survivor*. It takes all the elements of *The Art of War*, something I reference here from time to time, and puts people in an extraordinarily strange environment. Sound like fun, right, so I tried my best to get on the show. I had made a video each year and mailed it in with the paperwork. Year after year I never heard anything back but since I rarely give up I kept trying. One of the questions they asked on the application was "Name one personal item you'd like to bring with you." Okay, I wanted to make my video stand out once and for all so I grabbed my son David and off we went to a specialty shop on Walnut Street in Philly.

We looked and looked at all the cool gizmos and gadgets they had strung out all over the shelves and racks. "Put that dildo down," was something I never thought I would *ever* hear myself say. It was an adult toy store of course and I was looking for something very specific. Baaaaa! There she is. So we make the purchase and head home to film the video. With David holding the camera, there I was with a silly grin on my face, asking the *Survivor* casting people if they could regard the inflatable sheep I was standing beside as my "personal item." Now this time I would definitely get a call right? *Nada.* So what's next? How about mailing a letter directly to Mark Burnett's office in LA? He's the executive producer and this was my Hail Mary. In it I suggested that I was known for some perfectly timed one-liners and that I thought (now this was for shock value only) that people with IQ's below 100 shouldn't procreate. Off went the letter and months went by with no response.

Life kept moving and before long I was on yet another overnight flight from Philly to London Heathrow with meetings set up for the next morning and then another flight on to Munich or who the hell can remember where at this point.

If you haven't flown on a red-eye flight across country or eastbound on a transatlantic flight I can assure you that it needs to be on your bucket list. If you go to the right country or countries then you'll have a blast and the cramped quarters and jet lag will be well worth it. For me, on this bright sunny morning in London as we taxied to the arrival gate I turned on my cell and checked for messages.

"This is Eric (I think that was his name) from *Survivor* casting. We got the letter you sent to Mark Burnett and wanted to know if you can be in Los Angeles on Tuesday for an interview." Now this is a true, swear on my eyesight, story. Okay, after about a minute of quiet happy dancing in my head I thought, *how the hell can I pull that off?* I had meetings and more meetings scheduled there in the U.K. and then on to the Continent, meetings that took a long time to secure and could not be taken for granted. Believe it or not, and to this day I can't either, I called them and had to decline. I asked if they would consider me for the next round. He said sure but chances like that don't come along very often so I was pretty sure my name would go down in casting infamy. Looking back, what I should have done was called in sick to the meetings and jumped on a flight straight to LAX. But I didn't. I did my job. After all, getting that call for an interview is rare, getting picked is tougher and at this point only thirty or so people can make the claim that they actually won the damn thing. To me, to a degree, I had won already. I've always tried to get what I want and if conventional methods don't work then I usually come up with something that will.

Let's jump back to a race at Maple Grove and it's still raining. While I was sitting on the top of a race fuel drum inside the back of the trailer, begging for any sign of sunshine and warmth, my day lit up. Here comes Bob in his little white Chevy pickup. There's something or someone riding with him but I can't make it out through the wave of the windshield wipers. He's honking the living hell out of his truck horn so of course everyone is looking at him and then us. As he rolled to a stop he jumped out laughing and pulled a present for me out behind him. There she was, all blown up and ready to go.

When someone tosses you something you catch it right, unless it's on fire, dog poop, or an arrest warrant. This air-filled beauty, complete with flowing red hair and more inputs than the Holland Tunnel, came flying up to me. Everyone within sight or sound of the occurrence burst out laughing hysterically. Bob's always been a good friend and I want to thank him again. She was a good kisser.

On the occasion of another rain out, this one during the U.S. Nationals drag race in Indianapolis, we found a fun way to pass the time away. The weather had been bad all day and we knew they were going to cancel. We just had to wait it out. Sometimes I think they're really optimistic. Other times I think the decision makers are just trying to sell as many burgers and coffees and t-shirts as possible before calling it a day and sending everyone home. On this particular day at Indy, the NHRA's weather station must have been working just fine but for the guys and girls working the two fuel trucks we were sure the day was a goner.

"There's a liquor store right down the road," someone said. You'd have thought someone said Santa Claus is coming! Within an hour we had made the excursion, brought back a good amount of beer, ingredients for "buttery nipple" shots, and all the ice, solo cups, and munchies to get this party started.

Five-gallon plastic jugs came four to a box and those boxes came in handy. We set up a bar along with a six-foot tall privacy wall in the nose of the trailer and in no time the crew and a few invited guests were feeling little pain. All of a sudden something was really wrong though. Crap, my eyes were starting to hurt! Did we accidentally get hold of some grain alcohol like the old days at Penn State? Was I going blind? Uh oh, it was the sun! There she was, in all her glory, burning through the clouds and very quickly drying up the track and all the paved access roads. The race would be back on soon and we were struggling to make sense of it all. Troopers that we were, we got our acts together pretty quickly and by the time people were standing in line with their jugs needing fuel, we were taking good care of them as always.

At day's end, headed back to the hotel, the nipples and the Budweisers were all flowing again. Sales were good despite the crappy weather and everyone was ready to get cleaned up and find some real food to eat. I have to give old Joker some credit. I thought I could knock back a few beers but hanging with him, you were expected to down a six-pack before you made it to the hotel, even if the damn place was right down the street. It got to the point where we were going through a case of beer per person per night. Jose would again find his way to the party and before long everyone would be unconscious and dreaming of the sunny day of racing to come.

Taking care of our existing and potential customers was very important to us and kicking the competition's ass was equally the case. But when it was time to have fun, we did. Don't get the sense that we drank all the time. We didn't but life on the road, working race after race, can get monotonous. We might have been working at a race but we weren't out on the track going fast, we were behind the scenes fueling the action. Take into consideration that this all took place way before the miracle of iPhones, Wi-Fi, FaceTime, and all the modern day technology.

Dealing with customers, especially the rare one who felt he might have bought bad fuel, was always interesting. I have mentioned before though, I always found humor was a good way to deflect tension and get people breathing again. One time this racer said he had some green C12 that didn't make it through tech. We were closing up for the day and his sample was way on the other side of the track. I asked him if he would bring it by in the morning and we'd run a few tests on it.

That night, in addition to picking up more beer and munchies at a local grocery store, I picked up one of those little boxes of food dyes. The next morning I put some water in a new white plastic jug caps and dropped a bit of green food dye in to make it resemble green C12. Eventually the customer came by and I invited him into the nose of the trailer where I had set up my hydrometer kit, dielectric meter and a few other gizmos to make things look like we knew what we were doing. Actually, we *did* know how to check fuel in the field and would, once we had some fun with this guy. With everything going on I managed to pour his sample into another new white jug cap and then pulled a switch. As an aside, jug caps used to be white plastic until someone at VP realized ultraviolet rays could get to the fuel and damage it so eventually even through that small lid opening and made the change to black. White jugs are the easiest to see through to check fuel levels but just like you can see through it so can the ultraviolet rays. Left out in the sunlight, the lead or other chemicals in race fuels can be knocked out of suspension by the rays and render the gas useless. I picked up the green water I had made and smelled it for a few seconds as if I was checking a fine wine. As the customer and my truck driver watched intently I then took a big swig of it. His face might not have changed expression and neither did mine but the driver turned away and went back to work so his laughter wouldn't give it all away. I swished it around and down it went. "Yep, that's C12." I offered him a sip and he looked at me like I was crazy. Then I showed him the food dye, offered him a donut, and went about testing the sample he had brought me. It was off. We determined that one of his crew guys had used the same fuel jug to get pump gas for their generator and once good clean race fuel was pumped into the jug the good fuel became tainted with gasoline residue. Case closed. By the way, food dye can be fun for the whole family, just ask my kids. They grew up on my Saturday morning breakfasts of green French toast, blue scrambled eggs, red milk, and so on.

As anyone in racing or many sports events for that matter knows, rain delays can drive you crazy and for a variety of reasons. In some events we rented RVs so we'd have somewhere to get out of the elements, cook some food, have hot coffee or cold drinks for our guests and ourselves. I love movies, and back when DVDs were the rage I'd travel with a handful of my favorites and some new ones so I'd have something to keep me out of trouble. At one race, I got to share one of my favorites with Joker and the rest of the VP crew. It was raining its butt off and the forecast looked bleak but since they didn't cancel the schedule we piled into the RV to wait it out. Before long, grilled cheese sandwiches were being served and I popped *Monster's Ball* into the DVD player. If you haven't seen it I do recommend it for a variety of reasons but mostly it's for Halle Berry and her erotic adventure with Billy Bob Thornton. It was pretty hot and for some strange reason included a birdcage. After we watched the entire film and saw that the rain was far from over, we wound up watching the birdcage scene at least another eight times. Nothing like six guys crammed in an RV watching a sex scene. The only thing that afternoon was missing was Bob Kaiser, his plastic girlfriend, and my sheep.

It wasn't all fun and games though and one morning after forgetting to set an alarm I got a very real wake-up call that almost cost Joker and me our lives.

Rockingham Dragway in North Carolina was holding the Winston Invitational drag race. This was back when cigarette advertising was still allowed and that brand was a series sponsor. The southern pine trees of that region were everywhere and the well-known golf course at Pinehurst was just thirty miles up the road.

"Damn it," one of us yelled. We'd overslept and needed to get our butts dressed and to the track! The last thing I ever wanted to do was let a customer down, and when you're providing the on-site race fuel supply, you didn't want to have anyone miss a qualifying round because they couldn't get fuel from the truck. *Das ist verboten*!

I gulped down as much coffee as the baby coffee maker could brew and washed up and dressed as quickly as possible. Off we went down the road. Traffic was backing up and one of us thought we could drive down a back road across track property we had just passed. It had to lead to the track so we hoped we could get into the facility quicker that way. Remember now, we might have been slightly hung over. I was driving and hauling ass like a rally driver through the pines. In an instant, our lives flashed before us. There it was, a heavy steel cable that was hanging from two pine trees, at hood height, across the road. I slammed on the brakes and as the car slid to a halt the cable came to a rest just above the hood at the windshield wipers. If we'd been screwing around another second we were both sure our heads would have landed in the back seat. My kids might have won the court case since there was no flag to warn their daddy of the hazard but I think, at least I'd like to think, they'd prefer to have kept me around instead. Joker and I realized immediately how close we had come to losing weight the hard way. We also figured out how to get into the track and take care of our customers. Luckily we weren't *that* late. I thanked God a lot that day and continue to thank Him for the luck and the blessings I've had. Joker and I agreed that night to tune it down just a smidge. Now don't think we cut back on the partying. We just made sure every hotel we would stay at from then on had a bar and restaurant. If not, they needed to be within walking, perhaps stumbling, distance. We cut back on the tequila and with the help of some friends, at least on one race weekend we got in trouble without drinking a drop.

John and Dottie DiBartolomeo own DRC Race Products in Beaver Springs, Pennsylvania. When John's not engineering new products he's covering drag racing with his camera and his keyboard. On this one weekend in particular he was off working an NHRA National Event and that left his wife Dot to work their display at the NHRA Division One event at Maryland International Raceway in Budds Creek. Dottie, Joker, and I were staying at the same hotel if memory serves me correctly and when we saw she was flying solo we had dinner together and might have taken in a movie that night. Years earlier I had convinced her to join the VP team at the Autosport trade show in Birmingham and had a great time. She has this unforgettable laugh that endears her to so many in the racing community. We ate, watched the movie, and worked the rest of the event before heading back to our home bases. It was refreshing to wake up without any grogginess for a change. Then, about two months later, John came to the VP truck I was working out of and with a very unhappy look on his face said, "We have to talk." Okay. To the best of my knowledge I didn't owe him any money so maybe he's just having a bad day. I finished up with my race fuel sale and stepped to the nose of the trailer so we could talk. The conversation went something like this; "Dot's pregnant!" I was thinking congratulations should be in order but his expression was not a happy one. I learned a long time ago, thanks to lawyers and some people much smarter than me, to keep my mouth shut and not to say anything that could be used against me. "I don't think it's mine," he went on to say. Okay, I'm still clueless. "Remember that weekend you guys were together in Budds Creek?" Holy shit! My mind was racing at 300mph! I looked at his accusing face and he'd have to tell you what mine was doing but all of a sudden he burst out laughing. Yeah, this one wasn't mine, thank God! My keester would have been welded to the top of a flagpole if that had been the case. Many months later John and Dottie had little Christina and years later she'd come to work with me at VP in Delaware before going off on her own to start The Design Joint. To this day, we still laugh about that encounter in the race trailer. Whew.

Back to life on the road, it turned out Joker and I had a lot in common. He was lonely and far from his home in Texas. When I was home, my kids might have been just a few blocks away but because of the divorce, many nights I felt like I lived on the moon. Bored and lonely is a perfect formula for getting into trouble. We'd drink a lot on the road but I wasn't really into drinking at my house, especially by myself, and pretty much never at the office. I had watched my father fall asleep after dinner as a result of his many scotch and waters and I just didn't want that for myself. So if you're bored but can't or don't want to drink there are two things that can pretty quickly liven up a party; guns and starting a fire.

Chester wasn't in the best shape and the singlewide office trailer we used was a target for thieves way too many times. We had bars installed on the windows and the doors, but the burglars decided to just peel the faded, ribbed aluminum away from the exterior and try to climb through between the beams. The front of the trailer was lit up by a complex street light but the rear was in the shadows and vulnerable. Yes, eventually we'd get some lights installed but that would take time. Landlords don't like to spend money, especially when it's a county authority. I remember the would-be burglars must not have been overly bright because one time when they peeled back the skin they encountered the back of a large four-drawer filing cabinet. Now me, I would have moved over to the next area and tried again but luckily, that time they gave up and went away. We had already lost three or four desktop calculators and yet another answering machine so we tried to come up with something that would not allow them to push their way in again. I was smart enough to unplug the fax machine and take it home every night. That little machine was my lifeline to European business. It cost us $600 back in the day so it was precious. Svensk BP, the only overseas distributor we had in the early days, wanted us to send faxes so they could be interpreted and responded to quickly. Overseas couriers were very expensive and nobody wanted to wait for the postal services to get it done.

Since rail was on the premises we looked around and found a stack of very heavy railroad ties. An hour later we had a few of them inside the office and laid them horizontally against the wall. Now remember, we're bored and it's winter so there's not much racing, little phone activity, hardly any work to do during the day, let alone after hours. We were sitting around talking or watching television and I had an idea. Maybe it was something we saw on TV, I can't recall. "Joker, let's set up a shooting range inside the trailer!"

Yeah, okay, it was a crazy idea but what the hell. I carried a 9mm Beretta at work and also had headphones that I wore at the range. We took a piece of paper and drew some circles on it and then stapled it to the massive railroad tie. The office had three rooms and a small bathroom in the center room. The target was at the back of the trailer and I stood perhaps twenty feet from it. Headphones on and have at it. I emptied the clip and changed it out for Joker. It was just the two of us standing in an office trailer in a desolate part of town with nothing going on outside but the winter's cold wind. I remember distinctly that he waved off the headphones and took his turn. *Bam, bam, bam, bam, bam* and within a second he stopped and for good reason.

We noticed immediately that while my bullets had found their target none of his seemed to have. Oh shit, that meant only one thing! We quickly inspected the railroad tie and found some of the bullet holes but there were a bunch missing. Seconds later, standing outside the trailer, we found the "exit" wounds. The damn wall looked like Swiss cheese. Acting like two crime scene investigators we carefully reconstructed the trajectory that the bullets must have traveled as they passed through the thin trailer wall. "Okay, we're good." They must have gone into the ground. The abandoned, burned out buildings on the other side of the railroad tracks were clearly vacant or at least we hoped so. The VP Firing Range went out of business twenty minutes after it had opened and Joker went and got a pair of glasses.

Like two little kids with nothing else to do, what other kinds of trouble could we get into? There were some old trash drums lying around and since it was a bit chilly we decided to fire one up and get some heat going. We could have just gone inside but what the hell, nothing like a campfire and in Chester this was the closest we were going to get to living in nature.

Thanks to the racing fuel we used to get things started, the fire was going good now. We didn't dance around like Tom Hanks in *Castaway* but there was something primal about it, I guess, plus it was cold and we were bored. We fed the flames with parts of broken wooden pallets our former neighbor had left on the property line. Okay, now we have fire. "I wonder if we could see any difference between race fuel and pump gas?' Joker asked. Well, what the hell. It didn't take much to entertain us at that point. We probably had twenty different fuels inside the VP warehouse and storage trailers along with pump gas for lawn mowing and snow blowing. With a basic knowledge of chemistry, knowing about initial boiling points and flashpoints and all sorts of things, there was a chance we might see something interesting. After all, some of the ingredients to these race fuels had different characteristics and reasons for being there but they all had one thing in common. They were flammable liquids and we were curious. Take a second now and consider what Ben Franklin must have been thinking when he sent a kite up into a storm in hopes of attracting some lightning. We're two grown men. "What's the worst thing that could happen?" By the way, we were both trained in HAZMAT and actually knew what we were doing but to anyone that might have been watching who knows what they were thinking.

C12 is a leaded race fuel, dyed emerald green in color, and is one of the most popular race fuels used in the world. We used the plastic cap off the top of a fuel jug to pour a very small stream of fuel into the fire. Okay, that was cool.

Then we tried a larger amount. Okay, that was cool too. I'm thinking as I write this that Joker and I, twenty-five years later, need to reenact the scene and put it up on YouTube.

We tried larger amounts, different race fuels, and for the most part we thought we could tell some seemed to flare up more or quicker but since we were in an open area with winter breezes, who the hell really could tell. "What do you think propylene oxide would do?" one of us suggested. "Prope" aka "PO" was a chemical that was used in fuels to enhance ignition. Man, did that stuff like to catch fire. When mixed with some other chemicals, the right chemicals and in the right proportion, it made for a really nice race fuel. The P in CMP, the ass-kicking race fuel from VP, stood for prope. We wanted to see if we could observe anything different on the flame.

One of VP's early octane boosters was packaged in metal quart cans and it was thought that delivery method might be the safest way to introduce the prope to flame. Now remember, we were curious and weren't drinking. We actually had a 20-pound fire extinguisher nearby in case something stupid happened. Really, with this big Texan and a Pennsylvania Irishman working together nothing bad could happen.

The stuff sizzled. That's my recollection and the best way I could describe it.

We had grown accustomed to handling the jug caps full of fuel as we poured small amount into the flames. We actually got to the point where we could watch the flame travel up the stream and head for the jug cap. Cool. Just don't try this at home. Leave it to us knuckleheads, I mean professionals. We were pros actually. We had Commercial Driver's

Licenses with HAZMAT Hazardous Material Endorsements and training.

If you haven't seen an NHRA nitro-burning Top Fuel or Funny Car I suggest you get to a race or watch some action on YouTube. In particular, watch video taken at night when one of those bad boys is making a run under darkening skies. If all goes as planned, the eight exhaust pipes spit flame much of the way down the track. It's really impressive. The sight, the sound, and the smell are memorable. For us back at the fire drum, the full-on propylene oxide experiment was about to take place. It was getting late and you can only play with fire so long. We opted not to light any nitro. The police might be stopping by at some point to see what we were up to and if they wanted to see a nitro show they would have to go to the races like everyone else.

We filled one of the quart cans half full and threw it in the fire. Remember the flames erupting from the exhaust pipes on the funny cars? The same damn thing happened to the quart can. It remained intact but the flames charged out of the can opening until the material completely burned off. It might have only taken second to burn off but it was worth it. One Mississippi – okay, that was cool! Now let's add more fuel and then let's add a few more cans. Thankfully we were getting hungry and with all of our attention on the bright flames we might have lost track of the fact that we were playing with fire in what some might call not the safest environment in the area. "Nitro – should we try some nitro before we go?" That had to have gone through our minds. We were intrigued but the fact that our luck had been pretty good so far we decided to try that some other time and called it a night.

Not every night in Chester was fun and games though. I still remember one where I thought I might be in big trouble. With warehouse workers coming and going and orders increasing exponentially it was pretty common for me to work all day, drive home to have dinner with the kids, and then drive back down to Chester to load a truck or drum up some fuel. The area was typically very quiet aside from the streetlights that lit up most of the dock. In the daytime you felt pretty safe but at night that wasn't always the case, especially if you were alone. Parts of the development's cyclone fencing had been peeled back or had holes cut in it. The guardhouse at the open front gate was often left unattended too. I had a concealed carry permit in Pennsylvania so I kept something in the office in case of a robbery, something in the car in case of whatever, and a 9mm on my hip when I was working alone late at night.

I'd push a drum dolly into one storage trailer, grab a drum, turn and roll it out of the trailer's darkness and into the dock lighting and then into the VP rig I was loading. There might be ten different storage trailers and twenty different products that would contribute to the 123 drums I had to load. If the driver needed to leave early in the morning then this might be what needed to happen. I'd walk into the darkness and then turn to see the light again and again, until one time as I entered the VP trailer I thought I saw someone down on the ground in the darkness walking toward me.

I stopped dead and called out to the person. I shouted something like, "This is a secure area, you need to go back!" No response. I let go of the drum kart and watched as the person continued toward me. Okay, that's it; I'm not going to become another Chester crime statistic. I pulled my gun, thumbed the safety, and pointed it at him. He kept coming. "Dude, you need to stop or it's gonna get loud!" Nothing. He kept coming. My mind was racing. Do I put one in the ground in front of him or one in the air toward the river? At the time it never occurred to me to look behind me but I should have. Suddenly he stopped and raised his arms. "I'm the security guard," he called out. I couldn't understand why the hell he had kept coming. I kept my gun on him until he walked into the light. He'd had his headphones on and his head down watching where he was walking, without a flashlight! This had become a recipe for disaster I know he won't forget. He'd have his flashlight with him from then on and I'd continue to try my best to get home safe every night. "Enough already with tight budgets," I argued the next day. In no time we spent some money to light the place up like a ball field.

Eventually Joker's wife Nona finally moved north to Pennsylvania and they got an apartment about halfway between my house and the plant in Chester. She was a special lady, with a sparkle in her eyes that lit up the place. She also had a slight and somewhat adorable twang to some of her words, clearly identifying herself as a proud Texan. I learned really quickly that she could drink both me and her husband under the table. What I particularly enjoyed was her warmth and her cooking. Man, could she make a dinner! Other than visiting some Taco Bells and Chi-Chi's in my travels, and authentic restaurants in San Antonio, my familiarity with good Mexican cooking was vague. My first taste of it came when I was in the sixth grade in the Philly suburbs. A family moved into the neighborhood from Texas, and to help introduce themselves and their children to the rest of us, the mom cooked us all homemade tortillas! What the hell's a tortilla? Just a few years earlier, some bastard named Lee Harvey Oswald had killed our President Kennedy in Dallas. That's all any of us knew about Texas but those tortillas won us over and they blended into the neighborhood really well.

Nona and Joker were back together and setting up house. They invited me over for dinner quite a bit and we continued to party there and have fun on the road but there was a void in my life. At an amazing New Year's Eve dinner that Nona prepared we toasted the night away and shortly after midnight I made the quick drive home wondering what the New Year would bring my way. Little did I know that same night, at a house party just three doors down from where I lived, my future soul mate was asking herself the same thing.

Chapter Ten

NOW THIS IS EXCITING

You've already read about some of our exploits in the Great White North but if you're still with me here are a few of my all time favorites. On one trip things got kind of hairy and while on others we got to see something really weird. We were headed up to Sanair from Philadelphia to make a fuel delivery to a distributor and then take the rest of the fuel to the track to work a race event. I had flown into Trudeau Airport just west of the city and got to hang out on Crescent Street just above where it meets St. Catherine. The alcohol content of the Canadian beer was a bit higher than the U.S. blends back then and I was enjoying the atmosphere that makes things there so much fun. It was the start of one of their national holiday weekends so everyone was happy and without a care in the world. The next morning, my truck driver would have to stop at the border and wait for word from accounting that the distributor's wire transfer had hit our bank. We didn't like to take fuel outside of the U.S. without it being paid for in advance. It's tough enough to repo racing fuel in the States. It's a whole other thing to try it where you are a visitor. Even though Canada is like a sister to America, she's still a foreign country.

The only word my driver or I received was that they money had not hit the VP account. Our distributor wasn't answering his phone but since I knew where he lived, right off the interstate on the way to the track, I figured it best to go there and make sure he was okay. I told my driver to sit tight and I'd get back to him. When I pulled up to the man's house his car was in the drive so I knocked and after a short time he came to the door and invited me in. Everything looked okay and he made me a well-needed coffee while I got comfortable and took a seat at his kitchen table. Okay, things were still good. Maybe he was out late last night just like I had been.

He excused himself for a moment and then walked back into the brightly lit room with a large framed .357 caliber revolver in his hand.

The look on his face was somewhat threatening but for some strange reason I didn't feel at risk. I was more curious and wanted to see just where the "F" this was going. He was built like a bull but he had always acted more like a friendly teddy bear. We had spent a lot of time hanging out together so who knows, maybe he was off his meds. He started to pat his other hand with the gun and just stared at me. "Did I say something wrong?" and "I didn't know she was your girl-friend" went through my mind but neither of us said anything. It was just awkward. He began to point the gun at me. The nice thing about a revolver is when it's being pointed at you the bullets, if there are any, should be visible. Yep, it was loaded.

"We're going to have to talk about your prices, Mr. Kelly," he said with a deep voice and French accent. *Okay, I'm not dead yet. He's just being a dick.* He placed the stainless steel gun on the table with a clunk and started laughing. Yep, he was definitely a dick.

He poured himself a cup of coffee, pulled up a chair, and suggested that he had not wired the payment because he wanted leverage to negotiate a better price. I was aware with the holiday, St. Jean-Baptiste Day if I remember correctly, the banks would be closed and at this point no wire could happen until we got through the weekend and the race. If we brought the fuel in and made the delivery to his warehouse it would then be outside of our control and potentially a mess that I'd have to deal with. We needed to get into the country, get his fuel off the damn trailer, and head over to set up to service a race. Despite everything else, I hated keeping customers waiting. What a company guy, I'm in a foreign country with a guy holding a gun and my main concern is to take care of the racers. If only this was happening back home. I could have introduced him to a few of the hand-held toys I have and perhaps a few of my friends with badges.

I heard him out. His argument for getting better pricing was somewhat justified so I agreed to a slight discount. At that point it was better to move on, get the money, and retaliate later. Within minutes, I had $25,000 in American cash in a bag and was calling the driver to tell him to come across. We got rid of his fuel, worked the event, wired the cash to VP's bank in Texas, and headed home. Within months we found another distributor and wouldn't you know, I heard that guy wound up in jail. I wonder if the closing of the jail cell door sounded anything like the clunk on the table that day.

Years back but still fuelin' around in Canada, once that government announced they were going to impose a national ban on the importation of leaded racing fuel we moved quickly. One distributor ordered a full truckload, 120 drums, of one of the most popular leaded fuels available. We pulled the rig into his barn and spent a few hours unloading the trailer. It was late and we were tired and all that was left to do was go down the road to a hotel that had ample parking for big rigs and then find some food and drink. But there was one problem. We got stuck in the barn!

As we removed the 43,000 pounds of race fuel from the trailer its height rose up a bit and as the front of the trailer slowly came close to the top of the barn's doorway we weren't going to clear. It was tight going in and looking bad trying to leave. So one guy thought we'd have to put some fuel back into the trailer to drop it back down. I was wondering where the guy's chainsaw was because I was thinking about customizing his entryway. "Well, how about I just let some air out of the suspension and tires if needed?" was my driver's suggestion. Okay, pass me a Molson. I climbed up the stationary ladder that was mounted on the front of the trailer and watched the clearance as the driver just barely inched his way out. Minutes later we were down the road and cozied up to the bar. I hadn't paid much attention to the rigs before that night but I can assure you I did from then on. Being almost stuck in that barn was interesting but what happened after a race one time was flat-out weird. While packing up the rig after working a big drag race we saw this Canadian race fan walking through the pits upending every empty Nitro drum and collecting whatever leftover liquid he could into a dirty rag. I guess to him it was like sniffing glue but to the rest of us this dipshit needed to go back to the home. We warned him not to do it and got moving a bit quicker picking up the empties before closing the trailer doors and heading out. So Canada has many memories. Some good and some, well not so much. Luckily, thanks to science and common sense, in the years to come that ban would be amended and leaded fuel would continue to flow in the Great White North. Regardless, whether it was leaded or unleaded, that part of my territory grew stronger and stronger. Thanks to great people like Randy Lungal in Ontario – who put VP on the map up there – VP is THE race fuel in Eastern Canada.

Chapter Eleven
YOU TAKE YOUR MAKEUP OFF

OVER THE YEARS I would be asked many times by Steve Burns and eventually by the new owner in later years to move to Texas and take a much bigger role there. My answer would always be no thanks. The reality was that PA is where my children were and I would never move away, whether it would be for love or weather or money. Jet planes and access to phones and email were all I needed to do the job they had for me. I didn't need to move to Texas and for that matter, I didn't want to. I really liked having the separation from the owners. I always did. I liked the freedom and independence to do as I saw fit, when I saw fit without anyone up my kazoo about it. Yes, it might have been passing on an opportunity to make a lot more money and have more power but it also came with much greater responsibility, more stress, and even more time, whether it be physical or emotional, away from my kids. Burns would always just tell me to be profitable and keep us out of lawsuits. Okay, I can do that. In all my years at VP I never got us in a lawsuit. I knew the laws and used them to protect VP rather than having to defend it or myself in court.

At home, every spring, months after the sun seems to have abandoned you for a long, cold winter, it is really exciting when that first burst of warmth hits you. At work, the change was palpable. The first day the temperature climbed past 60F, racers would open their trailers, race cars would be rolled out of garages, and the phones would start ringing. Hibernation might be over but my personal life wasn't all fun and games. Late one Saturday night at home, after pizza and beer and binging on *Cops* for four hours, I took stock of where I was in life.

My parents were gone, the adopted siblings had all gone their own ways, and my kids were living with my ex. I had chosen to keep some distance from our mutual friends for the simple reason that I didn't want to hear any grief about what I had chosen to do. My kids loved me, I had a dream job that truly was an adventure, and I had good health. I wondered that night if I would ever get into another serious relationship. Nobody wants to spend the rest of their lives alone but with three kids and a crazy schedule, it would take a very special woman to accept me as I was. After taking inventory of my situation I found myself at peace. I liked who I was and was happy, for the most part, with where I was at that point. If there wouldn't be anyone special in my life from then on, so be it. I really figured I had been blessed enough already. Some people have a fear of being alone but I didn't. Part of me rationalized that I probably would be and it was the universe's way of paying me back. If that were going to be the case then I would accept the sentence. I might have gone out for more beer at that point but something tells me I called it a night.

On one of the many trips to Texas the girls in the office had taken us visitors out to dance halls to "two-step" as they called it. Most of the dancing I had done was to disco music in Philly and at a bank-turned-disco at Penn State. This was totally different and it was a blast. I had gotten kicked out of one of the dance halls down there and the reason was pretty simple. While a bunch of us were standing around, striptease music came on. In a split second, I was climbing up on the bar. Okay, it was with one of the receptionists. There we were, slowly unbuttoning our shirts to the beat of the music. If you think race cars and pit crews are fast, let me tell you something; dance hall bouncers are faster. I was pulled down off that bar and put out in the parking lot faster than the old Gatorade crew could execute a pit stop. It took some talking but I assured them it wouldn't happen again. They let me back in but I had to button my shirt to the collar first. It was just another fun night on the road. Once back in the Keystone State I wanted to practice my two-stepping and went to a place called the KP Corral in King of Prussia. It's right next to Valley Forge and was adjacent to where Lenny Sammons held his very popular Area Auto Racing News Motorsports show for so many years before it found a good home at the Philadelphia Expo Center in Oaks. The Corral might be gone now but what started there certainly isn't.

There she was, a familiar face that I hadn't seen in years. Lisa and I had met through a mutual acquaintance but that had been the extent of it. She recognized me at the Corral too and we hit it off. Neither of us went there very often so the rare chance of our meeting makes it special. My weekend race schedule was crazy but before long we agreed to get together midweek and go out to dinner. This particular day, Joker and I took a heavily loaded tractor-trailer up to Maple Grove and set it up for the drag race that was scheduled for that weekend. We then picked up a rent truck at Penske's in nearby Reading, loaded it from the trailer parked at Maple Grove, and ran it over to Nazareth Speedway to get set to service the Indy Lights race there. After that we drove the VP Ford Van back down to Chester where I'd finish up my office work and he'd head back to Reading in the van. My date with Lisa was that night and I needed to clear my desk and get home to get ready.

The plan was for me to pick her up at her condo in Bryn Mawr, have a drink, and then go to dinner. We laughed so much that the first drink turned into the third or fourth and I think at that point she had Chinese food or some pizza delivered. I still had to drive to Reading, get some sleep, and get up early to work the drag race. We laughed and caught up and agreed to see each other soon. It was late, it was raining heavily, and I had some miles to go. Little did I know what would be waiting for me at the hotel in Reading.

I checked in and they gave me the room next to Joker's. I knocked on his door to make sure everything was cool but the look on his face wasn't a happy one. "Come on in and sit down," he said somberly. He sat on the side of his bed and went back to pulling windshield glass out of his forearm.

"I wrecked the van," he said unsure of whether it was going to cost him his job. "I left my briefcase in the truck we took to Nazareth. I thought I had left it in the rig at Maple Grove but it had my logbook and the cashbox money in it.

I drove back to Nazareth, got it, and then headed here. It was raining its ass off and I lost it on one of the back roads." That didn't matter. I just wanted to make sure he was okay. He passed me a beer from his cooler and went on to tell me the full story. The van wound up lying almost on its side, at a 45-degree angle, in a ditch. He hadn't been drinking but may have been a few mph over the speed limit trying to make up some time.

"The damn cop that came along wouldn't let me get in his cruiser and kept telling me to get back in the van. I kept reminding him it was almost on its side but he didn't give a shit, get in the van!" I started laughing and eventually Joker did too. I could just picture this big old Texan sitting almost on his side behind the wheel, windows all smashed. The new turbo diesel white van was totaled. Joker had been able to reach our good friend and VP dealer, Craig Von Dohren, who gave him a ride back to the hotel after the cop told him he was free to go.

Joker asked me about my date and I told him it had been fun and that we were going to go out again soon. "That's it?" he asked. "You must really like this one because you're not giving me any details." I just smiled because he was dead on. "You know what we need to do now, don't you?" I asked. Ten minutes later, after finding the hotel lounge closed early on weeknights, we were in my car leaving the parking lot in search of a bar. The fact neither of us noticed the WRONG WAY – ONE WAY signs as I turned left didn't faze us until we saw the headlights coming. Thankfully we were able to hang a U and get on with the evening.

The van incident did actually turn into a bit of a

nightmare after all. Turns out the insurance agent neglected to put the coverage through and so we were left with a junk van and a heavy note due Ford Motor Credit. Luckily those agents have essentially what doctors do in the way of malpractice insurance. Everyone got paid, Joker kept his job, and eventually we'd get a new van. Someone was looking out for us that night and all the others. Thank you, Lord.

Back home, Lisa and I dated more and more and before long it was time to introduce her to my kids. She'd had no real experience with children but her enthusiasm and love of life had her dive in full force, literally. It was Friday night so they were set for a sleepover. After the introductions we took them to the local Burger King where they polished off their nuggets and fries. As we cleaned up we saw the kids jump into the plastic ball area and without blinking Lisa dove right in. An hour later we were up the road at my house and my two daughters were playing with Lisa's makeup while my son and I were watching them and something on TV. Within an hour, the kids had removed all of their future stepmother's makeup. Strangely, they also took her knee-high socks off. Now this is where it gets weird. The girls proceeded to tie Lisa's wrists to the coffee table legs. All she could do was laugh and look at me wondering what the hell I was teaching these children. Like I said, we hit it off from the start and that night showed she'd fit right in!

It was great to see how everything progressed. One thing Lisa made sure of was that she would never encroach on my time with my kids. She understood the impact of the visitation agreement and my extensive travel and was determined that she would never compromise that. One night, I wished she had. Standard operating procedure on Monday and Wednesday nights had been to grab my son and two daughters and head to the mall for dinner and some time together. So the four of us finished up the kids meals and such at the Roy Rogers and headed off to the escalator to check out the lower level. The signs say don't take strollers on those things but I figured I had this covered. I had one in my arm, one holding on to the side of the stroller, and the other holding on to me. One problem, my oldest decided to break off and wave as his sisters and I slowly headed farther and farther away from him. Now you try grabbing two kids and running back up the escalator to get the little bugger standing up top. Worse yet, he was smiling! They, whoever "they" are, say you shouldn't curse around children and I agree but I may have said "fudge" or something like that. As the physical distance between us grew, I asked God to lend a hand and just then a woman who was approaching the launch pad simply put her hands under my little guy's arms and lifted him right up and rode the stairs down together. I was tempted after that to zip tie him to me after that but it was probably against the law.

The holidays were tough though. Once your parents are gone, no matter who else is at the table, Thanksgiving and Christmas dinners just aren't the same. I'm not experiencing or writing about something exclusive to me, everyone gets to experience this in life but that doesn't make it any easier. After my parents were gone and since I had moved out, family gatherings and traditions all changed. No matter what, I would be there to get them ready for bed on Christmas Eve and I'd be knocking at their front door early Christmas morning before they were allowed to come down to see what Santa had brought them. I'm happy to say that despite my decision to move out I always made their school functions, got to sit and watch practices and ball games, and never ever missed a birthday. Hell, I flew to England for a weekend race, flew home for a family event and then flew back to Germany for another race the next weekend. The joy on their faces when I showed up to see them, whether it was just an average weeknight or for something special, was the best feeling ever. It was priceless. Sometimes when I'd bring them home to their mom the look on *her* face though might not have been as happy. Case in point was a particular Saturday before Easter.

I'd suggested that to make our annual Easter egg hunt even more memorable we should have a raw egg fight in the back yard at my house. The dads might be laughing right now but in hindsight I can see why most women are probably cringing. All I had in mind, truly, was something fun. Perhaps it could become a tradition. The day went great and I am still impressed with how well my three could throw. There was egg yolk everywhere! Time was running late so we shot inside to get cleaned up before taking them home but things don't always go as planned. The damn hot water heater had died. In Quebec the French phrase is "*tabernac!*"

Ice cold water showers didn't seem like a good idea so I thought taking them home, where they could get hot baths or showers, would be best. The look on their mother's face when she opened the door wasn't necessarily a good one. I think that was the first and last annual egg fight. We had agreed, no matter what, that the differences that broke us up, either during the break or afterward, would not be aired in front of the kids. They were the most important things in either of our lives and we stuck by that rule since Day One. But bringing them home coated in raw, scrambled eggs definitely caused her to voice her opinion. For the most part things worked out but obviously it wasn't always all fun and games.

There was one of me and three of them. As they got older their personalities and individual needs really evolved so I wanted to get one-on-one time with each of them. Yes, I was aware I had jeopardized that time by moving out but if it was good for the kids I thought it made sense to do it. Well, you can't always get what you want. Their mom refused to modify the schedule and to this day all these years later I still resent it. She said she "wasn't a babysitter," and it was "all or none." Now I was working my ass off to sustain the two households. I didn't want the kids looked after by strangers at a daycare so I gave my ex extra money, a good bit of money, so she could stay home and take care of them until our youngest was in first grade. Even with that she didn't give in to my request. Yeah, I did this all to myself but I was thinking of the kids and I think she was just still pissed at me.

Once a particular September came, the first two kids were already in elementary school with my baby now ready to start first grade. For some reason it meant a different bus schedule and she was supposed to wait for it by herself as her mom went off to work. No, that wasn't sitting well with me in any damn way so every morning, regardless of what was happening at work, I'd drive to their house and pick her up. We went to the local diner every morning for a cinnamon bun or a corn muffin and then I would drop her off at school when it was time. I finally got the one-on-one with at least my youngest. I would still spend as much time as I could at home with my babies but they weren't babies anymore. All three were growing into these incredible young people that I am so proud of. They each got into playing baseball. My son had an arm that was like a rocket launcher and my daughters could hit. I remember whenever one was having a dry spell at the plate I would whisper, "Just picture the #@&! teacher that gave you a C instead of a B." And there goes another home run!

Many summers we'd retrace the steps I had taken with my parents and travel to Quebec City to visit my aunt. The kids embraced the travel and that made me very happy. Not only did I like to travel for work but also that's what I'd do on vacation. Remember my nickname.

My son David went with me to England, Ireland, and Spain, and my oldest daughter Melissa got her grown up one-on-ones with me in trips to Jackson Hole and Yellowstone. When I offered my youngest, Kristen, a trip to anywhere she wanted to go as long as she graduated college with good grades, she nailed it. Off we went to Australia and an incredible journey the two of us will never forget. In our travels we got to spend such really good one-on-one time together, together now as adults. Nothing like watching your son try to pick up a girl after he's had way too many Guinnesses or flipping a coin with Melissa on whether to ignore the "Go Back, Bears Present" signs on a trail in Yellowstone. I've always believed in gut feelings and instincts. A very dear friend once said that is when God and your Guardian Angels are talking to you deep inside. At the Great Barrier Reef Down Under one afternoon my gut was screaming. My youngest and I were out in about eight feet of water a good way off the beach and something kept telling me it wasn't safe. After a few minutes I told her we should go in. "Shark!" someone yelled as they pointed to the *really* big fish swimming nearby. Over the years, Steve Burns had always said some pretty interesting things. I can still remember his telling Zander Burns off the coast of Key West, "remember, when you jump in the water you become a part of the food chain." Not today, Jaws, not today.

CHAPTER TWELVE
ON ANY GIVEN DAY

IN THE BUSINESS, sales were growing significantly. I am proud to say that we blew Fred's 15% comment out of the water again and again. Each year he would set out sales goals and 25% growth was always the target. He preached then, and I agree, that if you set low goals some poor performers would only work to that end. I, in turn, would argue that the poor performers didn't need to be on the team. It was those types of comments that endeared me to my peers.

Sometimes the sun shines bright and other days it rains. On special days, the sun breaks through the clouds and the frowns are turned upside down. Corny, I agree, but on this one particular day, the sun *really* made us smile. As I wrote earlier, Sunoco had been marketing their racing gas products under CAM2 brand name. And then it happened. Someone at Sunoco decided to abandon the CAM2 name and market their race gas products under the parent company brand. Sunoco Race Gas was now on the market.

"Since I can't get CAM2 anymore I might as well start

selling your stuff," was the type of call we got in Chester and at the other offices. I might have gone outside and yelled a few things like "OMG," and "WTF," and on and on. Happy days were here again! I still can't thank whoever made that decision enough. Long term it might have made sense for Sunoco but short term it propelled VP into another growth spurt.

At work, things were good. We still struggled to do more with less. Couldn't afford a forklift so we tried everything else. With the better trailers we were able to acquire, the ones with eight tires, we could actually load 120 or so drums on each trailer. More tires could bear that much more weight. In forty-eight foot long trailers we'd load eighty drums on the floor and twenty on top of the floor load in the front of the trailer, and then twenty more on top of the floor load in the back at the rear doors. Those forty drums had to go UP on top! No big deal. I can usually figure things out. Remember the motto the U.S. Marines use? It's amazing how easy it is to drop a heavy drum from the back of a trailer onto the ground. Gravity does 99% of the work. You just need to lay it on its side and then have a big truck tire lying on the ground waiting to cushion the landing. If you timed it right, the drum would bounce and you could guide its path upright and beside the tire. Getting that drum up on top of the other ones was the tough part.

We went to the local lumberyard and collected two lengths of 4" x 4" wood studs. We laid one end of each on top of the drums already in the trailer and dropped the other end on the ground. Position them about two feet apart. Grab hold of the drum you want to put up, lay it down on its side, and you are set. You could walk inside the two-foot gap as you rolled the drum farther and farther. As the drums kept coming and the heat kept building it got harder and harder but we did it time after time after time. You just had to stay focused because if 356 rolling pounds wanted to do something different than you had planned you needed to be ready to move. Oh, and remember, once the drums reached the top you – or someone – needed to stand it back up and roll it into place. Another really cool thing I implemented was leverage. It's amazing how much you can lift or dislodge if you've got the right lever and length to it. Leverage isn't a bad thing to have in business either.

Eventually that all gave way to buying a foot-operated hydraulic lift. None of us knew they existed but I can guarantee you I would have paid for the damn thing myself if I had known. Thank God for Grainger Catalogs! Now that's an example of being so busy that you can't step back and see what you need to. One drum would go straight up. One guy would throw it on the lift plate and another would remove it once it reached the top. That still called for manpower and if someone didn't show up for work, it wasn't fun. No matter what, it got done and not just in the Northeast. That same dedication made things happen with all the key, loyal people at VP no matter what office or plant they worked out of. Whatever it took and then some – that's one of the ways a David can take on and beat a Goliath.

I could find myself loading a truck and sweating my butt off only to come inside the office trailer to check messages and have to switch into sales guy mode. I would dream of the day that we were much bigger and I could focus all of my time on making money and hiring a larger staff but the sense of accomplishment was enough satisfaction for now. One afternoon I got a call from an Englishman by the name of Roger Bailey. He ran the Indy Lights Series and he was unhappy with their fuel supply situation. Within no time I was sitting across the table from him up in Dearborn, Michigan if I remember correctly. I was skeptical. Being from the Northeast might have made me a certain way. Was this guy truly unhappy with his Sunoco fuel supply or would he use my offer to improve his deal with them? I had seen it happen with race teams and race tracks before so my cautious optimism was warranted. Thankfully, some of the Sunoco distributors had given Roger quite a headache and change was indeed needed. Okay. Let's do this.

On-site, trackside fuel supply is a very simple concept. The race teams roll into the race tracks and temporary street circuits set up all across North America. Sometimes they bring fuel with them but those rigs are usually loaded to the maximum weight allowed with cars, engines, and equipment. Rigs are only allowed to weigh a certain amount and usually 80,000 pounds is max. They, like all rigs, are subject to scrutiny by the Department of Transportation. If you are carrying hazardous materials, like race fuel, there are a bunch of other requirements and restrictions that go along with that. The easiest thing to do is have a race fuel company bring the fuel to the site with their trucks and dispense it to the teams as needed. That gives the series officials, race promoters, teams and tracks the peace of mind that fuel is one thing they can forget about. There are two things you need to race, and those are tires and fuel.

Imagine you have a million dollar race team and you've towed all the way to Cleveland from your home base in San

Diego. It's 8am and your team engineer wants to scale the race car as he sets up the chassis for that first practice session. The gopher, the go for it guy, heads over to the fuel truck but it's locked up tight and there's nobody around. Except for the 12 other gas-gophers in dire need of fuel.

The story I was told was that some of the regional Sunoco fuel distributors – and this was a very long time before 2017 – who were assigned the fuel service duties, might have gotten the fuel truck to the site but that didn't mean the person who was supposed to be there to open up and pump fuel would make it there on time. Roger provided me with quite a few of the excuses he'd been given and perhaps the best one he received from the fuel pumper that showed up late was, "I looked out the window and it looked like rain so I went back to bed". Roger proceeded to show the knucklehead the rain tires that were being used that day. In another instance, the fuel attendant would pack up at 5pm and go home. Many times the practice and qualifying schedules, which were always posted, ran past the 5pm hour.

So the deal was struck. Sunoco was out and VP was in. For me, it was the first North American touring series I signed and I was happy to have learned all about the failures of our competitors. *The Art of War*, or at least my own playbook version of it, says find your opponent's weaknesses and exploit them. We agreed to show up early, stay late, communicate directly with an on-site contact person for the series so whoever was working the events would be aware of schedule changes, etc. I got to learn a lot myself. For example, while the on-track action might be done for the day the engineers would continue to work on the cars. They might make changes that would affect the weight distribution of the race car on its four tires. If the car needed to have fuel on board to be set up properly then we needed to be available to them. We agreed to remain open for sixty minutes after the last on-track session. The bonus for me personally was that just as there would be an on-site person for the series, Roger wanted consistency with an on-site person from VP. That would be me. I was excited to look at their schedule and realized I'd finally get to see the events at Phoenix, Vancouver, Denver and so on. I knew right off the bat that if VP was going to pick up the tab for me working an event in British Columbia that I'd gladly pick up the tab for flying up to Anchorage from there for a few days off after the event. It was a great deal for the "Ramblin' Man" in me but the dad in me was conflicted. It's like I had a good/stay at home dad angel on one shoulder and the bad boy work/travel dad one on the other.

Phoenix hosts a NASCAR race each season and is located in the Southwest part of the United States. That's Union 76 country and on arrival at the track on set-up day I had my first encounter with an overzealous track employee. "You can't bring that VP rig in! We have a contract with 76 and it states we can't let any other race fuel company sell fuel here or display their logos or advertisements here." Okay. Within a few minutes we got Roger Bailey involved. Engineers who were setting up their paddock areas and wanting to scale their cars needed fuel and we were still parked outside waiting to get in. After a few hours it looked like things would be worked out. We rolled in and started delivering our big blue VP drums to every paddock. Then the fire marshal stopped by to inspect our operation. This wasn't our first rodeo and even though I had flown in from the East

Coast and was working with a truck and driver from the Texas plant we knew we had it covered. All the fire extinguishers were fully charged and recently inspected. The ground rod and wire were all attached to the rig. Since this was my first race at that venue I wasn't sure if the fire marshal's appearance was SOP (Standard Operating Procedure) or if the track had called him on us. We passed his inspection and then the same grumpy track employee came by the truck. "Okay, we let you in but you have to cover up both sides of your trailer." In my mind, this was a crazy request but in actuality it was the deal that had to be struck. Off I went to a local hardware superstore and returned with enough material to cover the large VP logos. That was where we met in the middle. He might have thought he won that war but I can guarantee you that every paddock had a pretty blue VP drum in it and every race car in the series had VP decals on them and every bar in the area was decorated in our red, white, and blue as well. The Union 76 boys and the track didn't stop us that weekend but it pissed me off and that usually has consequences for somebody.

Their next race would take place in Long Beach, California on a temporary street circuit set up close to where the Queen Mary ocean liner and Howard Hughes's massive Spruce Goose airplane are parked. There was a celebrity race as a preliminary event to the Indy Lights and then the Indy Car race, so between the atmosphere and the environment it was a great place to work and watch some racing. The only glitch was when someone suggested they needed to sand bag in our fuel truck. What they neglected to see that first year we were there was the massive sewer drain open and within our diked area. If we'd had a leak, the sand bags would have kept the fuel from the paddock but not from flowing into the sewer system. Got it fixed, applied the sunscreen, sold some gas. I mention sunscreen for one reason, plain and simple. It can save your life. I used to go without for years until a malignant melanoma caught my attention. Growing up and burning at the beach in the 60s and 70s might have been in vogue but not anymore.

Phoenix and then Long Beach were soon behind us and we were back East for another stop on the tour. It's funny. I grew up spending time in Quebec City, Canada each summer but other than overnight stops in Lake George, New York I never spent any real time in between Quebec and Philly. Funnier yet is the fact that I grew up in Philly and never got inside Independence Hall until I was nearly sixty years old. People say you tend to take for granted what's right in front of you. Once I took on the VP gig, and especially the ARS Series, I got to see a LOT of New England and realized how much I had missed. Picture this, for example. The ARS had a race date at New Hampshire International near Loudon. Everyone said get motel rooms on Lake Winnipesaukee, so we did. Looking back on it, one of the scariest moments I can recall happened there but on the flip side, for the fan in me, that weekend was one of the coolest of my career.

My truck driver and I were standing at the check in desk at the lakefront motel. There to our left, lying comfortably in the sunlight coming through the huge floor-to-ceiling bay window was a beautiful grey and white huskie. We continued to exchange pleasantries with the front desk clerk until I noticed a little boy quickly walk behind us. In an instant and without hesitation he put his hand on the sleeping dog's head. In the blink of an eye, the startled dog reacted and locked on to a large part of the kid's head with his mouth! While it wasn't biting down hard it was clearly holding the kid in place by the face. Now I didn't have a lot of experience at the time with dogs but I did know one thing. I wasn't going to try to pull the kid away. The kid started screaming, the kid's parents started screaming, and as quickly as it had started the owner ran from behind the counter and punched their huskie. Within a minute the lobby turned into a three-ring circus. If there had been an ambulance-chasing lawyer around, the kids' parents would have signed him or her up on the spot. The parents were crying and yelling, the kid was crying, the dog owner was crying, and I was just happy to see that the little guy was fine, just startled. For the truck driver and me, we had seen and heard enough and headed for the beach bar. Later that evening, I got to appreciate another one of the perks of the job.

We opted to have dinner in the hotel restaurant. We'd already enjoyed happy hour out on the beach so driving was out. The hostess sat us without delay and once I got adjusted and blew through the menu I noticed who was sitting at the very next table. Paul Newman was an avid racer as well as an awesome actor. He and his beautiful wife Joanne Woodward were right there, straight out of Hollywood, having dinner with Mario Andretti and Emerson Fittipaldi. Mario and Emerson are world famous race car driving champions and the four of them were just enjoying a quiet dinner together. I was in heaven. I've loved movies since I was a kid. At the funeral home, we actually got to make one while I was in the 6th grade. My father got hold of an old-style casket, the type Hollywood might have used for a Dracula movie set in Transylvania. With Dad's help we used dry ice to fog the area and only had candles and very dim lighting around the casket. One of our classmates was inside and slowly opened the lid. I think there were three of us involved in the project. It went over well, the kids at school got to see it, and we had a blast.

There I was, sitting at a lakeside restaurant with beer and food and these four were within arm's reach. I was thrilled and just soaked in the moment, hoping this VP thrill ride would never end. The only thing missing was a hot date. That would have made for a happy ending to a wild day and night but all I had was this big, hairy truck driver to look at. Okay, hopefully they have HBO.

The season progressed and things went pretty much as planned. Before long, Vicki O'Connor of the Toyota Atlantic Series was ready to abandon her Sunoco deal and sign with the old VP red white and blue. She had noticed our impeccable service. The teams liked our products and the financial arrangement between us was amicable. She had the same requirement that Roger did. VP employees must staff the events. They didn't want us handing the labor or equipment off to local dealers or regional distributors. They trusted VP and that's who they wanted fueling their events. VP was growing a reputation for providing top quality products and excellent, professional trackside fuel service. Not allowing the locals to service the events caused some internal friction. Some looked at it like we were taking sales away from them. Others, the non-shortsighted, realized this was just another good thing for the brand and anyone affiliated with it. We got them all pit passes to the events and that made many of them happy. Getting to walk up to celebrities like Ashley Judd and David Letterman and ask for a photo or an autograph made them happy. It was a pretty cool gig and I'm proud to say I negotiated both deals and would go on to do many more. The truth is that while I may have negotiated them, it couldn't have been possible without the hard work of all the people at VP who had built a great reputation for high quality products and equally as important, for providing professional, reliable trackside fuel service.

To most people, some of what I have described so far might make the job sound incredible but nothing's perfect and it did get to be boring at times. Not all races were busy, busy, busy. Sometimes the drum pumps inside the race trailer were still for hours and we had to do something to kill the boredom. If we were really bored we could wax the tractor and polish the wheels but in reality that needed to be done before we showed up looking all shiny and new. One time we sat on the side steps of the truck and held up scorecards for the ladies as they went by. We got some laughs from both the ladies and the men because we did it with a sense of humor. There was another time where despite the Employees Only signs that we posted, people would just walk up the stairs into the trailers full of highly flammable race fuel. Sometimes they would be holding lit cigarettes, cigars, or their checkbook to settle an account. Trying to keep control of things we bought a BEWARE OF DOG sign and a long piece of heavy chain. We padlocked one end to the ladder and laid the rest of it out so that it led into the darkness of the trailer. Between that and the new sign it seemed to keep people on the ground where they belonged.

I think the stunt that got us the most attention, though was another sign we put out. The track gave tours driving people around the garage area in tramcars similar to what you might see in the parking lot at Disney World. The fans and tourists would ride past the truck, taking pictures of us waving at them. We displayed a PLEASE DON'T FEED THE ANIMALS sign and that got us more laughs and I'm sure it got us a decent amount of brand awareness too. Just like I had done with Gatorade back in the #88 days I wanted to get the VP logo in front of as many people as possible. Before long it was time to get back to filling jugs and running drums. I had wrestled drums and other objects for years and never hurt anything. That was until a trip to Vermont and this time, I did it good.

Jason Rueckert, the Regional Manager for the Indiana office and VP's traction guru, flew into Philly and went on a road trip with me. First we stopped to visit Howard Commander at Lebanon Valley Speedway & Dragway just west of Albany, New York. Howard is one of the smartest and most experienced men I know in motorsports and spending time with him was always interesting and beneficial, especially if you chose to sit and listen. Howard is an amazing promoter and track operator. Over the many years I got to work with him he taught me quite a bit. His track continues to draw big crowds in the stands and large car counts in the pits while many others struggle and fail to succeed. Long before Hugh Jackman made the movie, one of Howard's earliest recommendations to me was to read P.T. Barnum's book. P.T. had been an entrepreneur, a politician, and a showman who went on to establish the very famous Barnum & Bailey circus. I got a kick out of Howard's recommendation because way back at the beginning, during VP's early growing pains, some days had indeed been a bit circus-like. With a small staff and large amounts of work many of us might have resembled the clown juggling bowling pins with one hand, plates in another, while balancing who knows what over our heads. From me, I would recommend everyone read the book *Good to Great*. Those lessons apply to everyone and everything! Once Jason and I finished visiting Lebanon Valley we drove further north to Vermont to visit Tom Curley at his Thunder Road Speedway. Curley, like Howard Commander, was one of those special people in motorsports. If he liked you and you were smart or lucky enough to spend time with him you could learn so much, and I sure did. In addition to running Thunder Road he owned and operated the ACT American Canadian Tour in New England and Quebec Province. It was a very popular asphalt oval track series that put on a great show wherever they went and featured top drivers like Brian Hoar, Jean-Paul Cyr, Wayne Helliwell, Jr., and Phil Scott, the racer and now Governor of Vermont. Just like I had gone after other tracks and regional and national racing series, ACT used a lot of fuel so I wanted it. The fact it was serviced by John Holland and Sunoco had nothing, okay it had a lot to do, with my decision to go after it. In actuality, that didn't really matter. I wanted it, regardless of who had it.

When I first went after the ACT business I tried and tried to get Curley to call me back but for whatever reason he never did. Sometimes people are busy, I get that, and I delegated a lot of return calls since there are only so many hours in the day, but at least people heard back from someone at VP. I'm tenacious so I kept at it, choosing to try something different. I left Curley a message that said, "Tom, I've found it easier to get Vice President Dick Cheney on the phone. Please give me a call if you can. I'd really appreciate it. Thanks." Believe it or not, he called me back the next day. Soon afterward we eventually met at his office in Waterbury, Vermont and made the deal. He had avoided calling me back originally because he said that he'd had a bad experience with another fuel company, other than Sunoco, and decided it was better to stick with what he knew. But when people do finally call you back it's an indicator there might be a chance so you have to go for it and we did. We got to fuel his track and provide fuel for his series, proving again that persistence pays off. It was there at the ACT offices that I got to say hi to someone I had first met almost a lifetime ago at Daytona. Ken Squire, who had called the "500" many times for CBS and conducted the famous post-race interview with President Ronald Reagan and '84 Firecracker 400 race winner Richard Petty, was still doing radio broadcasts and his studio was right there by Curley's office. It was either that first day or perhaps a dozen meetings later that I suggested to Tom that with all the stories he and Ken and Howard Commander knew from racing that they should sit down sometime and just talk and talk and talk into a recorder or on camera. Their stories were amazing. So many of us spend hours driving or flying and that would have made for a great audiobook.

So Jason and I were at Thunder that day to test a new traction compound, aptly named Two Groove, on the asphalt short track. It had rained overnight but the track was now sunning itself and drying up nicely. I needed to move a drum of traction compound from our shiny white

VP van to the track's pickup truck. The truck's bed was cold and wet and for the first time ever I messed up. I was talking with Curley and one of his guys as I slid the drum around and because I wasn't paying attention and did it right, I tweaked the crap out of my back. I figured in all the years at VP I had probably moved 40,000 drums. I think that's 14 million pounds. Not anything special but that number just looks impressive.

Despite hurting my back, the test went great. Curley had sprayed his track surface for years with one of our other products, one that was designed for use on drag strips, and had great results. Despite the product's name he would always call it "Goop." He had a spray apparatus already installed in his track pickup and we watched as he sprayed into the approach to each turn, through the turn and then eased off as he entered the straight away. He did the customary low groove first and then ran high to establish a second groove. If it all worked it would allow his competitors to run side by side, pass each other, and make for a more competitive show for the racers and more importantly, for the fans. If they like the racing they'll come back and maybe even bring a friend. Races that are single file, follow the leader ones, are boring and lead to snoring. The test car did fine where he'd normally run but now with the Two Groove he found he could run the second, higher groove. Everyone there also knew what that meant for the racers; less tire wear for the cars and that would save money. The series tire sponsor might not appreciate that since they're there to sell tires but plenty of racers have quit because they couldn't afford it anymore. Better racing puts more fans in the stands and gives them a reason to keep coming back. Increased ticket sales could mean track improvements, higher payouts to the racers, and so on. For a simple cash outlay, promoters might be able to accomplish all of this and it makes perfect sense right? Curley got it as did a few others. Very sadly, racing lost one of its best a few years later when Tom finally lost the fight and died.

After the test Jason and I continued the heading and went north into Canada to meet our truck driver at the Formula 1 at Montreal, and I was screwed. VP had fueled many of the support events on the Formula 1 weekend but it was clear I wasn't going to be of any help this time around. During the ride my back had tightened up and the shooting pains were starting to feel like internal fireworks. Best medicine when in another country and in pain? Canada's high-octane beer of course. That and a ton of Advil seemed to help but the next morning, when it was time to get up and get to the track I was stuck. I literally couldn't move. I tried for twenty minutes and then finally figured the only thing I could do was roll as best I could off the side of the bed and fall onto the floor. Worst-case scenario, the maid would find me face down, bum up.

I managed somehow to get up, got dressed, and inched my way out the door like a zombie. We got to the track and inspected the truck and setup but for the most part I was staring at my shoes all day. After driving 450 miles home with a bad back I listened to Freddie Turza's advice and went to a chiropractor. Knucklehead that I was, I never considered going to one in Canada or once we got back into the States. The doctor had me stand on dual scales that would measure the weight at each foot. I think I had 18 pound more weight on one side than the other. Talk about getting bent. Twenty minutes later, after a whole bunch of cracks and crunches I was like a new man. The final crack, the neck one, was something I had dreaded though. But my head didn't fall off and I wasn't paralyzed as a result. I hadn't felt that good in ages and I'd recommend that type of treatment to anyone who might need it.

In all, things were going good at VP. We had the typical employee issues that any company might grapple with. Some people didn't want to work hard. Some wanted more money and left if they didn't get it. The good ones, the ones I needed on my team to give me the steady foundation so I could work on the business, got what they needed. Whether it was a Kelly Hole or a work-around, I'd figure out a way. If I couldn't give someone an increase in their hourly rate fine; I'd bonus them instead. I'd always find a way to make things happen. If you were into motorsports this was a cool place to work but I was always looking for more.

CHAPTER THIRTEEN
SAY CHEESE

TRAVELING THE COUNTRY and the world, being around celebrities and models, racing champions, and all the trappings wasn't enough for me though. I always wanted more. In actuality, I needed more. Anyone that really knows me well will tell you that I bore easily. I have to have many projects in the air or things lined up. It's not an ADD thing; it's just the way I am. Back in the early years we had a very limited budget at VP but a young girl named Jill Ankele approached me at a race with an idea that helped keep the boredom at bay for some time. She suggested we should produce an annual calendar poster and for the first edition she wanted to be the VP girl. She handed me test shots she and a friend had taken one sunny day in a field near Maple Grove Raceway in Reading. There she was, looking great in a stunning bikini, screeching for the camera as she jumped off the top of the drum. She hadn't realized the hot sun had cooked the steel and her reaction was the same as anyone crazy enough to hop up on a hot stove.

At this point in time I can't remember if I did the shoot with budget or using one of the infamous "Kelly Holes". If you know what a loophole is, then just know that I exploited so many loopholes in the company's early rules and regulations that I did whatever I needed, did whatever it took, to get something done. To get something I needed. Sure, I could take the scolding but if we got the tools we needed to help wage the war then it was a win-win in my book. Oh, that's right. The whole point of shooting a bikini poster was to attract existing and potential customers to the trade show booths and give our sales team an opportunity to chat with the racers while they waited in line for an autograph. So what was the Kelly Hole for the inaugural poster shoot? I may have given a few free drums of sponsorship fuel to a team who in turn paid the photographer, model, and the printer to get the project completed. The next poster shoot was a blast. There I was in a studio outside of Reading, Pennsylvania and there she was, our beautiful model, unconscious and lying on the sofa in front of the photographer and yours truly. So what would any red-blooded American do? Yep, one of us shook her while the other grabbed something to fan her. Apparently, to be sure her stomach was flat and rock hard for the camera, she had decided not to eat for the two days before the shoot. Under the hot lights she just passed out. Some water and some fresh air got her nice sea legs back and she was ready to continue. The finished product was a beauty. Now this has nothing really to do with David, Goliath, or race fuel but it is an example of being resourceful and getting the most out of your buck. The photographer and I hit it off and so I decided to have him shoot a personal Christmas card for me and throw in his studio time as part of the VP gig. I wanted to dress up in a hooded robe, shepherd staff in hand, and be surrounded by a few sheep. Sunglasses in place of course as always but only because bright light really bothers me. I thought given my sense of humor it all worked but despite being in farm and livestock land we couldn't get one damn sheep let alone a half dozen. I sure wasn't going to use a stunt-double, blow up version but in hindsight okay, I should have. Baa!

The posters became very popular and the distributors, dealers, customers and race fans all wanted them. "I'll take one for my dad, one for my brother, and one for me," I remember this one excited woman saying. Many told us they had started a full collection on their shop walls and really looked forward to seeing what we came out with next. So it was time to step it up a notch. Are you familiar with Leeann Tweeden? She's an angelic beauty who has graced the pages of *Playboy, FHM*, and Frederick's of Hollywood lingerie, and hosted popular shows on television. I reached out to her and she agreed to pose for two consecutive annual calendar posters, both shot the same day. I flew to LA and when I met her for the first time I was stunned. She had barely any makeup on and it was then, as she stepped out of her car, I was certain there were angels among us. Wow. The coolest part was that she was a beauty inside and out. Over the years I've worked with a lot of models but this young lady was so genuine, so friendly and outgoing that it made the day a great one. She also introduced me to Panda Express long before that chain made it to Philly. Note that I got two years for the price of one. That was indicative of still having to do the most we could with the smallest budget. Money was coming in to VP but operating the rapidly growing company was an expensive proposition and the question often raised by ownership was a simple one. "Do you want a poster or do you want the highest quality performance chemicals in the products you are trying to sell?" Well heck, I wanted both so out came what my peers called the "Kelly Hole" again. Obviously over time these loopholes were closed up. Heck, I helped close plenty of them for the protection of the company. After all, my loyalty was to my high school friend and the guy who gave me the chance. I would protect him, Steve Burns, and VP with the same intensity I had applied to "whatever it takes." The Leeann shoot went great and we developed the Millennium 2000 and the red-hot 2001 poster calendars. She worked with us at a packed trade show in Indianapolis and drew a huge crowd to the booth. Thanks again, Leeann!

Now what can I say about Rhonda? The posters were becoming quite popular so I got the green light to continue producing them. My good friend and hard-working distributor in Ontario, Randy Lungal, was quite the ladies' man. Heck, on a bet a bunch of us sat stunned one time as we watched him lure a young beauty away from a guy who was clearly her boyfriend. I have to commend Randy as he had very good taste and typically dated only the most attractive women. The fact that most of them were main attraction strippers from the top clubs in Toronto didn't matter to me. I figure he must have gotten the looks and personality genes I was missing so whoever got them should make good use of them. Then after working the Toronto GP's Friday practice session he and I met up with his girlfriend Rhonda. There was a really cool hockey themed bar named Gretzky's, as in Wayne, downtown and it seemed like a good place to enjoy some drinks and wait for my wife's arrival. She and I had a good arrangement. Whenever I'd be working a race weekend in an exciting town she'd fly up to join me on Friday afternoon. I'd work the events during the daytime while she gave in to her shopping addiction. On Sunday night after the racing and the shopping concluded we'd jump on the same plane and fly home together.

So there we were – Randy, and his statuesque, Pamela Anderson look-alike girlfriend named Rhonda, and me. While we waited for Lisa to arrive we exchanged shots and laughs and enjoyed the atmosphere. Hockey memorabilia was everywhere. So the more sauced we got the better the stories went. I told Rhonda that when my wife arrived she needed to be sure to look straight at her when they spoke since my wife had a hearing problem. I'm partially deaf thanks to forty years of working races without hearing protection so I feel it's okay to have an inside joke as long as nobody is offended by it. So eventually my wife showed up. She jumped out of the cab, gave me a kiss, and sprinted to the ladies' room. Rhonda decided she needed to go as well and within a few minutes there they were, face to face in the ladies' room at Gretzky's. Taking her by the hands she said loudly and very slowly, "Hi, Lisa, I am R A N D Y' S friend. My name is R H O N D A." My wife looked at her and politely asked what the hell was the matter with her. Minutes later the two of them came back to the table belly laughing and having a good old time. The joke worked. The next day after their shopping concluded the two girls showed up at the track and it was like Moses parted the sea of people. Now my Mrs. is a beautiful Italian woman but as she described it, "I could have been naked and on fire and nobody would have noticed! Rhonda's look had people stopping in their tracks."

Later that Saturday night the four of us got together again to have some laughs and enjoy what downtown Toronto had to offer. Food, beer, shots, and what they call Bloody Marys up north, "Bloody Caesars." Early the next morning I made my way to the track only to find I had a problem and very limited solutions.

All fuel for the Canada races had to be pre-ordered and prepaid. Someone could order ten drums and only take five and we'd be stuck with them, including the big tax bill that's levied on race fuel that crosses the border. If they had to pay in advance then the engineers were damn certain to calculate the right amount of fuel they'd need based on scheduled practice time, etc., etc. Before we left the track the night before we had checked with every team engineer. "Got enough fuel for tomorrow?" Everyone said they were set. We didn't miss anyone and used the participant list to make sure. We're done. Time to have fun and watch some races.

"I need fuel," interrupted the coffee and beignet I was enjoying while trying to regain my senses. The Molson and the Cuervo hadn't completely left me yet and my thoughts of having a nice sunny day of actually spectating at a race quickly came crashing down.

One of the teams said they'd miscalculated. Suggestions of asking another team or teams for fuel fell on deaf ears. Everyone was close on fuel and besides that, the team that had miscalculated was embarrassed to let anyone other than me know about it. I was frustrated to say the least. We

ALWAYS brought extra fuel with us to races, ALWAYS. Only problem was, the two extra drums we had left over Saturday night had been loaded in Randy's pickup and sent home with him. The truck that had delivered and dispensed the fuel on site had cut out Saturday night too. Our drivers spent a lot of time on the road as it was and whenever they could leave early they went for it. Plus it saved VP another $300 in hotel and per diem costs. I knew what I had to do but the call would be a painful one.

"Dude, you need to bring a drum back." There was silence on the other end of the line. Randy thought that I was kidding but he was in no shape to laugh or get up for that matter. He wasn't hung over though. The seafood he'd had the night before didn't swim very well in his system and he was looking forward to a morning on the potty rather than a ride all the way back to the track. "And, they need it ASAP."

Two hours later, Randy arrived with a smile on his face and was ready to do whatever was needed to finish the transaction. Could the day get any better? "I'm sorry, we miscalculated. We are fine on fuel. Don't need the drum," was all I needed to hear. So after a half dozen more coffees and some promises to make good for his above and beyond effort, Randy prepared to roll out and head back home. Luckily the teams were parked outside the temporary road course otherwise the drum delivery would have stuck Randy inside the circuit for the duration of the event.

What came of the Toronto Cluster#$%! was simple. The team owner knew we'd done a great job and that his guy had let a few of us down. Beyond the apologies he offered, going forward, to help out whenever he could. At some races, we'd do "drop and runs." That's where pre-ordered drums are dropped at the team haulers and the VP truck gets to keep moving on down the road to the next delivery. No dispensing or manning the event for the duration. It's cut and dry but eliminates any marketing benefits had by parking a rig, our rolling billboard, and setting up a consumer display where we'd hand out decals and brochures, refer people to dealers, and talk to potential ones. Sometimes a team would be running late and our guy might have to sit for hours or even overnight to wait for them. This is where that team we bent over backwards for in Toronto lent us a hand. If someone hadn't shown up yet as a favor they'd accept the delivery from us and we'd communicate to the delinquent team where they could retrieve it. That's one of the many things I loved about working in motorsports. People are basically made of the right stuff. Back in Toronto though, before Randy got to escape the track, I had to pitch another idea; I just had to have Rhonda on the next VP poster!

The saying goes "Life's what happens while you are making other plans" and that's exactly what stopped the shoot from happening. She got sick and wasn't able to fly down. We were on deadline and were forced to go to Plan B. Needless to say I was disappointed but the tens of thousands of racers never knew what they missed out on. In a pinch because of a deadline, Bruce Hendel jumped in on the West Coast and shot the poster using another model. He went on to shoot those for quite a few years and eventually I took the project back. I'm not saying these posters had anything to do with sales, even though we hope they had some effect on it. But the cool part was that VP was a privately owned, edgy company. We could do things like that while other politically correct companies couldn't even consider doing a poster at that time in the culture.

Sunoco could afford to give away free decals to anyone who wanted them and often held contests that awarded free pump gas to the winner. All you had to do was drive into one of their gas stations or convenience stores (c-stores) and grab some decals and sign up to enter. For us, with 99% of the customers male racers, we made a bikini calendar. So what next? Rhonda had raised the bar pretty high. As an aside, when I was planning my first trip to Moscow I took the train from Philly to New York and went to the Russian Consulate. If you were in a hurry you could pay a bit more and get your visa to visit their country that same day. As I approached the consulate office that was located back then way up on 91st Street there was a line of women standing down the steps onto the sidewalk and there wasn't anything less than a "nine" in line. They were stunning, their eyes were icy blue, and I knew right then where my next model would come from. As it turned out, these Russian beauties all worked in New York doing everything from bartending and au pairing to escorting and dancing. There might also have been a few ladies there from findarussianwife.com but I wasn't sure. They'd make their money and then fly home to share in their wealth and perhaps come back here or head to another foreign land for more. Needless to say, the following two projects I did both involved Russian or Ukrainian models.

Typically, professionals know how to pose and pose and pose but one of the two best posters I did were a hit thanks to some props. For the 2010 calendar I filled a graduated cylinder with water and some green food dye and then the model held it up and gazed at it. Some thought it was a bit phallic while others saw it for what it was, just a really hot bikini-clad VP technician giving the fuel sample a visual examination. The winning pose for the 2011 calendar actually happened during a break in shooting. The model was sitting on the floor reading through one of VP's fuel brochures and I saw the shot. I told her *don't move*, handed her my reading glasses and *voilà*! It gave us the school teacher/librarian look that proved to be very popular.

VP continued to wage its battle for market share against big companies with deep pockets and if we didn't have the cash to compete we knew to do everything else with what we did have. When you are in an uneven, uphill fight that's what you do, even if it means getting "dirty."

Chapter Fourteen
GETTING DIRTY

EARLIER ON I wrote about Syracuse and Super DIRT Week but I have to admit my love affair with that type of racing had a very bumpy start. If you've never been to an oval track dirt race, where the track surface is dirt or clay as opposed to asphalt, then you really need to go. My first experience with dirt racing came at the very popular Grandview Speedway in Southeastern Pennsylvania. I think I lasted twenty laps. The racing is fast and exciting, and drivers and teams put on quite a show for the fans and promoters. I only lasted there a short time because way back in the day I wore contact lenses. As the race cars fly down the straightaways they turn left and pitch throw their rear tires into the turn. Sometimes a cushion of dirt gets pushed up and the cars can use that to hug the corner, keep the engine revs up, and launch down the straight. It's pretty exciting but as the tires spin for traction on the dirt surface they essentially rooster tail the dirt into the air and consequently onto everything and everyone on the outside of the turn. Now picture twenty to thirty race cars all doing this in four turns lap after lap. For me, my contact lenses caked up faster than a fat kid at a bakery and my night was pretty much over. First my eyes kept me out of law enforcement and now they were screwing with *this* job? It wasn't Grandview's fault. Dirt flies at every oval track race. It was a rookie mistake that I made. On the way home I stopped off to see the kids and they looked at me like I was from another planet. They laughed as I spent an hour getting the dirt residue out of my ears, eyes, nose, hair, clothes, and wherever else it managed to hide. Don't let that turn you off of dirt racing because that was a very long time ago and a lot has changed. Improvements have been made, and spectating at those great races is an awesome experience.

One thing I learned that night was that if you are legally blind and try to drive home without your contacts you're crazy, so keep a spare pair of glasses in the car. Second, I was introduced to a world of incredibly exciting racing and it happens at over 700 dirt tracks across the United States and Canada. The kings of that sport, the World of Outlaw Sprint Cars, run an extensive schedule, as do the touring Late Models, DIRTcar, and so many other regional and local series and tracks.

I attended that race at Grandview maybe twenty-five to thirty years ago and since then there have been dramatic improvements in the conditions at the dirt tracks. VP developed products that could be blended into the track surface or sprayed on it and it essentially cut the dust. Somewhere in the middle of all of that I got corrective laser surgery on my eyes and working dirt races got to be a blast.

While my first visit to a dirt track race ended rather abruptly, from a sales standpoint it was clear that this was an arena I needed to pursue. I had known nothing about dirt racing before that first night but those cars ran lots of laps and were thirsty for fuel. While other sales guys on the team seemed to pursue their passions in the drag, motocross and road race bike arenas I would focus on the automotive side of oval track and road course racing and eventually fell for rally cars too. Oval track cars consumed drums each week while a weekend MX rider or drag racer might burn only a pail. Don't get me wrong though. I didn't neglect anyone. I had great admiration for them and worked bike shops and engine builders just as much. Working the MX des Nations in the U.K. and in the U.S. at Budds Creek was a blast and my fascination with the spectacle known as the Isle of Man TT took me overseas to Douglas many times. I was so proud when the Tas Suzuki won the event not once but again and again flying the VP colors, and it was Philip Neill, the team owner, who put that bike and our logo on the front of the PlayStation game that was sold around the world. Two years before I retired I negotiated a multi-year deal with the event organizers, and VP became the exclusive on-site fuel supplier. If you've never been, or never watched the TT check it out on YouTube.

Back on dirt, eventually, at the conclusion of one of the Super DIRT Weeks, we got a formal letter from DIRT's attorney, the late Andy Fusco. DIRT had decided to seek bids from all the fuel companies to secure not just official fuel status but spec fuel status. Controlling the tracks is a good move, controlling the fuel, tires and other parts racers have to use is even better — at least for the series and the company that wins the bid. Racers typically get a piece of the action in point funds or track improvements so, for the most part, the concept is a good one.

We were invited to present the bid, aka the tender, at an open meeting the morning after DIRT's annual champions' banquet. The event was held at a Robin Hood themed facility up in the Adirondacks if I remember correctly, and after sharpening my pencil as best I could I thought I was ready and intended to win. That morning, as all the fuel company representatives were shaking hands and spilling coffee, we all counted the minutes until the formal meeting was to start. Everyone was gracious, after all it was just business. Just before we entered the meeting room, one of the representatives from Goliath's New York distributor, M&R, said to me, "Hey, we're not married to these guys so if you win, we want to be your track fuel supplier." That was interesting.

Donnelly greeted the participants and each of us handed over our sealed bid envelopes. There were only three. Turbo Blue, Goliath and VP in that order.

Talk about being on the edge of your seat. VP had never participated in a process like this before and we wanted to win it bad. We wanted to win everything. If you continued to whittle away at the competition's sales volume only a few outcomes could occur. They'd make less and less money and decide to do something else, they'd get pissed off and try to do the same to you, or everything would stay the same. Turbo Blue's offer was tabled for some reason and the Sunoco and VP bids, on an estimated 300,000 gallons of race fuel, were within $7,000 dollars of each other. Goliath won and it was clear the M&R boys quickly forgot their suggestion to me.

"That's okay, you can't win them all," is what I heard from Steve and Fred while trying to appease me. Yeah, "go sell that shit in Hong Kong" is all I wanted to say in response. If there's one thing I learned in life it's be persistent and don't procrastinate. In the coming years, DIRT put their fuel program back out to bid at again. This time they decided to open the bids in private. I'm sure they thought that if we had come within $7,000 of the winning bid last time, and we *really* wanted this one, who knows what number VP might bid. We submitted the bids and lost. Disappointing but two things were certain. The sun will continue to rise each morning and I would never give up.

CHAPTER FIFTEEN
SOMETHING IN THE WATER

ELF, A GLOBAL company based in France and now operating as TOTAL, decided to step into the lucrative North American power-sports market. They'd had great success in FORMULA 1, rally, auto and moto racing all around the world and taking a stab at the U.S.A. made perfect sense. They had been accustomed to playing for the most part in the cumbersome and expensive FIA and FIM regulation international competitions. To a degree, many of the American fuels were not necessarily highly technical so how hard, they must have wondered, could dominating the U.S. market be? The chronology and the basic facts of what happened next should be correct. If not, please remember that I'm old and gray now and this is all based on memory.

The easiest way to make your company or brand known in motorsports is to spend money. Tracks and series love money. Who doesn't? Some need sponsorships to help operate or even survive while others rely on it to advertise and to pay out point funds and championship awards. Some just see it as another revenue stream. In the case of the AMA, the American Motorcyclist Association, they sanctioned professional and amateur supercross, motocross and road racing for motorcycles in the U.S. In addition to the many types of racing each element might have classes that would differentiate them. The classes would be determined by weight, engine size, various technical regulations, and so on. Their fuel regulations, for the most part, were pretty simple.

In what I would call a smart, aggressive move on their part Elf offered the AMA some $$$ to sponsor one of their many classes and as a condition, the AMA changed their technical regulations on fuel specs and essentially eliminated C12 from competition. I hoped some day to have the $$$ needed to pull that sort of stunt on them. For now though, we'd just work hard. I got pissed off and started to really focus my time on growing the overseas business. I figured if they were coming over here, invading our shores, then it was only fair that I did the same to them. France helped the U.S. defeat the British during the Revolutionary War and we, in turn, helped drive Hitler and his German forces out of France and back to Berlin. My dad was a part of that effort as was Steve Burns's father. So now the French were the invaders and that's all we needed. While I went after their sales in Europe, Steve Burns knew exactly what to do here!

It took very little time to reformulate the C12 just a tad to make it legal with AMA again. To lead the charge in the field, Bruce Hendel – an avid rider whose passion for motorcycles and bicycles is intense to say the least – went after them. Bruce was the Regional Manager for VP's West Coast territory and was the ideal guy for the assignment. He, as did Burns, already had relationships with all the professional and top privateer or amateur teams and riders. Think back to VP's humble beginnings in San Antonio and remember the name Kent Howerton. AMA type racing was in VP's blood, part of our foundation, and up until the Elf incursion, VP was the fuel of choice for just about everyone who rode. Yes, there were some wannabes who would come and go but this mission was to make sure the French were sent home soon.

Elf responded by delivering a new product to the teams. They had extensive lab assets back in France compared to what we had in South Texas. I've been to their new facility in Solaize and it's pretty impressive. If the enemy lets you walk around their property there's no telling what you might learn. Remember, I'm kinda observant and spotting a supplier's drum here or a shipping label on a box over there might come in handy. Their reach was broad, global in fact, and they had their fingers on every performance chemical known to man.

With Bruce and Burns's passion and focus, Duane Minazzi's talents in the lab, and Wade Gray's ability to acquire whatever the VP needed to compete, it was on. VP responded to Elf's first fuel with something better. Then a month later France sent another blend. A week later, VP responded. A month later there was another new blend from Elf. In even shorter time, VP responded again. This went on for quite some time and there were those handy 5-gallon VP pails flying everywhere into the hands of everyone and anyone who wanted a performance advantage. It was like watching a professional boxing match. Round after round the two combatants would punch and jab and duck and swing. When it was over, VP had regained its position as THE fuel of choice for pros and amateurs alike. The AMA had reaped the financial benefits of a class sponsor and Elf shook their heads and went back to France to figure out what the hell just happened.

Interestingly, somehow "If you can't beat them, join them" translated in France pretty well. Before long, we attended a meeting in Indianapolis where the man who had led the Elf assault on VP in North America asked if we would be interested in distributing their products for them in North America. *Sacré bleu*!

The proposition was an interesting one. For me it was like Coke was asking Pepsi to handle their sales and distribution. The discussions at VP went back and forth and entertained all sorts of thoughts and theories. Some felt it was a way to make some money. Others thought it a good way to keep track, control, or influence what happened with their products here. Another was of the mind that it was better for us to control it than someone else. In the end, most of us, including yours truly, preferred to enjoy the victory and leave that as a lesson to all who might wish to play in our American home field. You're going to get your ass kicked!

I've referenced *The Art of War* many times and practiced much of its playbook in my years in the racing fuel business. But I am not sure if its author, Sun Tzu, ever addressed fighting a war on the other guys' soil. I don't think I ever got that far in the reading. VP was still a David, although we were getting much bigger, smarter, and experienced, which made our slingshots a bit better, but the French Goliath was pretty strong at least on its home turf.

I began to spend more and more time overseas. The

domestic business was doing very good and I had all the right Designated Hitters and reliable, enthusiastic staff at home to support the business no matter what country we were selling in.

The language barrier was an issue from time to time but for the most part, most Europeans learned to speak English in school. While in the U.S. we were made to learn French, German, or Spanish, the Euro kids got to learn all three. If anything, my contacts would be rusty but we would get by the longer we spoke.

I found a great distributor in France and that set the first steps for waging a war. The strategy was to do it quietly. Buying big series or advertising to promote brand awareness in a new market costs a lot of money and waves a big flag at the companies you are trying to displace. "Hey, we're coming for you," didn't make any sense. There's also the knowledge that sometimes the big guys won't take any notice of you until you've gotten your foot in the door and once that's happened it's on. They might step up and spend a lot of money to put the "new kid" back in his place or send them home altogether. We did that with Elf in the U.S.

The plan was to provide an alternative product or products to the people who only knew Elf and perhaps a few other local blends. If all you were familiar with was the one brand and the high price you were paying for it, then perhaps showing some smart people an alternative brand, more power and competitive pricing would get it started. But we would need so much more. So let me ask you this. How do you say Duché?

By now you have a sense of how small of a staff I had at VP's Northeast office and how large our territory was. We were on an even keel with the other offices as far as domestic market responsibility but having everything on the other side of the Atlantic to worry about was big. Yes, I knew it would get me free trips to far and exotic places but it also meant I had to make something of those for VP or someone else would. I believed at the time that internally, my area was safe, that nobody wanted it or would go after it. Not any of my colleagues expressed any interest in traveling overseas on business, other than Bruce Hendel. He had to worry about everything that was on the other side of the Pacific. I always wanted to see that part of the world but for now, my slice was way big enough and with that it was game on.

It was said once that VP staffed its regional management team using the common sense method. If you wanted someone to deal with fast paced, fast-talking, Northeasterners then you should hire someone from there. Brought up in Philly, commuted to NYC, traveled out of the country since I was a kid, had some business experience. I made sense. After many overseas trips it was clear I needed to change things up and apply the same logic over there. Otherwise, continuing to do the same thing over and over expecting different results is Einstein's definition of insanity. I had to do more than just search for good distributors and attend trade shows. I needed full time boots on the ground and they needed to be to Europe what I was to the Northeast – a local.

In preparation for yet another journey to the NEC in Birmingham, England for the annual Autosport International trade show in January, I placed a classified ad in their magazine stating we were looking for sales reps with sales and technical experience. The magazine had global circulation so I thought for sure we'd catch someone good. I received all sorts of inquiries but mostly from people looking to make money traveling around on the VP expense account. It was disappointing until I got to the show and passed the ETS Racing Fuel booth. There he was, the bearded and bespectacled Frenchman, Jerome Duché.

We exchanged pleasantries and then I proceeded on my walk-about only to be stopped a few aisles over by Jerome. "I need to come to work for VP," is all I heard and between a meeting there and then another at Charles de Gaulle airport in Paris we made a deal. He first needed to prove to me that he was free and clear of any employment agreements with ETS. Getting into a lawsuit is one thing but my record was clean and intact and I intended to keep it that way both here and there.

Jerome was a very likable guy, a very interesting character. He had played drums and sang in a band you can find on YouTube and was a technical expert for ETS' exotic and expensive FIA and FIM type race fuels. He knew intimately what fuels were on the market and what we had to compete against. His parents lived in Normandy, sacred ground to any American, so this guy had even more to offer. Most importantly, since relationships and connections are essential, he knew a lot of people in the industry and had already walked through some very impressive doors.

Jerome fulfilled every bit of my wish list when it came to finding THE guy to help wage our war. As he came from Normandy I thought it fitting, in a very loosely symbolic sense, that he help us Americans to liberate Europe. He'd be the guy who made sure samples got to where they needed to be and that they were tested, many times with him standing there to make sure it was a legitimate evaluation. So we were set. "Jerome, we'll make some race fuel blends and you get them in the hands of every qualified tuner and engine builder you can find." Sounds easy? One problem. "What do you mean you might not be able to get the chemicals we'll need?" is what I said with *enthusiasm* to our people in Texas. I finally had my DH, my European Designated Hitter, but someone just said we might not have access to the balls. You have to have balls if you want to play the game! Was there really a problem or was someone just busting mine?

My reaction was clearly that of a city boy from the Northeast. The point being, at times I needed to be deliberate and direct. Anyone who worked with me at VP knew that. I liked to laugh a lot but my plate was really full, while others might not have been, and I didn't always have the time or interest in mincing words. I prefer to blow stuff up and move on to the next target. That's why some people have referred to me as "that damn Yankee" and other times they've used shorter, four-letter words. But as I may have stated before, I had little time for bullshit. I had the largest region to work, a plant to operate, and no time for stupid mistakes. I always had a mountain of calls and things to look after. If you were wasting my time, making VP or me look inept, or whatever, I let you know it. My time was precious and I didn't like anyone else wasting it. If we needed chemicals then to me, anything other than "they're on the way," was an excuse. Did I ever mention I drink way too much coffee? I had a strategy in mind and needed the support to make it happen. As we chipped away at our domestic

Goliaths, one would eventually quit the business and provide a windfall of sales and profit for VP. I wanted to do the same overseas. More profit provides the weaponry to fight bigger battles and so on. In retrospect, perhaps I should have used more sugar. Not on the coffee but on the people I needed the support from. Lesson learned, but you'll see how things turned out.

To a great degree most of the racing fuels produced and consumed in the United States are regarded as commodity fuels. The typical 110 and 112 octane type fuels are found at most race track pumps and in the back of most pickups and race trailers at tracks and circuits. They are also basic fuels with basic components with basic prices. VP's chemist, founder and fuel designer Burns, and the supply people had always stepped up when we needed them. When the lead ban went into effect in Canada and then again when Elf crossed a few time zones and decided to go head to head with us in motorcycle racing, their focus and drive was trained on the mission and they got us what we needed to continue the fight. They had also continued to make NHRA Pro Stock cars in North America go faster than any one of the so-called Goliaths could. Now was the time for them to step up again but this time it would be much more difficult.

While everyone at VP, including yours truly, had been waging our domestic wars I was also trying to get a strong foothold overseas. The drag racers were all buying our drag race fuels but this would be a different world. One that would have global implications on sales and our standing if we could get it done. The Goliaths on those overseas fields were Elf, Shell, Petro Carless, and much smaller ETS.

VP continued to fight its North American battles with Sunoco and the smaller Renegade, Torco, and the pesky wannabes with basic chemistry. There were also some very productive excursions into some really cool products that kept us at the forefront of the domestic technology fight. Meanwhile, the big boys who fueled the international FIA and FIM competitions, including Formula 1, had elevated their chemistry games again and again and again. While we were making the Pro Stock cars go faster and faster, these guys were making Formula 1 cars run like cheetahs on very technical, very complicated fuels. To make it even more of a challenge, the fuels had to resemble pump gas in octane and composition. These fuel companies had large laboratories with big staffs and big budgets. They had acquisition departments that could source chemicals from anywhere and everywhere. They had buying power. They had friends. They also knew all the rules, all the players, and had long established histories and relationships. Okay, no biggie. We're up to it as long as we knew the rules and were given the chance to compete. Not having a level playing field didn't really matter to us, we were used to it.

These Euro giants were having their own little battles and VP, at least I, wanted in. Now what to do about the chemicals? What was the real problem? Was my passion making anyone work harder than they wanted to or were their plates already full? In some cases, people might get comfortable, complacent, or too set in their ways and in a sales organization that can be catastrophic. Over time, I got what I needed or at least I thought so.

The timeline might be off here but after Fred Morrison's retirement in 2006 and Steve's continued hit and run visits and calls, we all needed someone to make decisions. One of the many things that made VP different from the Goliaths was our ability to react and make moves very quickly. Big companies like to have meetings and move along with plans and budgets and such. One of VP's core advantages in the battles was that we were quick and decisive. If the boss were nowhere to be found, we'd stumble if we kept going the way we were. It was clear someone needed to be able to make decisions, and believing I was most qualified I asked for the job. I had the most experience, had full knowledge of plant operation, was successful, had a great team that supported me in my region, had done as Steve had said years earlier and kept us out of lawsuits, and understood the intricacies. On a conference call Steve let everyone know that based on what I just cited, along with my loyalty and passion, he was naming me Corporate Director of Sales & Marketing for the company. He might also have joked that I still had compromising pictures of him with livestock. Someone said, "At least we'll be able to find him and get quick decision on things," and we were done. Some people don't necessarily like change so I would recommend another book, *Who Moved My Cheese*, to anyone troubled by change or the prospect of it.

My wife worked at a Fortune 500 company that constantly strove to improve their people. Learning, self-awareness, opening minds to new thoughts, trends, and techniques could make for a better person and a better employee. I wanted to bring that culture to VP. In my thirty or so years at VP we had been given only one seminar but I learned something invaluable that helped VP and me for years to come. "Work on the business, not in it," Denise

Blanchard from the old Padgett Stratemann accounting firm in San Antonio told the team. With those words, long before I got the corporate gig, I began to look at my people, the plant, the region, and the way everyone operated – including me. I pictured myself looking down on everything I just mentioned from a helicopter viewpoint. The things I saw were amazing and allowed me to really get my business head on straight. Thanks, Denise, those words had a huge impact both on me and on the business. Steve Burns is a brilliant man, a self-taught chemist, and successful business-person but not everyone can learn or fix something on their own.

I told my managers to take time to consider what they felt they needed, or wanted, to be better. I assured them that their feedback would be confidential and treated with the utmost sincerity. For me, as a matter of sharing, I told them I hated public speaking and intended to take a Dale Carnegie course in New York to improve. I had done press conferences dating back to Darlington in 1979 to address rumors that there was a rift between Waltrip and the Gardiners and had made announcements to crowds in the funeral business but never felt comfortable doing it. Maybe one manager needed to take an Excel spreadsheet course. Maybe one might need management training. Everyone can improve on something otherwise there wouldn't be any pitching coaches in major league baseball. I knew the strengths and areas needing attention of every member of the team and just wanted to give them the opportunity to self-evaluate and to improve. Plus when you show people you are trying to help them, not hurt them, they should respond positively and everyone should be the better for it.

For whatever reason the initiative didn't get the support I needed to move it forward. I could push for sales but not train or replace a poor performer. If we had a turtle on board I couldn't entice him with lettuce or light a candle behind him. I knew the weak links but couldn't tweak them. I might have been put in charge of the ship but couldn't discipline or fire the knucklehead who ran us into the pier In time I grew frustrated by this and other rev-limiters; the inability to move as I felt was needed, and opted to step back into my very successful regional role. The stress, caused mostly by frustration, and of running the region AND the corporate responsibilities weren't worth it and I needed get back to having a life. When it's that obvious that you can't fix or change something, yeah, time to do something else. Unless you're on fire there's no point in pissing into the wind.

Getting back to the mission I had started overseas, in short order, Jerome shipped us samples of the Euro fuels we would need to compete against. We weren't interested in copying them. We were interested in making something better. But you need a benchmark and then you get to work. Once the lab was able to look at the fuel samples Jerome sent over, the chemist was able to do a ton of research and development and if our buyer was able to acquire what was needed we were almost ready to go. But if you wanted a one-gallon sample of an exotic chemical it might cost you $800. Need ten samples of different goods and now you might be out $8,000 and haven't made a drop of new fuel yet. If the product works you can then buy larger quantities at a lower cost per gallon – you hope. If a particular chemical is sought after by other industries, like pharmaceutical, or even by another race fuel company, that can drive the price through the roof. It isn't dependent on crude prices or stock market indexes; I'm told it's driven by whoever decides how much money their chemical supply division wants to make that year. Okay, let's do this.

Back in action with the Euro blends and our sortie into the European FIA/FIM fuel market. Samples were produced and shipped over to Jerome. He hand delivered them to many of his contacts and watched as the new VP blends were assessed on the dynos. In many cases, this would be the first time many of these tuners and factory engineers had ever seen one of our products. In some cases, results were very good. In others, not so good but it is there that the learning and real development begins.

Jerome did a fantastic job getting things moving and before long he signed up a young, enthusiastic Czech named Martin Popilka who was familiar with the fuel business. His father had been in the fuel business in Prague but Martin wanted to do something on his own and something more exciting. Jerome couldn't have hit a bigger home run. Working tirelessly doing something you are passionate about is very rewarding. Finding someone of that same mindset and ability is priceless. Together they followed rally circuits all across Europe. From the January cold of Monte Carlo to the heat and humidity of England in summer, they were there talking to racers and tuners and engine builders. The following year at the next Autosport event in Birmingham I got to meet the Czech and was astounded by the number of new visitors we had to the VP stand. What had been a lackluster crowd was now a bustling and enthused one.

There must be something about that trade show and the

Hilton Birmingham Airport hotel. It's an easy walk to the NEC where the event takes place and so after-show happy hours and dinners were not just easy, they were the standard. Despite all the good things that came from that show and the fun and business that was conducted there, all good things must come to an end, it seems. It's a shame. Both of those young men had everything I thought was needed to make a great Euro and eventually a great global team. Plus I liked them both very much. However, sometimes things don't always work and I wish them great health, wealth, and happiness wherever they may be today. Regardless of the roster shake-up, having the winning fuel in the Asian Pacific Rally Champion's car was something we could now boast about even more. Clearly we were on the map and people were noticing.

The standard VP fuels menu along with our now famous FIA and FIM blends were doing great. Customers were making the switch to VP more and more. The ones that could afford to change the mapping in their rally or circuit cars were going faster and the distributors were making more money. Things in England seemed on track at long last too. But just as the Germans did their best to sink every supply ship the U.S. sent across the Atlantic, something we had all thought could never happen did. In 2012, a container ship named the MSC Flaminia, stocked from deep in her hull to five high above the deck, was on fire somewhere at sea between the States and Liverpool. On that ship was a 40' long container stuffed to capacity with VP Racing Fuels. Normal sailing time between the two ports might be ten to fourteen days and now VP, and her thirsty customers, were adrift without power.

The reports were that a fire, unrelated to VP or its container, had started aboard and eventually the Flaminia lost power and was waiting desperately for help to arrive. More importantly, a crewman was killed and several were injured. It was the worst thing that could happen on a ship at sea and once we got word of it we knew it meant trouble for us as well.

Large, steel ocean containers, "boxes" as we'd refer to them, would ship every two weeks from VP to our Euro distributors during the late winter through to September or so. It was a reliable pipeline that we had been using for as long as I could remember. Our U.K. distributor would need another box on the water immediately and he'd have to scramble to help his customers make do with the inventory he had, or could beg borrow or steal from the distributors on the Continent, to get by. So we had $50,000 worth of race fuel somewhere in the Atlantic on a ship that was on fire and needed to get another $50,000 worth of fuel loaded on the next ship we could book space on and hope the disruption wouldn't be catastrophic to what we had been trying to build there.

"So once they get the fire out how long before she's towed to a port so we can recover our fuel if it's still intact?" was a simple question I'd ask but the answers were anything but. "Every port is refusing to grant the Flaminia access," I was told, "there are concerns about hazardous waste and fumes on the ship and nobody wants to touch it." Okay, well at least there was cargo insurance on the load so if we never got it back we'd at least get paid. Not so fast, you're talking maritime law, international law, and international insurance companies. I guess we missed the extremely fine print. "Okay, we're screwed but what about the next box. How quickly can you get it to England?" More delays took place with the replacement order. It was a perfect storm, one rarely experienced at VP.

We'd have to wait for the chemicals needed for some of the key fuels, then we'd have to force our overseas special order into the production line to get the fuel made, drummed off and loaded, and then we'd have to wait another week or so for the ship that would have room for us. Not all ships accept hazardous materials or perhaps ones with our particular UN numbers. So we're all thinking this will have a happy ending, right? It continues.

The distributor lost a bunch of customers during that nightmare summer and once the new box finally got to him in England it was too late for many racers. Those who didn't have many options went back to their old fuel supplier and in many cases back to their old mapping. Many did make do with what they could get hold of and came back to us when their fuel of choice was again in stock. But for the most part it was the end of the season. Not all of the fuels were FIA blends. There were plenty of other products in the order that would be okay in the next season. But we did have 2012 formula blends left over and the big question was would the FIA or FIM change their fuel regulations for 2013? What to do then with $20,000 worth of outdated fuel? We could look for a blender who we could partner with to make this fuel into something else if necessary. This, along with everything else started another discussion about blending all, or at least certain of our Euro blends, there in Europe. Faster delivery time to the dealers and customers would be one immediate benefit. It would also eliminate ocean transport costs, eliminate some of the import duties, and so on. Those are all great reasons to find a proper blender. Their costs, access to the chemicals needed, and so on were another issue. Either way, it would be months before the next racing season really got going. To top it all off, warehousing HAZMAT in England isn't cheap or easy. We could move some of the fuel onto the Continent to our other distributors but again, for the most part, 2012 over there was done for the season.

Despite the setback, VP had finally established a significant name for itself in global rally racing but there was one major engine builder that I *really* wanted to partner with. M-Sport is one of the best, and their reach and customer base is truly global. I rode up to their HQ in Cumbria, England for a meeting. The U.K. distributor at that time had been doing all the driving which for the first time gave me the chance to really sit back and enjoy the countryside. It's probably best to drive it in a rally car since the roads are very well suited for it. Cumbria sits just east of the Isle of Man and just below England's border with Scotland. I had a meeting with Nigel Arnfield to discuss a technical partnership. He had heard some good things about us but when he realized that VP was the company now fueling the Rolex 24 Hour endurance race at Daytona that helped even more. Hearing that Martin and his new fuel company had visited recently pitching a partnership idea motivated me even more to make something happen. Nobody likes to lose and business is business. This set the stage for a relationship and after I retired Freddie Turza continued the course and made a deal that has proven very good for VP. Never give up, mate.

On the trip back from that initial visit with M-Sport

and much closer to current day, the ride turned sour. "Let's stop there," I suggested as we passed a high-performance speed shop located somewhere between Cumbria and London. Before long the distributor and I were in full disagreement about how to carry on business in that country. I had wanted to stop and at least have a discussion with the shop owner. "Heard of VP, have any racing customers that use VP, know where to buy it?" were the type of questions I intended to ask. If a distributor has a territory, but a speed shop that sells aftermarket performance parts in that region doesn't know about our products or where to find them, then there's work to be done. My driver was annoyed that I suggested he lacked drive if he wasn't interested in taking a few minutes to talk up an easy lead. Perhaps he was afraid that I'd discover how little the shop owner knew of our brand and consequently how little the distributor might be doing to grow sales. After that I knew there had to be something, someone, better in Britain.

As time went by, and for a variety of reasons the U.K. racers familiar with the situation understood, VP wound up parting ways with the distributor. Although the area is much smaller than the United States there are a tremendous number of racers and racing in Scotland, Ireland, Wales, the Isle of Man, and England. Originally I had reduced his territory down to England itself. There's just too much territory and action for one man to attempt to service and cultivate. We went direct with Santa Pod Raceway and so many other great resellers. Thanks to M-Sport and everyone else that touched the various deals in one way or another, VP and the U.K. are working well together now with sales and customer confidence is growing significantly.

So what ever happened with the FIA regulations? In short, among other things, the FIA ruled one chemical could no longer be used and that essentially killed the VP fuel that won the Asian Pacific Rally Championship a few years prior. The fuel had been kicking everyone's butt in rally racing but probably more importantly for some it had been taking market share from the big guys. Don't piss off Goliaths too much; you can see what they can do, especially with home field advantage.

The team back in Texas went back to work and developed a pretty decent fuel. I might have prodded them a bit about not letting the French or whoever beat us. If I did I'm sure that helped motivate a few people. We did some testing and then more testing and when we thought it was ready to show we flew samples to Moscow. The plan was to have THE top tuner for the Baltic region test the two new fuel blends. Primarily in rally racing in Europe there are Subaru and Mitsubishi along with Skoda and many others. The Subaru and Mitsubishi engines both ran fast and were very popular but their construction was different. The fuel might not be able to be a one-fits-all blend like the outlawed one had been.

Now the fuel was in Moscow, where Freddie Turza and I had already done a bunch of dyno work on past visits that were usually followed by photo ops in Red Square's Cathedral or the Kremlin and Lenin's Tomb and decent amounts of Russian vodka and celebratory toasts deep into the night. I remember like it was yesterday standing at Russia's Kilometer Zero and exchanging Cold War grade school stories with Evgeny Doronin, our Russian distributor. In my grade school located in the suburbs outside of Philadelphia we not only did we do fire drills but we practiced air raid drills in the event of an atomic bomb blast. We were told to get away from the windows and get under our desks, heads down and covered. To my surprise, Evgeny related he had experienced the very same type of drills in grade school there in Moscow.

There certainly was a lot of tension between the U.S. and Russia during the Cold War and during recent political events, but I can tell you that the Russian people, the ones I got to spend a lot of time with both there and here in the U.S. are great people. Their country is an interesting one that given the chance I would recommend visiting, even if just to St. Petersburg.

The two fuel samples made it to Moscow but it turned out the tuner and the engine he wanted to test on were going to be in Riga, Latvia and apparently there was no room for negotiation. It seems after we had spent a year or two getting this top tuner to like VP, he got many of his customers to switch to it at great cost to them only to find now that the popular fuel was no longer legal. They'd have to either switch back to an old blend and remap or go with this new blend, if it worked, and pay for mapping again. Racers don't like to get screwed and I can see where a few might have thought either VP, the tuner, or the distributor, were bending them over so to speak.

Okay, I told the Russians, we'll fly to Riga for the test and we'll ask you to decant the two blends we sent to Moscow into smaller containers. Keep some for yourself and ship one of each to Riga. I might have mentioned that in the U.S. most of us have a can-do attitude that makes us the greatest in the world. In England and other Euro countries people would look at me in shock when I suggested they toss a few pails or a small drum in their car and do what you need to do. In Moscow and Eastern Europe you can usually make things happen though. The Russians would gladly split the samples as requested but someone would need to get them to Riga. They couldn't be put on an airplane for a variety of reasons and our Russians couldn't bring them to us since they were spread thin working race events in their territory. Okay, apply the "whatever it takes" mantra right? Can we pay someone to drive the 900 miles to bring the samples to us?

We flew into Riga, flying over the huge chunks of ice that were floating in the Baltic Sea below us. We enjoyed our first evening in the city that only twenty or so years before had been under the Communist rule of the former Soviet Union. We got to tour the former U.S. Embassy and enjoyed the local beers. The next morning, our Latvian distributor drove us to the chassis dyno shop and we were set. But wait, there's only one sample can! Doing business overseas and dealing with ten different languages might have had its challenges but the person who received and confirmed the instructions spoke and read English very well. No excuses for screwing this one up. I don't know how you say WTF in Russian or Latvian but what the f---! We had flown 5,000 miles and paid a big sum to get the samples, now sample, from Moscow to Riga. This was our big chance to look good for the top tuner and we would have to cross our fingers now and hope for the best.

They base-lined the engine on whatever the car was used to racing on and then drained the system and put in the new VP sample. Nothing much happened. A few more pulls and it wasn't looking good. They put the old customer fuel back in and things went right back to where they had been. So any or all of three things might be happening. First, the "old" fuel could be something hopped up or not FIA compliant. If you are going to compare apples to apples then do so. Second, we noticed that the tuner's assistant always made sure the garage door was wide open whenever the customer's fuel was being run. Whenever the VP went in, the door came down and the air wasn't the same. Third, maybe the tuner was flat out sabotaging the test. Strangers in a strange land can often be taken advantage of.

We had to do something. "What have you got in inventory at your shop?" I asked the distributor. He had something that we thought might do the trick and an hour later, one of the very popular FIA compliant VP fuels was on board and making very good power. The only problem was, this fuel would be illegal in the New Year.

We were pleased we showed them the good power but what to do about running an illegal fuel? It turns out there's a lot of rally racing that doesn't pay much attention to FIA's strict regulations and consequently we sold a lot of that product in certain parts of the world. But we wanted to remain a player in formal FIA racing so we set out to spend more time and more money developing a legal fuel that did not contain that banned chemical. Now this is where it gets hairy.

All but one manufacturer worked hard to get new blends to market, all but one. People kept asking what Brand W was coming out with and nobody seemed to know. We made legal fuels, as did the others. New tuning, new mapping, frustration from racers and dealers who had left-over and now illegal fuel added to the transition. But where was the new Brand W fuel? After all, they had a huge market share and a lot of racers were waiting to get the new fuel and have it mapped so they could go racing. Guess what, the new fuel never came. Instead, Brand W relied on a little known FIA regulation. I know it now by heart but was incensed when I learned of its existence. Apparently the local FIA regulatory group could defer to using last year's regulations if they deemed it necessary. That's all well and good but why didn't the FIA make that clear to the rest of us? Surely Brand W knew it existed or pointed out its existence in the areas where they had good distribution and relationships with the majority of the racers. Okay, this Goliath got one over on us. The only comment I had to offer the FIA at the next meeting in Geneva was simple; "What the hell do we need the FIA for if the regional organizations can opt out of your fuel regulations whenever they choose to?" I don't think I got an answer but if there had been I would like to have discussed it further. Sounded like a Damn Yankee didn't I?

Why bother trying to win an uphill battle? Because we're Americans and to me the European market was my moon and I intended to walk, drive, train, and fly all over it and our competition. It's how we rolled.

Years earlier, my first real experience with the FIA had been a very good one. They had sent out notifications to all of the fuel manufacturers they had on record. They were requesting bids on exclusive spec fuel supply for the next season's FIA Pro Stock Drag Racing European Championship. There were perhaps sixteen to twenty race cars competing in a handful of drag races in Europe. For the most part they were racing NHRA type Pro Stock cars using

American built Pro Stock drag race engines. The FIA had adopted the NHRA's technical regulations and so for us it seemed like this would be a perfect fit for VP. It would also serve as a first step into the FIA world. Sometimes better to crawl before walking and so on. The bids, which were typical of old-world European bureaucracies, were pages and pages long and had significant requirements. It was incredible. Bidders had to assure things like, if I remember correctly, season-long retail prices to be quoted in euros. If for some reason the fuel could not be delivered to the racers running the championship then the FIA would reserve the right to do whatever they needed to ensure the race went on. That meant if they needed to have 500 gallons of fuel made and shipped by private plane from wherever they wanted to wherever they wanted, they could do so and catch this, the winner of the bid would have to pay the bill. In other words, if it would cost $100,000 to ship that fuel from the U.S. to Norway then they could do it, order it done, and we'd have to pay the bill. The fuel supplier could have suggested less costly solutions but the contract left the final decision in the FIA's hands. I'm sure the FIA was accustomed to worrying about fueling larger, more high profile international series that traveled to stops on just about every continent. The drag racing element was much more local to Santa Pod in England, Hockenheim in Germany, and tracks in Sweden and Norway. Regardless, we weren't going to let someone we had no real relationship with at that point have the option to make a call that could hurt us financially.

After talking with Burns and Morrison our response would be simple. I prepared a bid that ignored the various entanglements the document had requested or mandated. I love being from America and doing things our way. We stated very simply and clearly that we would make a very good fuel, sell it to anyone who wanted it, quote a good and fair price, and be sure the distributors had it in their inventories and that the engine builders in the U.S. and Europe had access to samples for testing and tuning. I don't know if Sunoco or Total or any of the other big companies even sent in a bid. The Goliaths might not have been interested in making such a small batch of fuel with all the liability and little ROI but we were on our terms and guess what, we won the bid. The FIA announced VP was the spec fuel supplier and that marked the first time VP began fueling an international series.

I really had only one concern. The drag racers knew VP and our fuels and knew they could count on our reputation for quality and consistency. But I had seen instances here in North America when a spec fuel had been mandated that an overzealous fuel dealer might jack the price a bit. In national disasters they call it gouging and VP would not allow that to happen to its racing customers. If a VP dealer was going to make it tough for racers to get the fuel they need and/or charge a ridiculous price for it then you needed to sell someone else's fuel because as Trump has said, "You're fired." Sometimes when a racer is also the fuel dealer that can lead to allegations of collusion so I always investigated and resolved the matter if it came up. In one instance, I actually saw a racer go to a fuel truck to get his gas and ask how much of a particular fuel was on the rig. Once he learned there were five drums he bought all five and that would have eliminated his competition from running the fuel they were tuned to. The truck driver who sold the guy all that product let me know what had happened. I had to give the one racer some credit for trying to buy it all up but it wasn't fair and I assured him the same thing might happen to him someday if he didn't work with me on this. An hour later we had four of those drums back in the VP rig and ready for the rest of the racers who needed it.

Speaking of gouging and "fuelin' around" check this out. VP developed SEF Small Engine Fuel. It's ethanol-free fuel and is built to sit in outdoor power equipment for extended periods and always start and perform when needed. It was packaged in quarts, gallons, five-gallon pails and big drums. Norm Turnberg up in Massachusetts was the first person to bring that issue to my attention. A local fire company had responded to a car accident call. A tree or power pole had come down on the vehicle and the driver was injured and in need of emergency treatment. Their chainsaw wouldn't start and they had to elicit the help of the fire company in the next town to get the wood cut and the man extricated. The next day the fire company called Norman, told him what happened and an hour later he was on the phone with me relating the story. An hour later I was on with Steve Burns and our chemist and before long SEF was designed, tested, reformulated a dozen times and then released to market. Up until that time I had been struggling to find a product that could keep us busy in Delaware year round. The economics of a seasonal business is simple. If revenue only streams for seven or eight months but payroll and other operating expenses went on for twelve that created some difficulties. We had been forced all too many times to lay off some good warehouse workers and office staffers only to lose them when we called them back in the spring. It hurt to turn people loose, good people especially, and I understood when they found another job – a steady one – instead of sitting through the winter on unemployment waiting for the callback. If this new product line caught on, selling fuels for outdoor power equipment like generators, chainsaws and other cutting tools could be big for business and solve the seasonal turnover issue I hated.

To promote the new product I even used our relationship with World Racing Group and DIRT Northeast to sponsor the Super DIRT Week race, naming it the SEF 200. We gave out samples to the local fire department, the DIRT rescue crews, and samples to the races. It turned out everyone had the same issue with the ethanol in pump gas. It attracted moisture and in turn caused equipment to fail. I was so damn excited by it all. I liked making racers go fast but I cared more about keeping people safe. Generators need to start when a wife and kids are cold and in the dark when a storm hits. Safety tools need to start and run well when needed to pry a racer out of his race car or cut a vent hole in the roof of a house that's on fire. What became clear there too was that the fuel quality had to be dead on consistent each and every drop, just like our race fuel. You've already read examples of how important safety and specialty equipment is but consider the supercross motorcycle racer who is using Brand X. As he approaches his big jump at full speed the engine sputters and he lands short of the other ramp, both he and the bike in pieces. Again, my enthusiasm in promoting SEF came a bit early. The product was sound and the need was there but without it wouldn't matter if the distribution channels weren't in place. Sure the race fuel dealer network existed but to really have a sales impact and a benefit to non-racing consumers we needed companies like Home Depot, Lowe's, NAPA, and many more to help make it happen. Promoting the new product during the television broadcast of the race was cool but would have done so much better if everything else had been in place. It wouldn't until new ownership came along and applied focus and assembled the right team to take SEF and run with it. Looking back at SEF, from inception to the brand name on the race winner's hat on CBS television was still pretty cool. Brett Hearn did a commercial for SEF that ran during the race and as part of the contract with the WRG, sponsoring the "200" had been our option so I took advantage of it. The SEF 200 first ran in 2010 but two years later things got real.

When a disaster hits, like Hurricane Sandy did to the East Coast back in 2012, power was out for days and when power is out that means gas stations can't pump fuel and cars and generators run out of fuel. Home Depot was now carrying SEF in some of their Mid-Atlantic stores as a test. In Texas they worked round the clock to get the area the truckloads of pails that would be needed. In Delaware, we were shipping fuel to armored truck companies that needed to keep money flowing. The New Jersey Turnpike Commission sent a truck to the plant to buy every five-gallon plastic fuel jug they could take. We even had a Ferrari dealership north of us order drums of our 100 octane street legal fuel and the pumps to go with them to assure their customers they'd have something to burn.

We loaded tractor-trailers full of skids, thirty-six pails per skid, of SEF fuel and shipped five of them to the Home Depots that were testing the product. For the armored car company, the NJTPC, Ferrari and all other customers the prices were what they would have been on any other day of the year. You help out, especially when people are in distress. But for some consumers at one of the Home Depots near the Jersey beaches someone had another idea of what was going on. Because of its chemical composition, SEF is labeled and sold not as a gasoline but as a chemical or blend of chemicals. It is not labeled as gasoline; it wasn't before the hurricane either.

The truck showed up at the Home Depot store and quickly a line developed to start buying the pails of generator fuel. There's no ethanol in it like there is in pump gas so the product should start and run and run and run without issue. That's why it was first developed for that fire department in Connecticut who couldn't get their chainsaw started and get a fallen tree off the car and driver it had fallen on. It's not an inexpensive product but considering how it performs and a shelf life that is so much better than pump gas, it costs more. Coming in a steel five-gallon pail adds to the cost. Person after person grabbed a pail or two, paid the price, and got back to running their generators and chainsaws and other rescue and outdoor power equipment. And then this guy comes along. "You're price gouging!" he charged the store manager. "Pump gas only costs a little but you're charging a lot!" Well it wasn't pump gas, he and we explained, but it was too late. The guy called the police and they in turn shut the sales off. Lots of people were turned away and as a result may have had hard feelings toward the store and the police. It wasn't gouging, you dipstick! Lots of people were left cold and in the dark that night thanks to you whoever you are.

CHAPTER SIXTEEN
NICE GOAT

I'VE OFTEN JOKED that my biological parents must have been a traveling salesman and an airline flight attendant. Most likely, based on how much I love spending time in the air, I was a by-product of a get together by these members of the mile high club. I love to travel, love flying, and have found tranquility at 38,000 feet more than anywhere else. While so many travelers, rookies as us vets call them, complain about all the horrible misadventures they experience on air travel, I've rarely had a bad experience. I can think of one Nigerian woman in particular who had reason to bitch but a VP buddy and I might have had something to do with it.

Jason Rueckert is one of the funniest and nicest guys I know. He started out as a truck driver for VP's Indiana office and worked his way up and into the captain's chair to oversee the Midwest Region for the company. He's a drag racer and very knowledgeable tuner and his particular field of expertise is in traction compounds. Remember, he's the guy

I took to Vermont to test the Two Groove product on the asphalt oval track. Anyway, I had been working on Santa Pod Raceway in the Midlands of England and needed an expert's help to push them even further on to using VP's Lane Choice compound. Without traction compound the high horsepower cars and bikes there and at tracks around the world would simply spin their tires into oblivion.

The trip seemed to go pretty well. Our Russian distributor and his son came to the U.K. to meet with Jason and to see nitro-fueled dragsters and funny cars for the first time in person. The track's operations guy got to spend a lot of time with Jason talking traction and at night we'd get involved with taste testing every vodka the bar had on hand while Jason developed a fondness for a good bit of Speckled Hen beer. But all good things must come to an end so Jason and I said our goodbyes to the Russians and the Brits, and headed south to Heathrow and the long flight home to the States.

For anyone who hasn't flown that route overseas it's really an out of body experience. They lock you and 200 strangers into a flying bus and hurtle you through the darkness at 600mph high over the frigid water of the North Atlantic. Eventually, if you were lucky enough to sleep at all, you wake up thinking and feeling like it's 3am. You're dehydrated and weary but the excitement of arriving on a new adventure gets the adrenaline going and you move ahead. On the return, you usually fly slower because you're traveling against the jet stream and spend about eight hours in the air. The airlines will play movies and feed you a small tray of chicken or pasta so aside from that it's up to you to sleep or read or find entertainment in your electronics. For Jason, he had something else in mind.

"Dude," he said with excitement, "look at what I picked up in the gift shop!"

He was sitting across the aisle from me and handed over a thick magazine. From the look on his face I thought it was either *Mad* or *Playboy* but he had found something better. It was a British fetish magazine!

I always sit in an aisle seat. I hate bothering people when I want to get up and stretch or use the small closet most airlines call the toilet. It can be a bother if the person beside you wants up a lot but I want to be able to get up and go whenever.

I slowly opened the magazine, keeping it close to my chest so I didn't offend anyone nearby, and within a second it was yanked from my fingers. "What in the name of the good Lord are you looking at?" the flight attendant demanded. I hadn't felt like that since a parochial school Catholic nun yelled at me for one of her thousand reasons. When I looked up at the attendant I knew I was safe. She had a smile from ear to ear and asked if she could take it up to show the captain. I found it funny, the thought of her taking a fetish magazine to a cockpit.

Ten minutes later she returned with the magazine and said we were getting free drinks for the duration of the flight. Okay, they're cool. We're set. Let me turn on a movie, enjoy the free Budweiser, and settle in for an uneventful ride home to my wife and kids. Three hours later, all hell broke loose as a woman began to scream, "Help me, help me!"

Sitting behind Jason were two women from Nigeria and one seemed to be having a heart attack or a stroke of some sort. She went completely limp and fell to the floor between the rows of seats. If you haven't ever picked up an unconscious person they're typically limp like a wet rag and so getting her up and available for medical treatment was going to be tough. "We have a medical emergency on board," the attendant broadcast over the intercom, "if there is a doctor or anyone with medical training on board please let a flight attendant know immediately." Within a minute there were two doctors and three nurses attending to the unconscious woman. Her friend was still hysterical and when it was clear there was nothing Jason or I could do to help we tried out best to ignore the IV bags that they had hung from the overhead storage bins and the defibrillator they had at the ready. The woman was in bad shape. Her blood pressure was barely reading and it didn't look too good for her. At some point, Jason and I started to whisper across the aisle. "Do you think she saw my fetish magazine?" he asked. Now it made sense. The woman might have innocently looked between the seats but when she saw the photo of the goat with the leather choker and the spiked high heels that might have sent her into a tailspin. This might have just been our attempt at cutting the tension with a little humor injection but that might have been what happened. They stabilized their patient once and then when she crashed a second time they got her going again.

Interestingly, once we landed, the customs officials had to check her before they would let the EMTs remove her from the jet way. To this day we don't know if we had anything to do with that poor woman's plight but I can tell you that sure was a hot goat.

CHAPTER SEVENTEEN

WINNING

IN NHRA CHAMPIONSHIP racing they had seen some racers start down a dangerous path. Very exotic, very expensive and potentially dangerous fuels were showing up at fuel check. The NHRA maintains a list of Approved Fuels that can be used in the classes specified. There were probably fifty fuels on the list from ten different manufacturers and that could make tech cumbersome. As some of these exotics began to show up more and more the NHRA put their foot down and banned some of the ingredients that were being used. Citing safety concerns and reducing the skyrocketing costs of racing for the first time ever they put "Official Fuel of NHRA" title and entitlements out for bid. Spec fuel sales for many of the classes, requiring each competitor use that product exclusively, and exclusive on-site fuel sales rights at their National Events were part of the package. VP, Sunoco (World Wide), and Larry Coogle Industries trucks had been parked at many of those big races. The company that won the bid would be the only ones allowed at the Nationals to sell fuel.

Remember that big and boisterous rep from Union 76, Bill Broderick? Well there he was walking around one of the NHRA events we were all working. Union 76 did NOT have a rig on site and probably had only one or two fuels on the Approved List. The look on his pompous, confident face told it all. You could tell that this guy, who felt he was something special over in the NASCAR Winners Circles, thought he'd be there in our world soon acting in the same capacity. Apparently nobody told him this wasn't circle track racing. It was drag racing and considering VP had won ALL NHRA Pro Stock Car World Championships and 80% of the cars at the track were on VP, we had no intention of losing one race let along this bid.

Fred and Steve worked their butts off preparing the bid. They most certainly asked all of VP's good friends to show their support and encourage the NHRA to award us the deal and keep the highest quality race fuels they had ever seen available at the events. The clock ticked and ticked after the bids had been sent in. Now all we could do was wait, and hope. Sunoco had beaten my ass in the Northeast with the DIRT bidding twice now so I wasn't very optimistic. But guess what, VP won the NHRA bid! We beat out two major refiners, Union 76 and Sunoco. Little David was doing okay and he had friends.

Spec fuel for some of the classes meant that the NHRA tracks that held regional events would have to allow VP in to at least provide fuel availability to those classes. We had a lot of pushback from Sunoco loyalists but over time not only did they negotiate with us and let us in but eventually a great number of them switched their race fuel business over to VP once their renewals came up. Not only did the bid win us the notoriety but we picked up big sales in peripheral business. I'm sure Sunoco corporate wasn't too pleased with losing the bid or the sales but I've been told there was only one distributor who really cared either way and that was World Wide and Frank and Stevie Lesueur. They were accustomed to traveling the country and following the circuit. Nitro was a big deal for them too and now it was gone. I can honestly say that I never gloated. It's a karma thing and it's also unprofessional. I will admit however that I did give Bill Broderick a one-fingered salute and a smile the next time I saw him.

Everyone likes to win and accept the accolades but sometimes a race is won because the leader falls out and your second place spot takes the checkered flag. Racers win some and lose some that way and it occurs in business too. An interesting and timely case in point would be the eventual departure of a Goliath, Union 76 racing gasoline, from the U.S. market. Aside from race fuel for NASCAR and distributors in the southeast and out west, the Union 76 brand was known for gas stations on the West Coast, and perhaps Florida, and truck stops in parts of the U.S. One day we got breaking news through the rumor mill saying Union 76 was getting out of the racing fuel business. My belief is they got out because a bean counter finally pointed out to the decision makers just how much all the free race fuel, logistics, full-page ads in track programs, NASCAR sponsorship, and racetrack suite area rentals actually cost. Since all the race fuel to the teams at the track was free of charge they were operating that division at a loss even before they turned the lights on in that big red ball. Remember, Union 76 had limited race fuel distribution in the U.S. The day formal word came down the wire that Union 76 had decided to cease the production and sale of racing fuel and ending their NASCAR program, we went nuts.

In the Northeast we got a call from a Union 76 distributor in North Carolina. He told us his supply was going away and it was time to talk. Sunoco already had a distributor in that same area so going to them was not an option for him. There were others but partnering with VP made the most sense. Okay, let's make a deal. I had needed someone in that area to help establish the VP brand and get our products in the hands of as many engine builders, race tracks, and race engines as possible. This guy had all the connections and we had met before, trying to get him to add our VP to his already established pipeline. He hadn't accepted our offer that time but now that his world had suddenly changed and his options were very limited, we had him. As an aside, years later when the North Carolinian got fed up with the way "that damn Yankee" (me) did things, they decided to quit selling our products. Here's an example of what caused the strife. They'd mail us a check on the 10th but our statements would be mailed from corporate also on the 10th. The mail would cross paths somewhere in the postal service. "I paid you and you're telling me I still owe you," was the rant. "We're done and that's that," they said sternly. There was no contract between us so we were free to part ways. Within an hour, after I placed a call to Tommy Chapman at VP's Georgia office, we had a replacement distributor all signed up and ready to go.

We liked to move fast and wanted a seamless transition so not one sale, not one gallon, would be lost. The only problem we did run into pretty quickly though was two hours later when the original distributor had a change of heart and called to order more fuel. "Sorry, but you'll have to call David Taylor over at Bobby Taylor Oil in Fayetteville." Life got interesting in that part of the Carolinas for a while but all these years later, David is one of VP's rock stars and I think the former distributor stopped selling fuel years ago. Sometimes big decisions made when you're angry turn out to be bad ones. Making quick decisions in response to someone's mistake can make you look good.

Out on the West Coast, when Union 76 said 'we're getting out of race fuel', the business got a huge shot. A huge distributor for Union 76 had nowhere to turn but VP and all of a sudden sales skyrocketed out there too. Sure there may have been other options for these former Union 76 distributors but why play with smaller brands nobody knows? Calling VP, and us calling them, was the best thing to do.

Union 76 got out for business reasons and its departure led to Sunoco stepping up and becoming the official fuel supplier for NASCAR. It's a very expensive proposition. I had heard rumors that it cost over $10,000,000 per year. Seeming to expand their brand and satisfy NASCAR's desire for marketing partners with a truly national footprint, Sunoco opened a very large number of branded c-stores across the country. In short, that did two huge things for VP. Sunoco appeared to have sent much of their regional racing fuel budget to NASCAR in Daytona and that resulted in a huge surge in business in my region in the Mid-Atlantic and New England. Looking back, I can't even count the number of calls I received from tracks and teams expressing interest in switching to VP but first year sales in the Northeast grew by twenty-seven percent or so. First they abandoned the CAM2 name and drove sales our way and then this. I had already been to all the NASCAR tracks, suite areas, and quite a few Victory Lanes with old DW so for me, I was happy to take the sales growth and not add a ton of more race commitments to my already full schedule.

The NHRA deal was very special to all of us at VP as was 76's departure and Sunoco's taking over the NASCAR fuel deal. It was time to get back to work. In the Northeast, empowered by our NHRA win, and hopes of a better outcome the next time we had a shot at DIRT. Things had changed though. Donnelly had sold off to a South African entrepreneur by the name of Bobby Hartslief. We flew to Dallas and had a very nice working lunch to discuss what we could do together. The talks should have been productive but nothing happened. Then Brian Carter, Tom Deery, and Ben Geisler took over things at World Racing Group/ DIRT and that's when it got interesting for VP.

Brian had told me that they weren't totally satisfied with who took care of their tracks and drivers. A change might be imminent. I always thought it best to get the lay of the land before you buy something so I attended Super DIRT Week for the first time in many years and loved it. I hadn't been back up there since we lost the DIRT bid. There was no reason to. If I had been seen talking to any of the teams then the Sunoco or tech guys would have been all over them looking for cheater fuel. We *had* dyed some of our race fuel the same color as the Sunoco/DIRT spec fuel product and moved some gallons but over time a majority of the racers went with the Sunoco flow and that was that.

"What are you doing here?" one young DIRT racer asked me. "You guys only make drag racing fuel, right?"

That was the phrase we had heard way back in the day when we really started working to grow our business outside of the niche drag and motorcycle markets we had been building our reputation in. I'd go on to tell racer after racer some of the names of teams we fueled. We had won the 2000 NASCAR Grand National oval track title with Jamie Aube and the 2000 NASCAR Modified title with Jamie Tomaino and that helped. Reminding them that Brett Hearn, Joe Plazek, Kenny Tremont, and so many others had chosen to fuel with VP before spec fuel was implemented. All those names gave us credibility.

That was October and I'd meet with Brian and his team at PRI in November, and shortly into the New Year VP was named the new Official Fuel of World Racing Group, Sprint Car, Late Model and spec fuel for Super DIRT Car/ DIRT Northeast. We'd work out the contract details as quickly as possible but Speed Weeks at Volusia in Florida was upon us. WRG and I agreed on the products and the prices and that we'd have two trucks and ample staff down there to do whatever was needed. After Florida in February the Northeast DIRT modifieds wouldn't race again until April in New York so there'd be plenty of time to work out the rest of the details. Freddie Turza went down there to work with each and every team and engine builder to ensure a smooth transition from Sunoco to VP. For me, I had decided to finally have my torn rotator cuff operation and finished up the contract with Geisler while working from home and under the influence of some pretty nice pain medication. I had procrastinated long enough. That's one area that I usually let myself get away with it. Hell, I went around the world a few times with a bad gall bladder until a surgeon told me what it would be like if it ruptured when I was on an overseas flight. Okay, "cut it out".

There would be all sorts of battles and bumps in the road as we introduced the spec fuel proposition to twenty-five or so tracks and hundreds of racers that had only known the Sunoco brand for so many years. The added benefit to winning the spec fuel contract was also huge. If a team knew it had to have VP in the fuel cell for a DIRT race, and they didn't want to drain Brand X out of the cell when they weren't running under DIRT rules, they'd make the smart choice and just race with VP all of the time. So not only were we going to get all the DIRT cars but a ton of those who raced other events. Nice!

The local distributor had been a good friend to many of these same racers and track owners so it would get interesting at times but we persevered. I'll never forget Charlie Holland suggesting to Freddie Turza that he "give this pail of spec fuel to your mother!" Charlie's a great guy and I know he was just frustrated and disappointed. His son John had supplied spec Sunoco to many of the DIRT racers and a few tracks so the loss was going to take some money, a lot of money, out of his pocket. You'll remember that John used to be a VP guy until a combination of things steered him to Sunoco. Like I said, I never gloat. Karma can come back to bite you bad but I have to admit it was a very big win for me personally and professionally and a big one for VP. Now Freddie T, I had to remind him, "It's just business, don't take it personal." If you know Freddie, ask him how many times I had to repeat that or he had to say it to me as we got things going up there on the DIRT circuit.

John's always been a great guy. That is, when he and I

are weren't trying to take money out of each other's pockets. He's probably still out there trying to take back anything I may have taken from him now that I'm gone. If you want to hear a funny story though, ask him or Charlie about the time a VP drum delivery went bad. All I can tell you is a drum got away from Charlie and my driver and the two of them went rolling down the highway in front of their shop in Connecticut.

Bob Dini, an incredible person with a long history in motorsports, was the head tech person at DIRT and did a tremendous job working with us during the transition. He's quite a character and if you ever get the chance to buy him a cup of coffee or a glass of wine, sit back and ask him to relate a few stories of his past exploits. It's an amazing story.

CHAPTER EIGHTEEN

FORCE, GATORADE, AND SEF

I HAVE ALWAYS had a great passion for motorsports and am very much behind anyone who helps brings sponsors to the sport, fans to the stands, and viewers to their screens. It amazes me that I write screens rather than TV sets. Back in 1979 when CBS telecast the Daytona 500 live for the first time, I was there working with Waltrip and got to celebrate his second place finish behind the King, Richard Petty.

The King had been great for the sport, Waltrip would have his place of course and a young Dale Earnhardt was there as well. I'll never forget offering him some Gatorade after the event. At that point there were no cameras, just a guy offering some thirst quencher to someone who might need it. With a wink and a grin he said, "Nope, I'll stick with Hawaiian Punch." Television and the fans in the stands grew NASCAR racing to an unbelievable level.

John Force is to NHRA drag racing what The King was to NASCAR while he was racing. He's THE man! Incredible fan base, strong list of national sponsors, and ALWAYS ready with a great sound bite for the TV crew or a journalist or fan. Thirty or so years later I'd find myself sitting on a beautiful white leather couch in a luxurious motor coach owned by John Force Racing. We were at Maple Grove Raceway outside of Reading, Pennsylvania for the NHRA National Event and I had an idea for a TV commercial that I wanted to pitch him. VP's Marketing Director was happy to accompany me. VP was a major NHRA sponsor, providing on-site nitro fuel supply so John was a customer but also someone who always gave VP a shout out when needed. Earlier in the year when VP was sponsoring Lenny Sammon's Area Auto Racing News trade show and fan show at the Philly Expo Center near Valley Forge in Pennsylvania John had flown in to do an autograph signing for his sponsor. It was early that Sunday, the show had just opened, and John had just arrived on his red-eye flight from the West Coast. He took a second to stop in our booth space and was even happier to oblige a cameraman who asked what VP meant to him. Watch it on You Tube if you want to see his passion. "VP Racing, Can't win a championship without it. They've been there all these years. A great partner to the NHRA. John Force Racing thanks you for your commitment and for a product that's proven and I proved it with all these championships. Fifteen. John Force here."

From my experience with Gatorade on the NASCAR circuit I had been trained to get the Gatorade name or logo in front of every camera you possibly could. The brand had a nationally recognized name and was available in most of the c-stores and food chains across the country. When I came to VP I brought that mindset with me. So in addition to trying to take every bit of race fuel business away from

Sunoco, Union 76, Elf/Total and all the wannabes, I wanted VP and our logo to become a household name. The idea for a commercial was premature though. At the time VP only had racing fuel to offer and not much of anything for the general consumer. As a kid I had watched as STP made their red, white, and blue logo and brand name familiar to anyone with a car or truck. They sponsored cars in the Indy 500 and eventually partnered with Richard Petty's #43. But they even reached out to us as kids. If you mailed a self-addressed stamped envelope to STP they would send you back quite a few of their decals. In grade school, we had them on everything. Talk about putting STP in your head before you were even old enough to buy anything. I wanted to do whatever I could to make our logo just as well known.

Here was my pitch to Force. "I want to make a brand-awareness commercial with you in it." I laid it out for him. The camera shows a few racers in driving suits standing in line at the side of a VP Racing Fuels tractor-trailer. They have their race fuel jugs in hand and are waiting for the VP employee to finish making small talk with the young woman he's been waiting on. Two of the racers with speaking parts are NASCAR Asphalt Modified Champion Teddy Christopher and World of Outlaws Late Model and Super DIRT Car star Tim McCreadie.

McCreadie: Man, she looks great in that driving suit. It fits her perfectly!

Christopher: Yeah, she's really good looking.

Both men continue their attentive gaze and then a racer sitting very close to them in his golf cart speaks up. It's John Force.

Force: Yeah, she's my daughter Ashley. Any questions?

That was my very basic concept for the commercial. Knowing how Force worked with the camera I knew that once the general premise was established, he and Timmy and Teddy could ad-lib, improvise, and just let the camera capture it all.

Force was very interested in getting Ashley as much time in front of the media as possible. She was leading the second generation of Force racers and would be there, hopefully already well established and well sponsored, whenever her father decided to hang up his helmet. They had even set up a facility at John Force Racing in California for her to produce commercials, video presentations for potential sponsors, etc. So it looked like a win-win for everyone. That was until Force brought up his lawyers and SAG. Everyone that's well known and perceived to have money is an easy target for frivolous, pesky lawsuits. Worse yet, representation expenses even in preparing to respond to a nonsense lawsuit costs big bucks. One of John's concerns, or his lawyers' concerns, was that if he did a commercial for VP Racing Fuels and someone, even totally unrelated in every way to Force, filed a suit against VP then they could name Force as well. Yes, you just have to love our judicial system. It's there to protect the innocent and punish the bad guys but dipshits take advantage all the time. I've only been involved in a few legal matters over the years and luckily for me I was on the right side of a bad situation. So the legal thing was Strike One. Next there was the SAG issue. Force is a member of the Screen Actors' Guild and apparently whenever a SAG member is paid to perform in front of a camera there is tracking and reporting that must be done to the guild. VP certainly wasn't in a position to do that back then. Strike Two. Finally, John's fee was the final nail in the coffin. We never really needed to get there, so it was clear while my idea had merit we weren't in a position to move forward even if the lawyers and SAG weren't an issue. Bur he deserves every cent of the sponsorship money he and his operation commands. Force is the best of the best. We just couldn't afford it at the time.

As a postscript to this story, in September 2017 I received the heartbreaking news that Teddy had been killed in a plane crash. He was a long-time friend and after recovering from the shocking news I was able to reflect on how much I had enjoyed knowing him and his brother Mike. TC could drive the wheels off of anything he climbed into and we were lucky to have known him.

Remember that Gatorade was already a well-known national brand with appeal to professional and amateur athletes and everyday consumers who wanted to replenish themselves after a workout. VP, maker of race fuels for race cars, boats and bikes, had a very specific customer base and had yet to produce a product for the general consumer. Not just that, but they did not have a distribution network established, a pipeline to deliver the goods even if we had them to sell.

Our meeting with Force concluded after perhaps another half hour of storytelling and laughter. He's built quite an operation and hopefully the funding and the on-track success and off-track presence of his daughters Courtney and Brittany will continue for decades. As a postscript, some time after that discussion about the TV commercial, Ashley got married and started a family and chose to hang up her helmet. Her sisters are winning just like she had.

Chapter Nineteen
LET ME ASK YOU
A QUESTION

WHENEVER I NEEDED to fill a position at work we'd run the usual classified ads in the local print paper and then as the years passed we'd post on Monster and all the rest. The method for finding employees may have changed and adapted with the ages but *my* interviewing methods didn't.

"So tell me about the last time you yelled at a co-worker," was one of the curve balls I'd like to throw at an interviewee. Perhaps "what was the last thing you stole at work?" was another. Then the old "what do you do when a customer really pisses you off?" or maybe "if you saw someone stealing at work what would you do?" Finally, if the chemistry was good and the exchange was casual and flowing I might ask, "so do you drink beer, wine or mixed drinks?"

The looks on the candidates' faces sometimes were priceless. Their expressions, or the delay in answering, were often telling. The responses were usually even better. "Oh I worked with one guy who was such an asshole that I just had to put the phone down once I had finally had it and marched right into his office..." Next up might be, "I'd take some copier paper home for my printer. They had plenty and I since it didn't cost much I didn't think twice about it." Okay. What time's the next interview?

The whole idea behind asking "curve balls" or questions they might not expect was to not just get more info but to see how they handled themselves. See if they have a "tell" like most of us do. Interviewing someone for a position that could help or hinder your career and your company was very important. It was a critical decision at any level as far as I was concerned. Hire a dumbass to handle flammable liquids and expect a spill, a spark or a worse. Employ someone to answer the phone that hates answering phones and they'll chase your customers to the competition. Making sure they would fit into the office, a cultural fit was important too. That's why chemistry was so important. Everyone working together as one happy, productive unit was the goal. Anything else might be a distraction rather than a team builder. If someone refused to be around anyone who cursed then they might not want to be around a bunch of truck drivers on a bad day. Sounds pretty simple but those decisions and then managing the people you hired were very important.

By the way, for anyone out there who's ever been responsible for hiring people, I'm sure we could all write a ton about a candidate's references and checking them. People are so damn litigious these days that companies, particularly the HR departments who you call to verify past employment, will rarely say anything about a former employee other than verifying the dates. I always tried to joke a bit to loosen up the HR person on the other end of the line. Hell,

I'd been successful with my HR wife so a sense of humor goes a long way. If you did get as far as the candidate's supervisor, my last possible question when they were evasive on saying anything about the person was this. "So tell me this much, if you had to hire them again, would you? If you don't say another word then I have the answer." If I got the dial tone or found myself floating in a black hole I had my answer and went on to the next reference or most probably the next candidate.

As a hiring manager you also had to take note of what time they arrived for the interview, how they were dressed, how long it took them to complete the pre-interview paperwork, and their penmanship. I know there is a move in the schools to stop teaching cursive writing but I've even seen printing that was atrocious. I guess Ai will do all the writing for us some day.

Two things I did learn quickly. You have to check their penmanship and if they need to perform any math, you need to verify they can do both. If you can't read their writing that's strike one. If they can't do basic math, which someone who claimed to have accounting experience on their application could not, that's strike two. I've already listed a ton of ways people can strike out. So now that a candidate has passed all the scrutiny and they're hired, you have to train them properly. If you don't give them the tools they need then you've set them up to fail. If their supervisor isn't doing their part then that needs to be fixed. If the environment isn't a healthy, happy place then you need to fix it.

To me, racing is edgy and fast and I always felt our appearance should be that way too. First impressions are everything. I don't need to write that people dressing inappropriately for interviews don't get hired. That's a given. I'm now talking about what a customer or a potential partner thinks when they first pulled into the gates at VP. If the place looks dirty or outdated they might wonder about the quality of the product they are thinking about buying. Everything needed to be kept clean and professional looking – as well as possible given the available funds to keep things looking and working well. Don't let me see someone in the yard pass a piece of trash. Pick it up and drop it in the can. Don't let me see the top of a drum of fuel covered in dust from the yard stone. If someone's handing you $600 for that product it better be delivered looking good. And so on.

What about the first impression when someone walks into your office or perhaps even sooner, the reception area? I always felt the greeter should be attractive, courteous, and quick to acknowledge them. Not Waffle House chorus acknowledgement, just say hello and "how can I help you" or "I'll be right with you," yes?

What actually led to what I fondly called "The Boob Off" we could debate, at least with my office manager, Kyle Galuska. She had interviewed really well and started with us a few years before as my receptionist. True to form, I had enjoyed the interview and she responded well to some of the questions I had asked. She would fit perfectly into my office culture. We were fun, upbeat, pretty loose with the language unless a customer was present but also always mindful that we didn't take our humor or descriptive adjectives too far. Happy hours were the norm, sometimes weekly if the workload had become too crazy. When Kyle and I got into a friendly, funny debate about bodily functions at our first company get together I knew she was a perfect fit for my group. She excelled at reception and earned her promotions with hard work and dedication. She became my right arm and I relied on her to a lot, especially with all my traveling. One of the young ladies I hired to work the reception desk was particularly attractive. Okay, she was stunning. Great look, great personality, good resume, good references and the customers seemed to really like her. What could possibly go wrong? At this particular time all of the girls who worked in my office were single, attractive, and good employees. If they weren't good employees they wouldn't have been there. If I had a choice between two people with the same resume, fit, and references but one was attractive and the other grossly overweight and unkempt then I chose attractive. The reality, at least in my mind, was you might run the risk of hiring someone whose health would affect their production and attendance. On the other hand, the knockout might cause their own little sideshow that can have a negative effect on things. It's a fact of life but one that as I grew older I learned a life lesson from.

If a cute customer would come in the employees were free to talk, flirt, whatever. As long as the work was getting done and an overweight, balding customer wasn't being made to wait while Girl A spent too much time with the cute guy, I was cool with it. But a few of the girls noticed that customers began to ask for the new receptionist. They wanted her to wait on them. So over a very short period of time I noticed that the girls were starting to dress differently. The sweaters seemed to get a bit tighter. The cleavage began to deepen and it actually got to the point where it became a distraction. Not just for the other employees, and for the customers, but for me. I remember one day I had to talk with one of the girls at her desk. She was a great employee, my office manager, Kyle. To this day I consider her a very dear friend. Eventually, she dated my son David for a time and I had actually hoped she'd become part of the family as she fit in well with all of the Kellys. But at the time her new look was a distraction and I was supposed to be responsible and protective of everyone in the office so I addressed it.

"Okay, I see what's been going on here and we need to tone down the cleavage in the office," is how I broached the subject. The look on her face was priceless and my words went over like a bomb. We moved the conversation into my office and discussed everything that had developed. No, not that! It was a professional discussion. "I don't know what you are talking about," she insisted. The discussion went on for quite a while. Now to this day she and I joke about it but she still stands firmly on her position that the girls in the office did NOT ramp up their appearance to get the looks off the receptionist and divided back amongst them. We went back and forth on the issue but it forced me to address it and direct everyone to tone it down a wee bit. I don't think we ever drilled down to specifications. I don't believe that I ever stated only 2" of cleavage can be visible or any- thing like that but I thought everyone got the message. Remarkably, some companies actually do list measurements in their dress codes. They limit skirts to no shorter than 2" above the knee and so on. God, I loved working where I did.

Boobs aside, I was regarded as "a great boss" and work- ing there was usually a decent experience. I always believed in taking care of the people that take care of you. I might expect hard work but that was in exchange for good pay and some perks. Weekly happy hours, pizza lunches, Christmas parties (bring a guest) at the Borgata, Trump Taj Mahal, or Tropicana casinos in Atlantic City, New Jersey. Yep, we'd provide the team with round trip transportation, hotel rooms and chips for the table games. We'd have a two-hour happy hour in one of the lounges and then move everyone to somewhere really nice to eat. At the Trop we'd start at Red Square, the vodka bar where you could put on a full-length fur coat and enjoy some very expensive sips in a very cold tasting area. Then it was downstairs to P.F. Chang's and some very memorable dinners. Every year we hoped to find this one waitress in particular to work with us. She had developed an entertaining fondness for one of my main man's wives and so we would of course egg them on and hope for something special. We had door prizes. It was a great time.

Some of the other offices were taking their teams to Denny's while I was renting a stretch limo for the crew and shipping them to the Jersey Shore to party all night. That became a morale issue for the other offices. My take, of course, was if you really care about your crew and they worked their butts off for you then do something special. That seemed to go a long way in Delaware. Use a Kelly Hole to get the budget if you needed to. Eventually HQ decided they'd force me to tone it down and hopefully the other offices would stop complaining. The VP bean counters eventually said they would no longer pay for the hotel rooms. Kim Turza is one of my dearest friends and was also my travel agent. She had always done a great job getting a group price on mid-week rooms down at the boardwalk so it wasn't as if VP had been paying large for them. So rather than cancel the overnight party or keep it close to home I just picked up the bill. These people were working their butts off for me and they deserved it and much more. If the other offices didn't know how to take care of their teams, I could show them how. Some people don't know how to do certain things but with a diverse team you should have it all covered, especially when it comes to throwing a party.

Pardon the digression, but let's get back to the Boob Off! Months later, I was working a trade show in England and I got a call from one of the office girls. "Jim, I want to file a formal complaint!" she said. "The receptionist is wearing a bra; just a bra. No top!" Now I'm 4,000 miles away talking to a potential customer and need to be bothered with this nonsense.

So I told the complainant, who I really liked and appreciated, that I would take care of it. I called my office manager. She verified that the girl in question was scantily clad. "She's not in a bra. It's more like a lacy corset," is what I recalled hearing from across the pond. So my instructions were that the receptionist would need to put on a VP t-shirt or go home for the day. I intended to deal with this once and for all when I got stateside. With the time difference and entertaining our European distributors at a happy hour after the trade show, I didn't want to hear anything more about cleavage issues at the office. Now catch this. The next morning I learned that the receptionist had given the office manager her notice and walked. She'd had enough of the office politics, is what I was told. I heard from some of my warehouse guys that the girl worked nights as a stripper in the area. Now it all made sense. She had a great personality, great look, and was used to working alone. Case closed. Just wished they had shared that intel with me earlier. It could have made for an interesting happy hour. By the way, the debate over what started the alleged "boob off" was a simple one. Just recently Kyle told me I had asked her to cover up her own revealing tank tops long before the new girl came to work for us. Either way, yeah, it all came down to boobs.

Managing people wasn't all fun and games though. Sometimes people are just stupid. While attempting to fill an office position at VP I interviewed someone who seemed like the perfect fit, the complete employee wish list. Smart, said all the right things, resume and references all good. As little David continued to grow in size we incorporated all the proper HR hiring practices and procedures, and drug testing was one of them.

"You'll have to pass a pre-employment drug screen and background check," was Standard Operating Procedure. "Not a problem," the candidate assured me. Contingent on her passing the drug screen, she was told she had the job. I was really excited about this hire. She seemed very capable and also a good cultural fit for the office. My office manager had given me her thumbs up as well. Now get ready because you can't make this stuff up. She failed the drug screen. Once she was informed she failed and therefore didn't get the job, she showed up at my office with her irate husband. "My wife quit her job and walked off it because you told her she had the job!" he yelled at me. Not the first or last time I had a pissed off person in my office and I'm usually pretty good at talking people off the edge of the abyss.

After a few minutes of thinking to myself, *boy, did I get this one wrong. She's got to be the biggest dumb ass in town,* I made it clear the meeting was over. "She was told verbally and signed documents acknowledging the requirements," is what I reminded them both. "If it was a false positive, and only you know if it was or not, go back and take it again right now." I knew there were "blockers." There were pills and drinks people could take to pass a drug screen. Sometimes they worked quickly so if she drove directly to the test lab and produced a sample then maybe she had a shot at the job but I didn't want to give her any time, even an hour, to "block" it.

The manager of the testing center called me personally. He had been made aware of her declarations that she never smoked pot ever. Thinking about her claims and his phone call and comments all these years later still makes me scratch my head. "Her levels were so high," the manager related, "that she was probably smoking a joint in the elevator ride up to our floor." We offered the job to our second choice and she worked out just fine. I hate wasting time and have even more disdain for people who waste mine.

CHAPTER TWENTY
SERIOUSLY?

ENGLISHTOWN WAS THE site of so many good memories but two jackasses that worked for me really screwed up one of my weekends there. In preparing to provide on-site fuel service at an NHRA National Event we'd load up a tractor-trailer with all the fuel we thought we'd need. We'd load the pumps to dispense the fuel, the karts to deliver the drums, the grounding equipment, spill kits and fire extinguishers to handle any incident, tools to fix anything that could break, replacement parts, and the promotional materials like decals, brochures, banners, and streamers to promote VP. My rule was load up like you were on an island and had to be self-sufficient. Typically we'd load up on Tuesday and then drive over Wednesday morning to set up. Back in the early days we'd have that line of customers waiting for us once we opened so getting there early and getting as many customers taken care of before the qualifying rounds began made sense for us and made the racers happy too.

While most of the other VP offices had white pickup trucks I had insisted on enclosed vans. Living in the Northeast we had to deal with four seasons of weather so rain, sleet, snow, ice, whatever Mother Nature threw at us could screw up your day pretty quickly. Delivering pails and drums or heading to a November trade show in Syracuse, New York would be much easier and safer if everything was locked up safe and dry inside a van. I digress but one of the South Texas employees once told me the van wouldn't work down there, that Border Patrol or Customs would want to pull it over too often to bother with one. It would be pick-ups for the Lone Star boys. Jokingly, I guess the rest of the offices didn't know how to use their side mirrors to back up a van so they took the easy way too. That Wednesday morning I arrived at the plant to load the four-wheeler we used to deliver fuel drums and my bike in the van. I was surprised to see the big rig was still sitting in the yard. The guys had worked late to complete the loading and the driver had assured me he'd leave early to avoid the rush hour traffic.

"He's not coming," my office manager said cautiously as I walked in with that look on my face. She explained he had left a message on the machine saying that unless he got a raise he wouldn't be coming in to work that day. At this point I'm thinking the book should be retitled "WTF" right? Okay, so I called his home. This is before everyone had cell phones. It wasn't as if we had talked about a raise and I had said no, he just felt he had the leverage at that moment to force me into something. He wasn't due for an annual review or a raise for that matter for some time. In other lives I had been boxed into corners a few times before by similar, shortsighted behavior and I knew within a minute what I was going to do. Plus, my fearless leader Steve Burns in Texas had always suggested we consider this; "What would you do if they were dead? What would you do?"

I thanked the truck driver for putting me between a rock and a hard place and told him his personal belongings would be placed in a box and set outside the fence line within a few minutes. I then went down the street to an oil company we were friendly with and said, "I need someone to drive my rig from here to Englishtown. I'll follow whoever can go up in their car so they can drive home. Who wants to make some money?" Three hours later I was setting up the pumps and getting ready to service VP's customers. I never heard from that douche again and nobody ever called asking for a reference they wouldn't have gotten.

A few years later I was working the fuel truck at the track and my office manager called my cell. Yep, had them finally. The progression had started with the heavy black carry bag through to the ones that would fit in your pocket. The actual names have been changed to protect the innocent. "Dick Head just walked in and told me to tell you he was going home and taking Young Impressionable, the warehouse worker too." It was a Thursday morning and we were busy as hell both at the truck and back at the plant. Orders needed to be shipped. Customers needed their fuel delivered the next day so they could go racing. If the fuel didn't get there in time they might be forced to use another product. That meant three things.

First, whether it was out of our control or not, we let them down. Second, if they had to use another product they might not know how to tune it and that could cost them a race. Third, if they did have to use someone else's product and it performed okay then we may have just lost a customer. Luckily, our stuff not only made more power but it also burned cleaner and cooler than other race fuels so your engine might benefit long term by lasting longer and prolonging the need for an expensive rebuild. Regardless, I had to fix the problem and fast.

I called "Young" immediately. I expressed how much I appreciated him and his good work and cautioned him not to get caught up in Dick Head's maneuvers. "I just want to work. I need the job and I like working there," is all I needed to hear. I told "Young" to head back over to the office and get back to doing as much as he could while shorthanded that day and I'd get him some help ASAP. Then I called "Dick."

"I hear you are demanding a raise," I said. He said his piece and then I said mine. "Here's the deal. Nobody backs me into a corner. You abandoned your job and tried to take advantage of an impressionable young guy who just wants to work. You're fired and now I need to get back to people that matter." That was the last I heard of him. What a douche! I figured out all the Kelly Holes years ago about how to get things done when having to operate outside the rules or in an unconventional manner. I could have figured something out for either of those guys, the driver or the dockworker. I could have given them monthly bonuses or more paid time off in the off-season or worked something out. I knew firing him would mean I'd have to spend more time out on the dock loading and unloading tankers and drum trucks. That would take me away from running the business and also from making sales. It would also make me late for my kids but I just chose not to give in or get creative because one critical element was missing in both of their cases. From Steve Burns and all the way through the organization; we don't put up with that shit!

Chapter Twenty One
IT'S NOT ALWAYS SUNNY

YES, PROCRASTINATION CAN kill you, especially if you are part of a sales organization. Never put off until tomorrow what you can or should do today. I learned that lesson a few times during my learning period at VP. After one or two potential accounts told me "Man, I wish you had called me yesterday," or "I wish you had called me last week," that was followed with the knife to the heart; "I just signed a three-year deal with Sunoco."

Those words were the worst I could hear. I preached to myself and to anyone on the team, internal or external, to make calls and make trips now rather than later. When it came to renewals I was always pushing for extensions. What was a series or track's incentive for signing now rather than later? "Because I have the funding now and I might not in two years. You know you sell more race fuel when you are selling VP so why play around? Sign the extension." They always did.

Remember my writing about how proud everyone was

at VP when we were awarded the NHRA Official Fuel and Exclusive trackside sales contract? We had beaten our big domestic rivals, the ones with deeper pockets than ours, Sunoco and Union 76. Well, things went very well over the many years. Sales were good and they got better as we were able to leverage our relationship with the NHRA and their member tracks. Some track managers would offer, "I'm an NHRA track and we want to support the NHRA sponsors so we'll give you our business." Some local deals took a lot of work while others were pretty easy. It was a very good deal for us and opened a lot of doors that opened more and more. But as time passed and the termination date of the contract approached we started hearing rumors. Word on the street was that the NHRA was switching to Sunoco. The extension had been discussed but someone at corporate in Texas dropped the ball – probably procrastinated or worse yet took the extension for granted, and soon we might be on the outside looking in. Remind me to send them an Assume Nothing sign. It doesn't matter who it was, they aren't with the company anymore. The NHRA deal hadn't been my responsibility but I had been the point man on many big deals like Indy Lights, Toyota-Atlantics, Trans Am, World Racing Group and DIRT, Isle of Man, Watkins Glen, Lime Rock Park, ACT, Rally America, Santa Pod, and many more tracks and series. I volunteered to fly to the NHRA race in Florida to meet with their Tom Compton and Graham Light. The fact that this trip would take me from the cold of the north to the sun and fun of Gainesville in March meant something to me. It was something I had first done many years before with my high school buds Fred and Glen. The fact that I had a solid team taking care of things at the

Delaware plant allowed me to go wherever, whenever, I needed.

Before I got to the meeting place I heard the rumors first hand. Some racer must have preferred Sun to VP and may have felt empowered by what was flowing through the pits. There he was, standing at the back of the VP fuel trucks while our guys were filling jugs and preparing to deliver drums to customers, telling our drivers that they'd be out of a job at the end of the season so they might want to put their applications in at Sunoco. Was the deal already signed? Pretty cocky behavior if it wasn't.

After exchanging pleasantries with Tom and Graham in the conference room in Gainesville Raceway's new hospitality and operations tower, I got down to business. "We're hearing you've signed with Sunoco," I said. "No, that's not true," responded Compton. And so it went but it was clear something was up. I had that sick feeling that the deal was done and VP would be the last to know.

The attendance at the NHRA's national events, corporate sponsorship, and television audience numbers had been dwindling. Since the global financial crash of 2008 everyone's world changed. Money got tight and fans that couldn't afford the expensive race tickets would have to find something else to keep them entertained. What I, and many others, had once regarded as the greatest show on earth was in a slump and it needed help to survive. Either a large cash injection to advertise and promote the sport or perhaps a partnership that would attempt to drive more fans to the stands. For me, I was concerned that once the fans stopped coming to the races they might not ever come back.

At VP, the new ownership wanted the continued growth

of race fuel sales but also put a lot of attention on two sectors they saw as the next big thing for VP. One was in performance chemicals like the SEF small engine fuel product, octane boosters, and such. The other area was branding of gasoline stations and convenience stores, c-stores. It was at this point that I became fully aware of what was happening. Getting the VP brand into auto parts stores and gas stations all across the country would be good for our series and track partners. We could use those avenues not just to build our own brand awareness but also to help drive consumer awareness to the NHRA and its race dates. Help drive fans to the stands that could in turn influence so many things that were mutually beneficial to the sport, our customers, our tracks, and everyone's sponsors. Simple, right?

However, I think the aggressive incursion by VP into the gas station branding business was stepping very hard onto Sunoco's toes. When mergers took place, like Mobil and Exxon for example, stations lost their lucrative contracts with one of those parties. Where there used to be a Mobil station on one street corner and an Exxon on the other, now there would be one Exxon. The third corner might have had a Sunoco station for that matter. This left the remaining station without a brand and looking for a new dance partner. Stations that sat along the nation's streets and highways needed an edge over their competition. Some felt somewhat enslaved by their big oil partners while others wanted an edge. They wanted something to attract a driver into their station over the other one. A hot new brand in the c-store/gas station arena might be just what the doctor ordered.

VP's new ownership had formed a new c-store branding division and began attending all sorts of Petroleum

Marketer trade shows and advertising in their trade magazines. For years, VP had gone after Sunoco's race fuel market share but now we were in new territory, their prime business. Race fuels sales made up very little of Sunoco's overall business. A single station, one that moves 100,000 gallons of pump gas per month, grosses $3,600,000 at the pumps before taking into consideration the in-store sales of everything from lottery tickets and cigarettes to beer and soda. Gas stations and c-stores were what Sun was really known for nationally to general consumers, not their racing. That might be what they used as their marketing platform for their NASCAR pitch and eventual partnership. Now we were treading into deeper water, their water, and it was obvious they weren't happy. A month earlier I had watched as we pulled five VP Racing Fuels tractor-trailers into Daytona International Speedway, amidst all the prominent Sunoco signage, to service the prestigious Rolex 24 Hour Endurance Race. It was the first time in our history that we had been able to drive in there and start delivering thousands of gallons of race fuel to the international road-racing crowd. Sun wasn't very happy about that either.

As I sat across from the NHRA's top brass at Gainesville I knew we had finally made the big mistake. We had finally pissed off a sleeping giant, the one last race fuel Goliath in our way in North America. Sun was calling on our most high profile accounts and using their deep pockets to take them away from us. If you're a movie buff like me, take a look at Ron Howard's *Cinderella Man*. At 1:41, boxer Max Baer had tired of the troublesome Jim Braddock and at the bell came out of his corner with an expression and charge that told Braddock and the crowd that Max was done playing around. Watch the whole movie for perspective but you might get my point already. Figure Sun was Baer and VP was Braddock, at least for that round. The historic fight took place in 1935 but the one we were in was in the early rounds and is still being fought. Looking back, way back, I'll never forget the frustration and pride that I expressed to Sunoco's then race fuel guy, Jim Meisner, twenty years before this. "If we can ever take your money out of the equation we will kick your ass!"

We went through the motions in Gainesville that day. The NHRA asked me how many chains were distributing our performance chemicals. Not many. The NHRA asked me how the c-store branding program was going. They asked, "How many stations do you have now?" and I gave the same answer. The timing of the contract extension discussion, basing the enhanced partnership with VP on the new programs, couldn't have been worse. It was probably two to three years premature and these few years later that proved out. Today VP has tremendous distribution of performance chemicals across North America. The c-store branding program in the United States has a significant number of VP locations. At the time they made their decision, the NHRA appeared to have needed two things: more operating cash and a marketing partner who could immediately provide opportunities to drive more fans to the NHRA grandstands.

"We have 500 stores and we'll put your race schedules and free decals in all of them," was a selling point I had heard before. So when the NHRA needed money and Sunoco had their many c-stores across the country, outnumbering VP's by 20 to 1, it was an easy decision. Don't forget, NASCAR had wanted a truly national partner when they made their official fuel supplier selection. Sunoco had been regarded as an "I-95" brand. When the Sunoco presence spread across the U.S., I assume in part as a response to Daytona's wishes, they really appeared to have something to offer the NHRA too. In addition to that, it was rumored Sunoco offered them twice what VP had been paying for the contract. Case closed. So we lost that one and we were pissed. What's a lad to do? Go take more of their sales.

We went on to sign an extension with IMSA so we could continue to roll the VP trucks into Daytona and pump VP for the prestigious Rolex 24 hour race. I figured it pissed Sunoco off when we signed the first deal so an extension, especially post NHRA, would be great. So that's exactly what we did!

I would meet again months later with Graham Light at the NHRA race at Englishtown, New Jersey but to no avail. It was clear the deal was done and we'd have to lick our wounds, learn the lesson, and regroup. Also, I haven't seen any impact of their partnership with Sunoco on fans in the stands. The starting line grandstands on television and in person continue to be sparsely populated. My idea for really growing the crowd (in person and on television) and broadening their fan base was to have Travis Pastrana jump over the race track on a supercross bike while two Funny Cars raced underneath him side by side down the quarter mile. Okay, if that doesn't sound safe he could do it in his Red Bull rally car. Remember the 269' New Year's Eve jump in Long Beach! Now that's entertainment and after all, the NHRA is in the entertainment business.

I'm told the NHRA-Sunoco deal was a ten-year term and so it may be a long time before an opportunity to partner with the NHRA again happens. Luckily, there was still plenty of business to go after.

Interestingly enough there may be another lesson in this. VP had established itself primarily through its drag racing and motocross roots. VP was THE drag racing fuel. Sunoco may have tried over the many years to out sponsor VP or spend R&D time trying to make better fuels that could help racers win more races and championships for them. Before Sunoco secured the NHRA contract they had NEVER won an NHRA Pro Stock Car World Championship. Never. And that includes all the years before spec fuel when the competitors could run whatever brand they wanted to. Losing the deal hurt our pride but the world wasn't going to end. Lick your wounds, grow sales, strengthen yourself through diversification, then go kill – I mean take – something. Just a quick thought on diversity. With the exception of being married, it's always best to diversify. Imagine being a company that only deals in leaded fuel. If it were ever banned or lead ran out, where would you be? What about electric cars, ethanol, and so on? Yep, best to have spin-off or complimentary product lines. Once you've built the damn thing, it is best to make the machine operate at full capacity. That's why you don't just sell fuel jugs to racers. You sell utility jugs too. I keep oil-dry, rock salt, and dog food in a few. One last thought. If you haven't done a SWOT analysis, identifying the strengths, weaknesses, opportunities, and threats of where you work or the company you operate perhaps you should. It can be a lifesaver. Do it on your competition too. I did it for VP quite often and continue to perform that service for others. Heck, I used to do it back when I was dating too. Okay, enough of that.

CHAPTER TWENTY TWO
LOOKING BACK

I WROTE EARLIER on that I had enjoyed being part of a team with the Gatorade-DiGard #88 and was thrilled to get the chance to be a part of the VP party. I am very lucky to have had such a great team first in Chester and then in Newark. They were what made up such a successful regional effort in the Northeast. People like Kyle Galuska, Ron Bradshaw, Tom Braksator Sr., Ralph Dominquez, Fred Oat, Mike Farr, and of course Frank Friske. They and so many others who worked behind the scenes or out on the front lines were part of what made VP the great place it was to work for so many years. They did their jobs above and beyond what was expected of them and that in turn helped provide me with this great ride and the success I achieved. I hope that through naming them here, thanking them for their contributions and achievements, they might get the additional recognition they deserve. Obviously there were many others and a few got good mentions throughout this tale. Perhaps the most significant to me in this story though are my children.

While they were growing up they may not have understood what I was doing or why I was doing it, *why I had to do it*, but they do today as adults. Whether they understand, forgive me, or hold it against me, what I did deprive them of will be with me until the day I die.

For those of us lucky enough to pursue our passions and do something really cool for a living I've expressed more than once that it comes at a price. Every time Lisa would kiss me goodbye she prayed I would return safely but also behave myself while I was away. Other than that covert trip to Jerusalem, there was this one time in Boston.

Way before cell phones were strapped to us like a vital organ we had toll free numbers to use to make calls from hotel phones when traveling. I had set up the VP booth for a trade show in Boston earlier that day and then took a tour of the John F. Kennedy Presidential Library. I headed back to the hotel to change into my VP shirt and call my house where the Mrs. was hoping to hear from me and then to call the kids, hoping they wouldn't blow me off to play with their friends. When I got to the room the maid was just finishing up so I jumped over the vacuum cleaner cord and started dialing the phone. My wife answered and we started our conversation until the shit hit the fan. "Who was that?" she said. "Was that a woman's voice?" she demanded. *Oh crap.* "It was the maid, honey, she was just asking if she wanted me to close the door," I offered. She wasn't buying it. To her, there was no reason in hell for a woman to be in my room while I was in there too. I tried to explain but she wasn't buying it. She had always been a bit concerned that my "party and panty days" on the road were behind me as I had declared they were when we began dating. This was the first time it seemed like I had given her any reason to doubt me.

I told the wife, "Hold on!" I jumped out of the chair and ran into the hallway hoping the maid hadn't disappeared because if she had my marriage was probably going to follow suit. But there she was, two doors down, wondering why I was approaching her with a crazed look on my face. "You have to do me a favor, you have to come back to my room and tell my wife who you are and what you said to me as you left the room!" She understood and followed me back in, making sure to flip the latch so the door wouldn't close behind her. In her strong Jamaican accent she explained to the Mrs. exactly what had happened and within a minute she was smiling and laughing and signed off with, "Everything irie!" Everything alright.

We still laugh about that incident to this day. The Jamaican maid and I got married and – no, I'm kidding. She went on with her job and I went on to the trade show thankfully never to cross paths again.

CHAPTER TWENTY-SIX
WHERE'S THE BEER?

AFTER ATTENDING AUTOSPORT in England this year I had
the honor of touring the historic sites of the Normandy
region of France. I continued to be amazed at the stories of
the bravery the American and allied fighting men demon-
strated on those beaches, in the air, and in the fields and
villages. I got to spend time on the Utah and Omaha
Beaches and in places like Sainte-Mère-Église and Carentan.
I got to retrace the steps that so many brave men from
America, Canada, and the U.K. took as they fought their
way across France to defeat Hitler and his forces. My father,
like Steve's, fought in Europe during World War II and I can
see where Steve and so many of us got some of our inspira-
tion and pride in America.

At VP they gave me everything I wanted. All I was supposed to do was grow sales, make money, and keep them
out of trouble. I had been entrusted with a big responsibility
and I ran with it. It was the closest thing to being my own
boss and I loved it. At a managers' meeting one time Burns

related how much he liked his team and went around the room saying a few nice things about each of us. When it came to me it was simple. "He makes me laugh my ass off, doesn't get us into any lawsuits, and all he wants is to be left alone to do his job. That works." Thinking back to the frustration I had felt with regard to my failed self-improvement initiative I have to say that I now feel fully vindicated. I enjoyed hearing the following story and am very happy to share it. Some time ago I had hired a very personable young man regarded as a traction compound specialist. He would be my DH in that field and his mission was to contact every asphalt track in the region, oval or drag, and get them to try our products. He had the green light to offer them free product and to be there to show them how to apply it. Unfortunately, not much happened. I had hired him while the racing season was in full swing and admittedly I was way too busy to spend much time teaching. His personality and experience alone should have made it work. Instead, with little success and missing his family in Michigan, he left VP and moved closer to home. A few years later he was winning all sorts of sales awards at NAPA Auto Parts. Turned out they had liked what they saw in him, put him through their excellent training program, and set him loose to sell. Eventually he returned to VP and since that time, partnered with Freddie Turza, he's been setting all sorts of sales records and making quite a name for himself. Congrats to Marc Wesler and anyone who is willing to take advantage of opportunities and to improve themselves.

To win a battle and eventually a war, you have to eat, sleep, live, and breathe the mission with unrelenting passion and focus. Whether you're competing on the field, track, classroom, or boardroom that's what it took to succeed.

Every dedicated member of the team that was present at VP years ago put everything they could into making the effort a success. It was a culture reflective of an old school, pure American work ethic. Work hard, play hard, and then work some more. Either Steve or Fred had given each of us a chance to be part of something special and we paid them back and then some. In Texas, people like Keith Simmons, Bubba Corder, Darryl Zoblosky, Veronica Martinez, and my dear friend Rebecca Sapp Koen, put incredible effort into the campaign. Susan Gray, our in-house attorney and CFO, kept us out of trouble or at least tried her best to. I must have received at least one, okay maybe twenty or more calls that started with a particular inflection when she said my name. "But, Mom," was my usual response. My "Get It Done" mentality would bring me some heat from time to time but in all my years at VP I never got us into a lawsuit or had anyone call HR on me. I may have pissed off a few people but at least they know I was there. Damn Yankee.

Wade Gray and Ed Marvin were also very much a part of the VP story in making things happen. Sadly, Wade and Ed left this world too soon but they will always be remembered fondly, usually with a laugh and quite often with a toast to them before shots. There were plenty of others that worked hard in Texas and at the other regional plants, like Tommy Chapman in Georgia and Kelley Hendel when she was in California. Freddie Turza might be based in North Carolina but he continues his work with everyone from the Saturday night racer at Grandview to the top engineers at the most famous engine companies in the world. If VP ever to follow his passion with his Crossmen Drum & Bugle Corps. He had studied education in college and was back working with young people. His wife Maureen right there with him.

I'm so aware and appreciative of the service and sacrifices of our veteran fathers who fought overseas so that Steve, Fred, I and so many of us got the chance to live out our dreams.

As for what I've learned and shared from my life experiences and being a part of a classic David versus Goliath tale, I hope you enjoyed reading about my journey and the behind-the-scenes glimpse into a world you may not have known much about. JK

THE END